# this is the
# saint
# bernard

**by
marlene j. anderson
and
joan mcdonald brearley**

Distributed in the U.S.A. by T.F.H. Publications, Inc., 211 West Sylvania Avenue, P.O. Box 27, Neptune City, N.J. 07753; in England by T.F.H. (Gt. Britain) Ltd., 13 Nutley Lane, Reigate, Surrey; in Canada by Clarke, Irwin & Company, Clarwin House, 791 St. Clair Avenue West, Toronto 10, Ontario; in Southeast Asia by Y. W. Ong, 9 Lorong 36 Geylang, Singapore 14; in Australia and the south Pacific by Pet Imports Pty. Ltd., P.O. Box 149, Brookvale 2100, N.S.W., Australia.
Published by T.F.H. Publications, Inc. Ltd., The British Crown Colony of Hong Kong.

# ACKNOWLEDGMENTS

The authors wish to acknowledge with thanks the cooperation and help of those who contributed in their own way to the production of this book. A special thank-you is due to Bruce Chapman for his tremendous help in correcting spelling and grammatical errors; to Robert R. Shomer VMD, for his unending counseling over the years; to Albert de la Rie for allowing us to reprint his excellent interpretation of the Standard, and to all the other Saint Bernard lovers who have in any way shared their photographs, their knowledge, and/or their experiences with us to make this a better book on a magnificent breed.

## PHOTO CREDITS

The authors wish to acknowledge the expert photography of the following people whose work appears in this book: Joan Ludwig, William P. Gilbert, Evelyn Shafer, Ritter, Norton of Kent, Tauskey, and William Brown, plus all the private photographers and proud owners whose work so enhances this book!

**Cover:**

Champion Beau Chevals Mt. Lesa Mardoug and the adorable puppy Softy, owned by Bruce Chapman. Photo by Bruce Chapman.

# CONTENTS

# ABOUT THE AUTHORS

Marlene Anderson

# MARLENE J. ANDERSON

Marlene Anderson was born into a family of dog breeders. She grew up in the dog business, surrounded by many breeds, which her mother and grandmother successfully raised. Young Marlene helped with the management of a large boarding and breeding kennel. It soon became the subject about which she knew most. Her grandmother's favorite dog was the Saint Bernard and she always kept some magnificent specimens of the breed. Thus, Marlene's constant companions were Saints, and they have remained very dear to her over the years.

Having a background in many arts, she joined the United States Air Force when she was 18 to work in Special Services. There she met and married Douglas J. Anderson when she was 20. She left the service several months later, and soon afterward became seriously ill. After a long hospital stay, close to death, her doctors finally diagnosed her disease as the dreaded and hopeless Multiple Sclerosis. With the impending doom of life in a wheelchair threatening her, Marlene's doctors prescribed a hobby or business that would keep her hands busy and her mind occupied. Her husband left the service, where he had been a career man, and the couple decided to raise dogs.

After they had traveled around the country a bit, with a brief stay in Alaska, their first daughter was born and the Andersons moved to the wilds of Western Maryland where Beau Cheval Kennels was established in 1957.

While Douglas worked far away from home and was gone for weeks at a time, Marlene busied herself gathering stock, studying standards, and working with dogs. German Shepherds were Douglas's favorite at the time and they were the breed decided upon. The little kennel shortly was filled with them. Although Marlene liked Shepherds, too, she was not content to raise them alone, and soon other breeds were racing about the property— Dachshunds, Pekingese, and German Shepherds were still not enough . . . something very big was missing!

After Marlene and Douglas purchased their first Saint Bernard, a large male (which later became their first champion) the couple decided they had to have more. They began breeding their own Saints in 1961.

Moving to Western Pennsylvania about that time to be closer to Douglas's work, the couple became interested in dog shows. On one occasion, they were invited by another breeder to enter a show to build points so that the other breeder's dog could finish.

Douglas won a four-point major that first time he walked a dog into the ring, and both he and Marlene were hooked! Since that time, the Andersons have bred or owned 48 champions of record, none of which was purchased as a champion, or with any points, and most were bred by Marlene.

The family later moved to Bucks County, Pennsylvania, to be close to the East's largest and most competitive dog shows. Here their kennels house 50 to 75 Saint Bernards at all times.

Now as the mother of four healthy daughters, Marlene feels the doctors were evidently wrong about the disease they diagnosed 17 years ago. She probably would have raised dogs in any case, and Saints were bound to have been the chosen breed.

The Andersons' goal has always been to better themselves, their environment, and their dogs. Never satisfied with what they produce, they constantly strive to breed better Saint Bernards.

Marlene believes common sense is the secret ingredient necessary in any venture, and especially in the mad, wonderful game of breeding and showing dogs.

# JOAN McDONALD BREARLEY

Joan Brearley has loved animals since she was old enough to know what they were.

Over the years there has been a constant succession of dogs, cats, birds, fish, rabbits, snakes, turtles, alligators, squirrels, lizards, etc., for her own personal menagerie. Through these same years, she has owned over 30 different breeds of purebred dogs, as well as countless mixtures, since the family's door was never closed to a needy or homeless animal.

A graduate of the American Academy of Dramatic Arts, Joan started her career as a writer for movie magazines, and as an actress and dancer. She also studied journalism at Columbia University and has been a radio scriptwriter, copywriter for some of the major New York City advertising agencies, and a producer-director in radio and television for a major New York City network.

Her accomplishments in the dog fancy are many. She is an American Kennel Club approved judge; a breeder-exhibitor of top show dogs (and cats!); a writer for the American Kennel Club Gazette; author of "This Is the Afghan Hound," and co-author of "This Is the Shih Tzu," two outstanding breed books. She is also a book editor for TFH Publications Inc. For five years, she was the executive vice president of Popular Dogs Publishing Company and editor of Popular Dogs magazine, the national prestige publication that sets the pace for the entire dog fancy. Joan is as active in the cat world, and in almost as many capacities, as she is in the dog world, particularly in the area of seeking humane legislation for animals.

Joan Brearley

She is an avid crusader and speaker for humane causes and is a well-known speaker before Kennel Clubs and humane organizations on the subject of animal legislation. She has received many awards and citations for her work on behalf of the welfare of all animals. Starting in 1971, Joan was starred on national television in a series of commercials for Gaines Gravy Train. On behalf of animals, she has appeared on several major television shows, including Mike Douglas, Cleveland Amory, Captain Noah, the Today show, etc.

At present, Joan lives in a penthouse apartment overlooking historic Rittenhouse Square in Philadelphia with an Afghan Hound, a Shih Tzu, a Cavalier King Charles Spaniel and a dozen or more cats, most of which are Best In Show winners and have been professional models for television and magazines. Joan has the rare distinction of having bred a Westminster Kennel Club group winner in her very first litter of Afghan Hounds—Champion Sahadi Shikari—the top-winning Afghan Hound in the history of the breed.

In addition to her activities in the world of dogs and cats, Joan is food editor and feature writer for Metropolitan magazine, which is published in Philadelphia. She spends her "spare time" at the art and auction galleries, the theatre, creating needlepoint (for which she has also won awards), the opera, the typewriter—and the zoo!

# INTRODUCTION

The history of the Saint Bernard goes back to the dawn of man's beginning. The Bible tells us that the animals were created first, to work with man, and were also named by man. Through the centuries we have seen that dogs have been both used and misused by man; that even today dogs are either man's friend and companion, or the object of his inhumanity and often exploited for financial gain. We may not know exactly what the first dog looked like, but we like to picture him as a large, kind-eyed SAINTLY-looking creature!

# CHAPTER 1

# HISTORY OF THE BREED

The Saint Bernard enjoys one of the most legendary and romantic histories of all breeds, going back to the seventeenth century. The world first became aware of their existence through artwork and stories depicting their great size, strength, and beauty. There are numerous theories on how the breed originated, including the crossing of such breeds as Great Danes, Bulldogs, Bloodhounds, Mastiffs, and even Spaniels. Based on the historical facts available, we know that when Hannibal crossed the Alps, he brought with him great Molossian dogs whose size and descriptions best resemble Mastiffs. We also know that the Roman armies brought Mastiff-like Asiatic dogs, as drivers of accompanying herds, and as guards for military posts and stations. Many of these dogs were left behind, filling the mountains and valleys with animals that could be used successfully for herding over rough terrain, or as guard dogs for estates and castles, as draft dogs, and later as lifesaving foundation stock for the Saint Bernard breed, as we know it today.

Certainly, there were already Swiss herding dogs, and through cross-breeding in the high and low country, large dogs emerged that resembled each other. A similar situation exists in the United States today with the "farm Collie." It is not recognized as purebred, but remains a breed unto itself, and thrives because of its usefulness in herding livestock on American farms.

## THE HOSPICE

The Hospice of the great or grand Saint Bernard still exists today, high in the mountains of Switzerland, separated by a small lake from the Italian Alps. This monastery originally consisted of a cathedral, monks' quarters, and a simple structure that served as a resting place for weary travelers crossing the treacherous pass from Italy to Switzerland. It was in operation for years under the guidance of the Saint Bernard monks, and still serves as a place of rest for those who come to see the famous giant dogs of lifesaving legends.

Visitors to the Hospice must drive up perilous, steep, and breathtakingly narrow roads to the mountaintop, where it is a relief to find a level spot, be able to park, and get out on solid ground. The bleak monastery sustained a fire in 1967, while a group of Saint Bernard fanciers were on their first tour, conducted by Albert de la Rie. There are two hotels for overnight guests, one in Switzerland, and another just past the lake on the Italian side. Here, one will find excellent food, gift and curio shops, and most important, the kennels which house the typical Hospice-type Saint Bernard—making the whole trip up St. Bernard mountain worthwhile. This is one of the biggest and most commercial kennels in all of Europe today—few European kennels are large, and perhaps only two or three could be termed commercial.

A Monk and two Saint Bernards at the Hospice in Switzerland.

The Hospice in Switzerland.

The Hospice is approximately 8,100 feet above sea level, and, in such altitudes and weather conditions, a monk's dedicated services are limited to about eight years. Viewing the towering peaks of perpendicular rock mass, covered with ice and snow, dropping away from the Hospice buildings, one realizes that every step is dangerous, any fall could be fatal. The forbidding, rugged terrain of this birthplace of the beloved Saint Bernard breed is a most unusual setting. One's first thought is that Saints were created for important, specific purposes—to swim, climb over ice and snow, find lost travelers and protect them. The dogs had to be sound! Muscle mass must have been born into every puppy through a selective breeding program designed to eliminate the weak, inferior specimens. The huge dogs had to have superior strength for climbing and running virtually straight up and straight down, for there is little flat ground. This is where the first real land rescue dogs were developed.

Saint Bernards of the Hospice, a pen-and-ink sketch from Cassell's Book of the Dog.

The monks will insist that lifesaving dogs were used before Hannibal ever thought of coming to the Alps. However, Saint Bernards' most likely descendants were the Mastiff-type dogs that were used in ancient wars and left behind in the mountains by the Carthaginians and Romans. These warriors had much use for giant dogs that could be trained to do battle, and used in the arena to fight bulls and lions. They traveled in packs with the soldiers, guarding military outposts in the bleak, cold mountain passes. Few men chose to cross the path of a huge, snarling war-dog, chained in a mountain pass. Bred with local mountain dogs, the Mastiffs eventually fostered a giant new breed of Swiss mountain dog.

Since the earliest records of the Hospice and its rescue work were lost in a fire, we can only guess when the great dogs first took part in actual rescues. A 1695 oil painting of a dog, nearly all white with spots, hangs in the Hospice today, and is recognizable as a life-saving Saint Bernard. With migrant workers, missionaries, and travelers of all rank crossing the passes each year in all kinds of weather, loss of life was heavy from snowstorms, avalanches, and bandits who lay in wait for purses heavy with treasure. There was only one place to rest, the shelter of the Hospice of St. Bernard . . . and it was always humming with activity. The spit turned with fresh meat in the huge kitchen, and a giant dog even performed this chore for all who hungered.

The breed's name then was "Butcher Dog," since only a butcher was able to own such a large dog that ate so much meat. Even today, in Switzerland and Germany, these dogs are owned frequently by restaurants and butchershops, since their main food intake in Europe is meat. Commercial dog food is not widely used and is rather expensive for the average dog owner and his family.

## THE STORY OF BARRY

The most famous rescue dog of them all was called Barry and, since his time, there has always been a "Barry" at the Hospice kennels. This dog is credited with saving some 40 human lives in the freezing temperatures of the Alps. Many legends surround him, one claiming that he died while trying to save a man's life. This is not true, for we know that Barry was sent to the City of Berne, Switzerland, in his old age, and kept there in comfortable

17

Beau Cheval's Pope II Mardoug, owned by Darryl Hayes of Ohio. Pope was sired by Beau Cheval's Parish Mardoug and is out of Ch. Beau Cheval's Tralee. M. J. Anderson was the breeder.

style until his death. He was mounted and stands in a glass case in the Berne Museum of Natural History. The kindness that shows in his eyes often causes visitors to blink away tears, as the many stories about him become a vivid reality at that moment. Barry stands tall, and rather slight of bone and substance, compared with what we like to see in today's dogs. But he is unmistakably a Saint Bernard. His coloring, topline, tail, and overall structure are certainly within the Standard.

Other dogs have been cited for saving almost as many lives, but Barry remains in most Saint Bernard lovers' memories as the hero of all time, and certainly he should.

## THE SAINT-NEWFOUNDLAND CROSS

In 1830, most of the Hospice breeding stock was lost due to cold weather or disease and, in 1856, when the dogs were on the brink of extinction, two Newfoundlands were used to save the breed. This produced the long-haired specimens that were almost completely useless for Alpine rescue work. Heavy snow gathered in their coats, forming ice balls, and as they gathered more snow, they were unable to move across the fields. These long-haired dogs were given or sold to people below in the valleys, and when used for breeding, they produced both long- and short-haired dogs. The Saint breed was restored through the Newfoundland cross, which is the only cross recorded in all Saint Bernard history. This is where the dogs get the black mask, the dark ear shading, and black mixed throughout the coat.

## A NEW NAME APPEARS

After being known as Holy Dogs, Alpine Mastiffs, Cloister Dogs, Mountain Dogs, and Hospice Dogs, not to mention Butcher Dogs, or Saint Bernard-Mastiffs, the giants were referred to as Barryhundes in honor of the heroic deeds of Barry. In 1823, the name Saint Bernard was first heard, and by 1865 the name was well known. Although it implied that the dogs were all bred at the Hospice, this was not true, since many were bred elsewhere.

Beau Cheval's Peer Mardoug, owned by Julie Howard of Woodbridge, Va. Peer is a young teenage puppy of rough coat variety.

Nevertheless, the name was fully recognized in 1880 and justly so, since the breed originated at the Hospice and should carry the name of the monastery of St. Bernard.

## THE KEG OR CASK OF BRANDY

There is no record of any lifesaving dog ever carrying a keg around his neck, and this illustration did not originate at the Hospice. Sir Edwin Landseer, the English painter, depicted Saints saving lives in this manner, and it planted a picture in many minds. Even today, casks are sold and found in nearly every Saint owner's house, although strictly for show. You may see a cask on a Saint's neck at the Hospice, but this would be simply to amuse tourists who expect such a sight! It is true that the monks carried stimulants to awaken and arouse weary or unconscious victims lost in the blizzards, but the dogs never actually carried any such provisions around their necks. It is a legend kept very much alive today, and keg-making for Saint Bernards is big business!

An old print showing Swiss farmers delivering their milk to a cheese-making establishment.

An original lithograph owned by Lt.-Col. and Mrs. Paul J. Phillips, Alexandria, Va. The dog is Ch. Bayard K.C.S.B. 8447, whelped April 11, 1877, and his breeder was Mr. King of Everton, England. Lithograph is a copy of a headstudy done by English illustrator-painter Frank Paton.

## RESCUE DOGS TODAY

There is little use for rescue dogs in the Alps today, since tunnels connect roads and highways and travel by foot is almost unknown. However, the dogs still do valuable work. Skiers get lost and have accidents and are searched for by men on skis with the happy man-loving rescue dogs! A few are trained each year by breeders and monks for rescue work. Herr Rodel, of the famous Swiss Sauliamt Kennels, does this and owns dogs which are fully experienced and capable of actual snow rescue.

Monks on skis, followed by a pack of dogs, are a familiar sight at the winter Hospice, for the sport is both necessary and enjoyable to the dedicated men. Skill on skis is all part of a monk's training. Skiing out upstairs windows is not uncommon, since the snow is often as high as the rooftops.

The instinct to save humans in the snow is not completely lost in our American dogs, but this desire and actual act would have to be brought out through rigid training. In experimenting with the

Andringham Sparkle, the Saint Bernard which has been owned by three Kings . . . The late King George V, King Edward VIII, and King George VI.

dogs, owners have found that Saints will race around in snow, but really do not look for lost masters or strangers. In a television show during an Eastern blizzard, 20 Saints were used in a rescue demonstration. All dogs were let loose at one time. According to the script, the star of the show would be calling for help beneath a drift right in the path of the excited dogs . . . and a dramatic rescue would be filmed on location. The tall, lanky, bespectacled star lay spread-eagled as nine dogs came barking and stampeding over him, nearly stomping him to death, covering him with snow, fogging his glasses and pounding him deeper into his bed of white! Finally, slowly, and only because he was scared to death, one four-month-old puppy with a keg too big for his neck came slowly up to the star, stopped and fondly kissed the man's embarrassed face, sat down beside him and saved the show, the star and the legend of the lifesaving Saint Bernard! The scene was well worth all the planning, and the cameras went on to photograph the other dogs leaping joyously through the snow drifts.

Three Best of Breed winners owned by Mrs. Marion A. McDonald of Mukwonaga, Wis. Marcus Aurelius, Best of Breed at International Kennel Club show in Chicago in 1930, Pythagoras Junior, Best of Breed at Westminster in 1930, and Jason, Best American-bred at Westminster in 1930.

Other Saint owners have told of their Saint coming directly to them, crawling on top of their outstretched bodies spread over the snow, licking their faces, and doing all possible to arouse them from a pretended sleep. It's pretty certain that one could see the same scene at poolside in June, if the dog was invited to lie on his owner there. Saints adore people, especially their loved ones, and getting one to sit on his owner and lick his face is not difficult!

## AN INTERESTING ACCIDENT

We recently had a young maiden Mastiff bitch accidentally bred by an aged $10\frac{1}{2}$-year-old Saint Bernard of smooth variety. Although the incident was tragic in one respect, I looked forward to finding out which breed was dominant. I predicted that the Mastiff would reign supreme, and never doubted that all puppies would be smooth-coated with the coloring of the Mastiff. Eight live puppies were

Adelaide's Pal of Berncrest, owned by Dr. and Mrs. W. M. Bartlett, of Jersey City, N.J. Pal is pictured at 15 months of age on January 19, 1932.

The best smooth-coated Saint Bernard at the Westminster Dog show in 1935 was this male, owned by the Hercuveen Kennels.

whelped and raised. All had brindle or apricot coloring with velvet black muzzles. None had Saint coloring or markings, and all heads were chiseled, broad, and simply magnificent. The litter was so beautiful no one could believe they were half-breeds. Veterinarians insisted they were pure bred Mastiffs, and so did several Mastiff fanciers.

In following the litter's growth, no undershot bites have developed; fronts and rears are like iron and broad as a breeder's dream, and size is excellent. I'm quite sure these dogs could be shown and fool any judge or Mastiff breeder alive today! This, I feel, proves our Saint's ancestry. The Mastiff breed undeniably took the leading role in the development of our Saint Bernards of

International Champion Kavalier von Grossglockner, owned by W. A. Fisher of Detroit, Mich., and pictured here in May, 1929.

today. The two dogs are so similar in temperament and conformation, it's too bad the Saint can't help the Mastiff of today, like the Mastiff once helped the Saint of yesterday. For as old as the Mastiff is, he is in deep trouble in many areas. So too is our Saint, but interestingly enough, for very different reasons.

## EARLY SWISS SAINT CLUBS AND BREEDERS

Breedings were exchanged between valley dogs and the Hospice dogs from about 1670 until late 1800 and still occasionally carried on today. In 1884, Henry Schumacher printed the newly founded Swiss Kennel Club's first edition, which covered correct breeding practices. The short-haired Hospice-type Saint was more prized, better known, and sought out by Schumacher for the pure Saint characteristics. Some of these dogs were sold to England and Russia and eventually other parts of the world. Schumacher was a pioneer in the breed.

Nine-month-old Algonquin's Hob V. Schwarzwald and three-year-old John Foley, son of Sandra and Bob Foley, owners of the Algonquin Kennels, Plattsburgh, N.Y.

## SAINTS ARRIVE IN ENGLAND

The first Saint brought to England was Lion, in 1810. He was very large, light in color, and later painted by Landseer.

The first exhibition of Saint Bernards took place in England, and a long-haired dog named Plinlimmon won the prize, thus beginning the long-haired variety's popularity.

Von Lotten kennels was started in 1925 by Otto Steiner at Muhen, Aargua. At this time a bitch, Meta von Lotten, was considered faultless, and soon received the title of world champion. Mr. Steiner became winner of the title World Champion Breeder. Meta's future litters were sold throughout the world. Another famous kennel was Zwing-Uri, owned by Charles Sigrist at Fluelen.

On the bench at the Bryn Mawr Kennel Club show is Ch. Beau of Highmont, CD, with Mrs. Jane Sheahan.

The Ohio Saint Bernard Club show in Cincinnati, Ohio, on June 24, 1950 saw Also V.D. Roth win Best of Breed. The judge was Stanley H. Bussinger, and the handler was Paul Hertzbrun for owner John M. Friend of Milwaukee, Wis.

This kennel is responsible for good exports to most countries of the world, including the USA. The Von Rigi kennels, Von Sood, and von Immenberg also produced many excellent dogs.

## GERMANY AND ITS BREEDERS OF THE PAST

The first Saint club was founded in Munich in 1891. The promotion of the breed in Germany was due primarily to men like Dr. Caster of Winkle, Rheingau, Prince Albricht of Solmes and Premier Lt. Fink. Germany exhibited only long-haired Saints at this time. Smooths were barely represented, making quality at its lowest with none conforming to standard. Of 40 dogs entered in Hanover in 1882, only six were considered purebreds, and these left much to be desired.

Other famous breeders in Germany at that time were G. Schmidtbauer, Dr. Toelle, R. F. Curry, Bubat, Guerteler, Kohn,

The great Ch. Harvey's Zwingo Barri v. Banz (on extreme left) winning the Stud Dog Class at a National Specialty show under Judge Maxwell Riddle. Owner-handled by Grace J. Harvey.

Boppel, Max Naether, and Kempel. The first stud book published in Germany in 1894 listed 175 short-haired and 126 long-haired dogs. Germany deserves much credit in the development and improvement of the breed, while suffering great setbacks during World Wars I and II. Famous kennels in the late 1800s were Altoona, Von Falkenstein in 1909, and Grossglockner in 1914, among others.

It is remarkable that the breed survived in Germany during the war years, when money was worthless, food was nearly impossible to get and great dogs were shot or starved to death. A handful of German breeders is responsible for saving the finest specimens and getting them through at all costs—just like great art, the famous Lippizan horses, or a country's costliest treasures. That story is still untold, but the courage and determination of those men are evident in Germany's dogs today. The excellent type, size, soundness and disposition were not lost.

## ENGLAND AND ITS SAINT BERNARDS

England was importing dogs from Switzerland in the early 1900s. With Mastiffs reigning supreme in England, many Saints were crossed with English Mastiffs in the hope of getting a bigger and taller Mastiff. Saints with the fawn Mastiff coloring were preferred. Famous dogs of the day were Fred Gresham's Abbess,

Mr. Sone's Barry, Mr. Macdona's Tell, as well as Plinlimmon, Bayard, and Sir Bedivere.

Saints soon rose to first in popularity and Collies and Saints were considered the dogs to own. Thus, big prices were asked and received, with Sir Bedivere being sold to Americans for a reported $7,000. After the breed reached its high in popularity, it then began to deteriorate quickly. The Saints of Britain are quite different from those of Switzerland, Germany, and American dogs of today, since they conform to a different Standard than ours. Size is of utmost importance. Dogs of superior height are prized, regardless of soundness. The red haw is also correct in English

Champion Bryjon's Damocles von Kris, Saint Bernard owned by Dr. and Mrs. E. E. Breyfogle, is pictured winning Best in Show at the Essex County Kennel Club show on July 20, 1957. Judge was Mr. John Lundberg and the handler is Tom Ashburn.

dogs, where it is definitely objectionable in the Swiss standard. Some English breeders of today are trying to develop the true Swiss Saint, but England in general breeds its own type of Saint Bernard, and few of these are seen in this country.

## FIRST SAINTS AND BREEDERS IN USA

Saints began to be registered and bred in America as early as the late 1800s, and the breed soon began to attract big money and many fanciers. The staggering number of 151 was shown at New York in 1890 and some of the world's finest dogs were being imported into the United States.

A dog named Hector appears many times in early pedigrees. Hector was a smooth-coated dog, and was imported from Switzerland to the Hospice kennels of New Jersey. Most of the earliest kennels and breeders are no longer in existence. Better known kennels that have dogs around today are Sunny Slopes of Stamford, Conn. owned by Mr. and Mrs. Howard Parker; Highmont Kennels of Philadelphia, owned by Mr. and Mrs. Stanley Bussinger; the Edelweiss Kennels of Springfield, Ill., owned by Joseph Fleischli; Powell's Kennels located in Pittston, Pa., operated by Laurence Powell, and Sanctuary Woods Kennels in Drain, Oregon, owned by Mrs. Beatrice Knight. Of the above kennels, Sunny Slopes, Sanctuary Woods, and Powell Kennels are still operated by their original owners. Edelweiss Kennels is trying to make a comeback through the daughter of Joseph Fleischli, but the original stock is, of course, gone and Mr. Fleischli has passed away.

## FAMOUS AMERICAN FOUNDATION KENNELS

Edelweiss Kennels in Springfield, Ill. played a great part in the rock-bottom foundation of our breed here in America. It is identified with such imported and famous dogs as Franzi v Edelweiss, Champion Gerd v d Lueg v Edelweiss, winner of numerous Bests in Show. Champion Gero Oenz v Edelweiss was another Best in Show dog, as well as Helma Oenz v Edelweiss and Bella v Menzberg.

It's interesting to note that Mr. Fleischli brought considerable attention to the Saint Bernard breed when it was considered down and out, although all his famous dogs were imported and not actually bred by him. Mr. Fleischli was devoted to the breed, and if

American and Canadian Champion and Swiss import Kobi v. Steinernhof. Imported from Switzerland as a puppy, Kobi, now deceased, was owned by Charles Cawker of Kobi Kennels in Canada. A large, typey smooth, of deep rich coloring and majestic personality, he remains one of the breed's outstanding producers.

A rough Obedience trained dog, owned by Ed Rodel,
Von Sauliamt Kennels, Switzerland.

Scene from the famed Zwing Yuri Kennels (of the past) in Switzerland.

Arko, headstudy of rough Saint Bernard in Germany.

Swiss import International Ch. Anton v. Hofli, now deceased, was owned by Dr. Antonio Morsiani of Italy.

Beautiful kennels of Ernst Appel, in Germany.

Saints in the Kennels of Del Soccorso, Dr. A. Morsianni, Italy.

Ch. Lorenz v. Liebiwil, owned by Dr. Antonio Marsiani, Italy, was 36½ inches tall and weighed 215 pounds.

Zenta vom Bismarkturm, a German-bred bitch owned by A. Morsiani of Italy.

Saints in Germany prepare for entering the ring. Center bitch is International Ch. Ulla, who was later exported to the USA.

Herrn Koch with Ledoc, his companion, in Germany.

Saint breeders and how they transport their Saints to dog shows in Germany.

German-bred Saints traveling in a van to the shows.

Valdo vom Bismarckturm, Germany, stands 36 inches high and weighs 216 pounds.

Ed Rodel of the famous Sauliamt Kennels with one of his dogs.

Ch. Sanctuary Woods Gulliver with his breeder, Mrs. Beatrice Knight, in 1962.

At the Middle Atlantic Saint Bernard Club's Specialty held December 10, 1960, Ch. Morgan's Echo of Hillcrest (left) is handled by owner, Laurence Powell of Pittston, Pa. Morgan was an important sire and producer of quality during his lifetime.

At the Beverly Hills Kennel Club Show, January, 1970, Brood Bitch class winner Charlinore's Grand Ursula (left) is shown with her three sons, Patrich's Flaming Ember (also Winners Dog and Best of Winners at the show), handled by breeder Dick Wiggins, Patrich's Forward Pass, handled by owner Frank Aitken, and Patrich's Fat Albert, handled by owner Merry Prestidge.

Ch. Subira Casper the Viking, top winning Saint Bernard in 1968 and 1969. Subira is owned by Eleanor Keaton, wife of the famed and beloved comic Buster Keaton. Casper's record at the time was 126 Bests of Breed, 80 Group placings, 1 Best in Show win.

Pat Wiggins with her 1970 Winners Bitch at the National Specialty, Orange Empire Dog Club Show, Calif. Ch. Charlinore's Grand Ursula was judged by O. M. Capodice for a 5-point major.

46

American and Canadian Ch. Beau Cheval's Mt. Lesa Mardoug, owned by Bruce and Marilyn Chapman of Willow Point Saints in Milford, Mich., is daughter of Ch. Illo vom Vogelheim and out of Ch. Beau Cheval's Mt. Alisia. A huge smooth bitch, with heavy bone, substance and type, Lesa is now a proven dam. She was bred by M. J. Anderson.

(Center) Ch. Roca's Image of Zee, awaiting inspection by the judge.

Ch. Beau Cheval's Golden Ceasar, owned by Leslie Golden of Bala Cynwyd, Pa., was Winners Dog and Best of Winners at a National Specialty. Bred by M. J. Anderson, he was sired by Ch. Beau Cheval's Tablo and out of J.I's Little Gypsey. Judge is James Trullinger.

Portrait of another Saint Bernard from the kennels of Beatrice Knight—
Ch. Sanctuary Woods Four Winds.

Baron von Peppy, son of Ch. Kobi von Steinernhof II and Ch. Beau Cheval's Tia Maria, is owned by Fritz Haffner, Drums, Pa. Baron is a proven sire. Here, he's handled by David Saylor.

Ch. Beau Cheval's Della La Mardoug, taking a 4-point win under Specialist Judge John Stanek, handled by Harold Deitch. Ch. Della, a feminine splash-coated rough, was sired by Ch. Rogerlyn's Duke, and out of Mugs. Bred and owned by M. J. Anderson, Della is the dam of many show dogs.

American and Canadian Ch. Treu von Meister, owned by Bruce and Marilyn Chapman, Willow Point Saints, Milford, Mich., is a large typey male and proven sire. Treu possesses a rich red mahogany coloring, with black mask and shaded black ears.

Ch. Roca's Image of Zee, typey son of Beau Cheval's Tapan Zee II, handler-owner Michael Borheady, Flemington, N.J. Judge Gail Devine.

Ch. Powell's Jed-Loki von Erik, sired by Powell's Erik von Echo, and out of Miss Jill of Cedarwood, was bred by Laurence Powell and is owned by Margaret Hudson of Virginia. Jed is a tall dog of excellent substance.

Hans Zimmerli, head of the Swiss Saint Bernard Club, is pictured with two Saints at the Bryn Mawr Kennel Club Show in 1969. He judged for the Middle Atlantic Kennel Club Specialty that year.

New England Saint Bernard Specialty show in June of 1961 with Judge
Ben Hoyt officiating found Ch. Chriss Robin of Shady Hollow with
owner Martha Willard; Ch. Golden-Gal of Shady Hollow with Frank
Smith, handler for Shady Hollow Kennels; Ch. Mr. Sandman of Shady
Hollow with owner Richard Jackson and Ch. Queen O'Sheba of Shady
Hollow, CD, with owner Alfred Saba, Jr. Queen O'Sheba finished for
her Companion Dog title in three straight shows and was top-winning
Saint Bernard Bitch for 1961. Breeder is Phyllis Jackson Smith.

Best of Breed at the New England Saint Bernard Club Specialty show in
1958 at Framingham, Mass., was Ch. Otto Count von Langenbruck,
bred and owned by Club President Edward A. Poor, and handled by
William Trainor. The judge is Stanley Bussinger.

Champion Ridiculous Nicholas and friend, owned by Bruce Crabb.

he had lived, no doubt he would have made great contributions through breeding, since he was one of the most knowledgeable men in Saint Bernards at the time. He will be remembered as a pioneer in our breed in America.

H. Heilman of Vermillion, Ohio, started a famous line of Saints, beginning with smooth imports, Champion Aline v d Roth, Maida v Alpine Plateau, and others. Mr. and Mrs. A. F. Hayes are responsible for the importing of excellent Swiss stock. Their famous Alpine Plateau kennels provided the foundation for many leading kennels today. Mrs. Beatrice Knight started with a fine import and bitch from this kennel, and the Dolomount Kennels of New York also started with Alpine Plateau stock.

We must not overlook the great and much talked about elegant rough of the day, International Champion and Sieger, Rasko v d Reppisch-Waldeck, which was owned by the Waldeck Kennels of Pennsylvania. This male is still considered by many as the greatest Saint of all time.

Sunny Slopes Kennels of Mr. and Mrs. Howard P. Parker, Webbs Hill Rd. Stamford, Conn., owned two famous Swiss imports, Siegerin Fortuna vom Rigi, and Champion Falco vom Rigi, her brother. These two smooths were imported from the famous Rigi Kennels of Switzerland. Another beautiful smooth, Falco vom Rigi, was owned by a Kurt Diederich, of Allandale, N.J. Mr. and Mrs. Stanley Bussinger, who operated Highmont Kennels for many years in Philadelphia, owned two excellent imported smooths, Minka v Immenberg, and Champion Major v Neu-Hapsburg.

In the midwest, Miss Odessa Llewellyn, of Waukee, Iowa, owned a rough Swiss import Champion Joggi-Oenz v Edelweiss.

The first Saint kennel registered by the American Kennel Club is reported to be Carmen Kennels, owned by T. E. Kemp, a professional animal photographer. His daughter, Mrs. Harold

June of 1956. At the National Specialty held in conjunction with the Delaware County Kennel Club, Judge Arthur Hesser awards Best of Breed to the Stanley Bussinger's Ch. Faust von Melina and Best Opposite Sex to Mrs. Jacklyn Reidl's lovely bitch. Pictured in the center is the coveted Gould Perpetual Trophy, and as usual, the charming young ladies in Swiss costume.

Holmes, continues to run the Carmen Kennels which is highly respected for its long dedication to our breed, and still produces excellent stock for young kennels throughout the USA.

Gottlieb Zulliger, a Swiss, had Saints all of his lifetime, and traveled throughout Europe and America, finally settling in Monroe, Wis., where he started the Alpcraft Kennel in 1910. Mr. Zulliger and his wife owned many fine specimens of our breed.

In 1962, American Kennel Club registrations for Saints totaled 2,459 which was a 30 per cent increase over 1961. Our beloved breed has been rising in popularity ever since!

## EARLY SAINT BERNARD BREEDERS AND THEIR GREAT DOGS

Laurence Powell and his wife, Marian, (who passed away in early 1970) owned many great stud dogs that are behind some of America's greatest show dogs of today. Mr. Powell was a perfectionist in the ring, and handled his dogs like an artist. Even today, he instills fear into anyone who knows his fine record of finished champions: when he enters the ring . . . watch out!

Beginning with his famous champion King Laddie Rasko Whitebread, bred by Norman F. Keller, we see the beautiful type associated with the Powell dogs of today. This fine dog is seen strongly in Mr. Powell's most recent Champion, (the late) Powell's Magus von Echo, and his immediate offspring, thus proving his dominance in the Powell line. Powell's Romeo Rasko, a son of Ch. King Laddie, was bred and owned by Mr. Powell, as was Ch. O'Brien's King Rasko, and Champion Powell's Little John, a grandson of Champion King Laddie.

Champion Powell's Rolf of Riga was a magnificent smooth, little appreciated for his worth as a stud dog, yet prized in a pedigree today. Champion Rolf was bred by David and Sue Taylor, of LeRoy N.Y. owners of another fine kennel, "Riga." Rolf goes back to the best of Brownhelm Kennels in Ohio. Mr. Powell also owned the impressive Champion Lee v Alpine Plateau, bred by the famous Alpine Plateau Kennels of Oregon, that produced Champion Powell's Laurette Lee and Champion Powell's Lady Lee, both bred by Benjamin D. Hoyt, but owned by the Powells.

Champion Lion D'Or was another fine rough son of Ch. Lee, who was winning steadily in 1951 and 1952. Champions Powell's

Jack Sheahan and Bernardo Rasko of Highmont, photographed in 1949.

Nina B., Morgan's Echo of Hillcrest, and Powell's Tristan of Riga, could impress any visitor to the Powell's kennels in the sixties. Champion Morgan was bred by C. and G. Morgan, and went on to be Mr. Powell's favorite dog in more ways than one. His huge son, Ch. Tristan weighed in at 217, when he won Best of Breed at the New England Saint Bernard Club's Specialty years ago. He was also a consistent producer of champions, like his sire, Morgan, which continues to appear in champion's pedigrees across the country.

Mrs. Beatrice Knight of Drain, Oregon, remains the queen of dog breeders today, certainly reigning above everyone else in Saint Bernard champions, having produced 100 or more show dogs. She has always been devoted to her dogs and to the betterment of the breed.

Mrs. Knight is greatly admired, and a true pioneer in the breed. Her famous Sanctuary Woods Kennels is a must visit for all would-be breeders, and her humility and hospitality are unsurpassed. Famous dogs include Champions Sanctuary Woods' Gulliver, Sanctuary Woods' Fantabulous, Sanctuary Woods' Four Winds, Sanctuary Woods' Attaboy, Sanctuary Woods' You Lucky Boy, Sanctuary Woods' Sheer Genius, Sanctuary Woods' Going My Way, and on and on and on. The names are beautiful, to match the dogs, and I salute the great lady who dwarfs us all in breeding champions abounding with type.

Champion Harvey's Zwingo Barri v Banz's name still excites many a breeder, especially in the Midwest, where he served as the foundation dog for many a show kennel. Mrs. Grace Harvey

Ch. Dawrob's Lord Brandy, a tall, mantled smooth, owned and handled by Fred Andersen, Woodbury, N.J.

Ch. Sanctuary Woods Going My Way with his owner Mrs. Holt.

made great strides in the breed in the middle fifties, against much competition. Handling her own dogs capably and with professional air, Mrs. Harvey made her famous Zwingo a Best in Show Saint, when few Saints were winning such honors. I never saw the dog, but those who did say they will never forget his gorgeous red flowing coat and impressive stance in the ring.

Mrs. Harvey went on to breed many rough champions, since she did not use smooths in her breeding program. Some of her better

The Ohio Saint Bernard Club Specialty show held at Gates Mills, Ohio, in August of 1952 saw Dr. and Mrs. E. E. Breyfogle's smooth Heilman's Julia von Gerd take the coveted Best of Breed award. Handler is George V. Rood. The Breyfogles are from Massillon, Ohio.

known Champions are: Zwinghof Valerie v Zwing, Zwinghof Tawny Luck v Zwingo, Zwingh of Xesbo v Gero's Wonna, Zwinghof Moon Minx, Zwinghof Wonna Joggi, Zwinghof Jeannen v Xesbo, Zwinghof Jumbo v Xesbo, and Zwinghof Quicksilver. The most famous after his grandsire's death was her Champion Zwinghof Golden Eagle v Jumbo, who under the guidance of owners, Mr. and Mrs. William Cooley, went on to place in many groups and Bests in Show. Mrs. Harvey is reportedly no longer breeding Saints, but her name will live on through her many rough champions and their offspring.

Herman Peabody chose the name "Brownhelm" for his Saint Bernards, since it was the name of the county in which he lived.

He never bred large numbers of dogs, but owned many famous and important foundation dogs for our breed today. Some of the dogs he owned and exhibited in the fifties and sixties were: Champions Mr. Jody of Brownhelm, Queen of Brownhelm, Rebecca of Brownhelm, Hilda's Helga of Brownhelm, Sweet Sue of Brownhelm, Mr. Topper of Brownhelm, Subira's Crackerjody (which later became Subira's foundation stud dog), and Ch. Samson Redoubtable. Some others he showed and owned were Champions Heilman's Hilda v Gerd v d Lueg, Heilman's Kris v Gero, Heilman's Julia v Gerd, Lady Agnes of Agony Acres, Kristina Annabelle, and others too numerous to list here. Mr. Peabody remains dedicated to the breed and is active in club work.

Of the aforementioned greats in our breed, Mr. Powell and Mr. Peabody are active Specialty judges today. I would like to see all

Champion Cavajone's Prince Charming, owned and bred by Bruce Crabb, Cavajone Kennels, Merrimack, N.H.

these people judging and passing on their vast knowledge to younger and less experienced Saint Bernard owners.

## SAINT BERNARD CLUBS THROUGHOUT THE USA

Saint Bernard Clubs can be found in most parts of the United States, with some states having more than one to help our fancy and breed. One of the oldest and most active is the Middle Atlantic Saint Bernard Club, which was founded by Stanley and Sarah Bussinger of Philadelphia. This club is one of the few that holds two Specialties each year, and certainly the first to do so.

A complete list of Saint Bernard clubs throughout the United States may be obtained by contacting the Secretary of the Saint Bernard Club of America. The address may be obtained through the American Kennel Club.

Champion Little John and Champion Cavajone's Crabb's Queen, both owned and bred by Bruce Crabb, Cavajone Kennels, N.H. Full brother and sister, they are from the first litter bred by Mr. Crabb and are pictured above winning at the Eastern Dog Club show in 1961.

The Saint Bernard Club of America Specialty show on June 1, 1963, found Champion Switzer of Shady Hollow Best of Breed. Switzer was also Best of Breed at Westminster Kennel Club show in 1964. Switzer is handled to this win under Judge Alfred Le Pine, by Jane Kamp Forsyth, for owner-breeder Phyllis Jackson Smith of the Shady Hollow Kennels, Johnston, R.I.

## A BRIEF HISTORY OF THE NATIONAL CLUB

Earliest records of the Saint Bernard Club of America are missing. We do know, however, that the original club was organized on February 22, 1888, and that the International Standard of that time was adopted to govern the breed in this country.

The original club was still active in 1892, in which year there was published by the club a small book containing the Standard, By-Laws, and a roster of officers and members, totaling 68 in all. This club was dissolved on September 15, 1897, and a new Saint Bernard Club of America organized at Grand Rapids, Michigan on December

30th of the same year. Col. Jacob Ruppert, Jr., was elected president; Dudley Waters was secretary-treasurer.

At the club's first annual meeting in New York on February 21, 1898, Mr. Waters was instructed to send copies of Constitution and By-Laws to The American Kennel Club, with application and fee for membership, making the Saint Bernard Club of America one of the oldest "member clubs" of the A.K.C.

In the following year, Col. Ruppert gave a silver cup to the club, and in 1901 President Frank Jay Gould presented a silver punch bowl to be known as the Gould Challenge Trophy. Both trophies are still in active circulation within the club. The Gould Challenge Trophy is presented annually for Best of Breed (member only) at the national specialty show, and the Ruppert Cup for Best of Opposite Sex (members only) at the same show. It is interesting to note that Col. Ruppert served the club as president intermittently over a period of more than 30 years.

The club was again reorganized in 1932 under the guidance of LeRoy E. Fess, who became editor of The Saint Fancier. In 1933, Joseph H. Fleischli became president of the reorganized club. In 1935, the club held its first Specialty Show in conjunction with the old Morris and Essex Kennel Club in New Jersey.

Club activities gradually waned until still another reorganization took place in 1943, the By-Laws being changed to encourage the formation of local affiliated breed clubs. Membership of local clubs as such, however, was discontinued in 1962 when the present Constitution and By-Laws were adopted by the membership.

The Saint Bernard Club of America was incorporated as a non-profit organization under the laws of the State of Ohio in 1954. Its current membership is over 500. The breed itself currently ranks in the "Top Ten," based on annual registrations by The American Kennel Club.

# CHAPTER 2

# AMERICAN KENNEL CLUB STANDARD FOR THE BREED

GENERAL—Powerful, proportionately tall figure, strong and muscular in every part, with powerful head and most intelligent expression. In dogs with a dark mask the expression appears more stern, but never ill-natured.

HEAD—Like the whole body, very powerful and imposing. The massive skull is wide, slightly arched and the sides slope in a gentle curve into the very strongly developed, high cheek bones. Occiput only moderately developed. The supra-orbital ridge is very strongly developed and forms nearly a right angle with the horizontal axis of the head. Deeply imbedded between the eyes and starting at the root of the muzzle, a furrow runs over the whole skull. It is strongly marked in the first half, gradually disappearing toward the base of the occiput. The lines at the sides of the head diverge considerably from the outer corner of the eyes toward the back of the head. The skin of the forehead, above the eyes, forms rather noticeable wrinkles, more or less pronounced, which converge toward the furrow. Especially when the dog is in action, the wrinkles are more visible without in the least giving the impression of morosity. Too strongly developed wrinkles are not desired. The slope from the skull to the muzzle is sudden and rather steep.

The muzzle is short, does not taper, and the vertical depth at the root of the muzzle must be greater than the length of the muzzle. The bridge of the muzzle is not arched, but straight; in some dogs, occasionally, slightly broken. A rather wide, well-marked, shallow furrow runs from the root of the muzzle over the entire bridge of the muzzle to the nose. The flews of the upper jaw are strongly developed, not sharply cut, but turning in a beautiful curve into the lower edge, and slightly overhanging. The flews of the lower jaw must not be deeply pendant. The teeth should be sound and

Beau Cheval's Rommel Mardoug, short-haired son of Ch. Illo v. Vogel-heim x Beau Cheval's Toffe Mardoug. Owned by Juan Gonzalez and M. J. Anderson. Rommel resides in Michigan with his owner.

strong and should meet in either a scissors or an even bite; the scissors bite being preferable. The undershot bite, although some-times found with good specimens, is not desirable. The overshot bite is a fault. A black roof to the mouth is desirable.

NOSE (Schwamm)—Very substantial, broad, with wide open nostrils, and, like the lips, always black.

EARS—Of medium size, rather high set, with very strongly developed burr (Muschel) at the base. They stand slightly away from the head at the base, then drop with a sharp bend to the side and cling to the head without a turn. The flap is tender and forms a rounded triangle, slightly elongated toward the point, the front edge lying firmly to the head, whereas the back edge may stand somewhat away from the head, especially when the dog is at attention. Lightly set ears, which at the base immediately cling to the head, give it an oval and too little marked exterior, whereas a strongly developed base gives the skull a squarer, broader and much more expressive appearance.

EYES—Set more to the front than the sides, are of medium size, dark brown, with intelligent, friendly expression, set moderately deep. The lower eyelids, as a rule, do not close completely and, if that is the case, form an angular wrinkle toward the inner corner of the eye. Eyelids which are too deeply pendant and show

Head study of Ch. Alpler's Fancy Dandy, 16 months old. Owned and bred by Alpler Kennels, Leavenworth, Kansas.

conspicuously the lachrymal glands, or a very red, thick haw, and eyes that are too light, are objectionable.

NECK—Set high, very strong and in action is carried erect. Otherwise horizontally or slightly downward. The junction of head and neck is distinctly marked by an indentation. The nape of the neck is very muscular and rounded at the sides which makes the neck appear rather short. The dewlap of throat and neck is well-pronounced: too strong development, however, is not desirable.

SHOULDERS—Sloping and broad, very muscular and powerful. The withers are strongly pronounced.

CHEST—Very well arched, moderately deep, not reaching below the elbows.

BACK—Very broad, perfectly straight as far as the haunches, from there gently sloping to the rump, and merging imperceptibly into the root of the tail.

HINDQUARTERS—Well-developed. Legs very muscular.

BELLY—Distinctly set off from the very powerful loin section, only little drawn up.

TAIL—Starting broad and powerful directly from the rump is long, very heavy, ending in a powerful tip. In repose it hangs straight down, turning gently upward in the lower third only, which is not considered a fault. In a great many specimens the tail is carried with the edge slightly bent and therefore hangs down in the shape of an f. In action all dogs carry the tail more or less turned upward. However it may not be carried too erect or by any means rolled over the back. A slight curling of the tip is sooner admissible.

FOREARMS—Very powerful and extraordinarily muscular.

FORELEGS—Straight, strong.

HIND LEGS—Hocks of moderate angulation. Dewclaws are not desired; if present, they must not obstruct gait.

FEET—Broad, with strong toes, moderately closed, and with rather high knuckles. The so-called dewclaws which sometimes occur on the inside of the hind legs are imperfectly developed toes. They are of no use to the dog and are not taken into consideration in judging. They may be removed by surgery.

COAT—Very dense, short-haired (stockhaarig), lying smooth, tough, without however feeling rough to the touch. The thighs are slightly bushy. The tail at the root has longer and denser hair

EARS: Size medium; rather high-set; strongly developed burr; flap tender; stand away from head at base, drop with sharp bend, front edge clinging to head; square, broad appearance

TEETH: sound, strong; even bite or scissors (more desirable); undershot not desirable but overshot a fault; black mouth roof desirable

EYES: Size moderate; dark brown; lower eyelids form angular wrinkle toward inner corner; not too pendant

STOP: deep, sudden

NOSE: substantial, broad; nostrils, well-dilated; black

MUZZLE: short, depth good; does not taper; bridge straight; flews on upper jaw strongly developed; gracefully curved, overhanging; furrow from stop runs length of; muzzle bridge; lower flews not pendant; lips black; clearly noticeable

CHEST: well-arched; moderately deep; not below elbows

FEET: broad; toes strong; well-closed; hindlegs rather high

FOREARMS: very powerful; extremely muscular

HEIGHT (minimum): males 27½; females 25½

COLOR: White with red, red with white; red various shades; brindle patches; w/r markings. Never one color or without white

BODY: powerful, strong, muscular

FORELEGS: straight, strong

HEAD: powerful, imposing; fairly over forehead skin imbedded between eyes; runs back toward occiput

SKULL: massive, wide, slightly arched, sloping at sides; cheek bones well-developed; occiput slightly developed; forehead skin wrinkled

WITHERS: strongly defined

BACK: very broad; straight; gentle slope to rump

SHOULDERS: sloping, broad; very muscular, powerful

NECK: very strong; set on high; carried erect in action or horizontal; muscular; round at sides; distinct indentation marks junction of head and neck; dewlap well-pronounced

TAIL: long, heavy; bushy; root broad; tapering to blunt end; straight down in repose; lower third gently curving; more or less turned-up in action but never too erect or rolled over back

HIND LEGS: slightly bent at hocks; dewclaws not desired; if present, must not obstruct gait

COAT: dense, shorthaired; tough, lying smooth; not rough to touch. Two varieties; longhaired and shorthaired

HINDQUARTERS: well-developed; thighs powerful; very muscular

which gradually becomes shorter toward the tip. The tail appears bushy, not forming a flag.

COLOR—White with red or red with white, the red in its various shades; brindle patches with white markings. The colors red and brown-yellow are of entirely equal value. Necessary markings are: white chest, feet and tip of tail, nose band, collar or spot on the nape; the latter and blaze are very desirable. Never of one color or without white. Faulty are all other colors, except the favorite dark shadings on the head (mask) and ears. One distinguishes between mantle dogs and splash-coated dogs.

HEIGHT AT SHOULDER—Of the dog should be $27\frac{1}{2}$ inches minimum, of the bitch $25\frac{1}{2}$ inches. Female animals are of finer and more delicate build.

Considered as faults are all deviations from the standard, as for instance a sway-back and a disproportionately long back, hocks too much bent, straight hindquarters, upward growing hair in spaces between the toes, out at elbows, cowhocks and weak pasterns.

## LONGHAIRED

The longhaired type completely resembles the shorthaired type except for the coat which is not shorthaired (stockhaarig) but of medium length plain to slightly wavy, never rolled or curly and not shaggy either. Usually, on the back, especially from the region of the haunches to the rump, the hair is more wavy, a condition, by the way, that is slightly indicated in the shorthaired dogs. The tail is bushy with dense hair of moderate length. Rolled or curly hair on the tail is not desirable. A tail with parted hair, or a flag tail, is faulty. Face and ears are covered with short and soft hair; longer hair at the base of the ear is permissible. Forelegs only slightly feathered; thighs very bushy.

*Approved* May 12, 1959

# CHAPTER 3

# A EUROPEAN STANDARD
# OF THE BREED

Albert de la Rie in his book *One Hundred Years of the Saint Bernard*, wrote a marvelous description of the breed characteristics of the Saint Bernard dog, which we feel is worth reprinting in this book. With his kind permission we reprint it in its entirety:

**BREED CHARACTERISTICS**

(With permission of Albert de la Rie, from his book: Pages 18–25 *One Hundred Years of the St. Bernard.*)

The Swiss breed of St. Bernard dog is named after the St. Bernard mountain, the location of the breed's historic activity. The St. Bernard dog's characteristics were fundamentally advised by the Kynological Congress on June 2, 1887 in Zurich for the breeding of such, were established, accepted, and were officially published in SHSB 1889. The official Stud Book of the Club is the SHSB.

1. GENERAL—Powerful, tall, in all parts strong and muscular figure, with mighty head and most intelligent facial expression. In dogs with a dark mask, the expression appears more stern, but never ill-natured.

We do not find herein anything about proportions or relationships between the various body parts, even though this is very important. The relationships must be the same, whether the dog is tall or small, and they are difficult to present. The length must be at least 75 cm for a minimum height of a dog of 70 cm. The height is understood from the highest point of the shoulder to the ground, the length is the distance from the chest to the rear end. Bitches may be somewhat lower, but they have to have the correct relationship as already mentioned. An "intelligent facial expression" is also difficult to define, similarly a "noble facial expression." These two characteristics are noticed exclusively by good breeders and judges. Probably "stern expression" (serious expression) is the correct description, although more than only the facial expression goes with the so-called "nobility." It is remarkable that the word "noble" does not appear in any description whereby every breeder and judge must know that "noble" is the singular quality, which can make a champion dog. In my opinion, it is of lesser importance that the expression must never be ill-natured, but it is important that the dog is not actually ill-natured. This characteristic must never be allowed and leads to disqualification in the ring.

Under this heading also belong the descriptives "TYPE" and "NOBILITY" which are not mentioned in the Standard.

*Basic Form* is meant, when one speaks of type. Thus not only the head is decisive for the type, but the head is certainly a measure for the determination, whether the dog has a good or a bad type. Further determining type is the structure, because for the St. Bernard this is fundamentally different from other breeds due to the bones, the front and the hindquarters. If the head type is not quite correct, the dog will never belong to the best and he will never become a champion, even if he gaits ever so nicely. Just as important is the so-called "Nobility." Nobility is a summary word, the sum total of all good qualities in an animal. Eyes, eye color, and expression belong in this absolutely. St. Bernards have a wise and friendly expression. The eyes are located moderately deep. The lower lids do not close completely as a rule and form angular folds toward the inner corners of the eyes. This is clearly described under item 5 of the STANDARD and should be considered much more. A somewhat lighter eye should not be a reason for a disqualification, mainly the expression should be considered, which can still appear very friendly and noble even with light eyes. The mask is desirable, but the animal remains, even without a mask, a St. Bernard who will be judged in a show on the basis of his other qualities. We find no word in the Standard about dogs with white or almost white heads. This is probably due to the fact that many good early dogs had either white or half marked heads. This should not be a reason for disqualification even today. It is left to each judge to give preference to the better, nicer marked head, the deciding quality being the correct shape of the head. A white or half white head with the better type is to be preferred to a dog with a nice mask but with not as good a head shape.

A nice head study of Sandra and Bob Foley's Algonquin's Hob V. Schwarzwald.

2. HEAD: like the whole body, very powerful and imposing. The massive skull is wide, slightly arched and the sides slope in a gentle curve into the very strongly developed, high cheek bones. Occiput is only moderately developed.

The famous Swiss import, Figaro v Sauliamt, an American and European CACIB champion, pictured with his ten-day-old son, which was later to become the Canadian Champion Mardonof's Echo of Figaro. Owned by Mary Lou and Donald Dube, Mardonof Kennels.

The supra-orbital ridge is very strongly developed and forms nearly a right angle with the horizontal axis of the head.

Deeply imbedded between the eyes and starting at the root of the muzzle, a furrow runs over the whole skull. It is strongly marked in the first half, gradually disappearing toward the base of the occiput. The lines at the sides of the head diverge considerably from the outer corner of the eyes toward the back of the head.

The skin of the forehead, above the eyes, forms rather noticeable wrinkles, more or less pronounced, which converge toward the furrow. Especially when the dog is in action, the wrinkles are more visible without in the least giving the impression of morosity. Too strongly developed wrinkles are not desired.

The slope from the skull to the muzzle is sudden and rather steep. The muzzle is short, does not taper, and the vertical depth at the root of the muzzle must be greater than the length of the muzzle. The bridge of the muzzle is not arched, but straight; in some dogs, occasionally, slightly broken.

A rather wide, well-marked, shallow furrow runs from the root of the muzzle over the entire bridge of the muzzle to the nose.

The flews of the upper jaw are strongly developed, not sharply cut, but turning in a beautiful curve into the lower edge, and slightly overhanging.

The flews of the lower jaw must not be deeply pendant.

The bite should be strong and is only moderately developed in relationship to the head structure. A black roof of the mouth is desirable.

Where the expression "powerful" is used, the word "imposing" goes with it automatically; thus a dog with too light a head is less desirable. Bitches have a less pronounced head build than dogs, although the head can be as massive under the assumption that the expression must really be sufficient and the skin on the head must not be disturbed by folds, which in the dog are also a minus point, when they are too strongly developed. When the skull does not suddenly slope steeply, a less marked impression is given, and the imposing feature of the head is lost.

A dog without steeply sloped head lines should not be allowed to get into the upper ranks in a show, whereby bitches again may have a less pronounced "STOP" (as it is called), without it being too weakened.

Danny V. Regensberg, a Swiss import owned by Edward Poor.

The muzzle must be short and the given relationship (about 11:8) is important. It must form a nice whole picture in relation to the skull together with a straight bridge of the muzzle. The bridge of the muzzle must not be arched and must not become narrower (conically). Nicely formed round lips improve the quality of the head picture, whereby sharply cut off (pulled back) flews are disadvantageous. The roof of the mouth should not be white, a black roof is desirable. Nevertheless, one sees St. Bernards with a white roof often, and it is the judge's duty to notify the breeder so that he can breed to avoid this drawback. Similarly unesthetically low hanging flews of the lower jaw are to be avoided.

3. THE NOSE: is very substantial, broad, with wide open nostrils, and it should always be black, like the lips. The broad, strong nose must be black inside and any other color results in a disqualification.

4. THE EARS: are of medium size, rather high set, with very strongly developed burr at the base. They stand slightly away from the head at the base, then drop with a sharp bend to the side and cling to the head without a turn (twist). The flap is tender and forms a rounded triangle, slightly elongated toward the point, the front edge lying tightly on the head, whereas the back edge may stand off somewhat, especially when the dog is at attention. Lightly set ears, which immediately at the base line cling to the head, give it an oval and too little marked appearance, whereas a strongly developed ear base provides a squarer, broader and much more expressive appearance. The happy medium is the best here. Too low set ears are to be rejected absolutely, whereas too high set ears (which produce the appearance of a narrower skull) also destroy the whole head image.

5. THE EYES: are set more to the front than the sides, are of medium size, dark brown, with intelligent, friendly expression, set moderately deep; the lower lids, as a rule, do not close completely and form an angular wrinkle toward the inner corner of the eye.

Eye lids, which are too deeply pendant with conspicuously prominent lachrymal glands, or a very red, thick haw, and eyes that are too light, are objectionable.

The eyes provide essential points during the evaluation of the dog, as well as shape, color, and position. They provide the main

Eminent European Judge Albert de la Rie, with Missy, owned by Jack Sheahan, and Poppers, owned by Carol diRosa, when Mr. de la Rie visited the Harrisburg Kennel Club's Show on March 20, 1971.

ingredient of the so-called "nobility," such that every eye fault weighs double of a fault of any other body part.

6. THE NECK: is set high, is very strong and is carried erect in action, otherwise horizontally or slightly lowered. The junction of the head and neck is marked by a distinct furrow. The nape is very muscular and rounded at the sides, which makes the neck appear rather short. The throat and neck dewlap is well pronounced; too strong development, however, is not desirable. A steeply erect neck is undesirable, even in action. I find the American habit of pulling up on the neck disadvantageous, since the neck is normally carried horizontally or slightly lowered. It may be correct for other breeds, but a St. Bernard with a neck and head stretched high up gives a worse impression than one with a slightly lifted or even lowered head. Too strongly developed throat and neck dewlaps are absolutely undesirable.

7. THE SHOULDERS: are sloping and broad, very muscular and powerful. Withers are strongly pronounced.

8. THE CHEST: is very well arched, moderately deep, must not reach below the elbows. It is not mentioned that the chest must be broad, which can be read between the lines from the "general appearance," since when the back has to be broad according to the rules, the same has to apply for the chest. The chest must not reach below the elbows for correct proportion. An insufficiently deep chest results in the whole body not being low enough, and the dog loses much of its imposing appearance. This is also the case for too narrow a chest.

9. THE BACK: very broad, only in the lumbar region very slightly arched, otherwise completely straight up to the hips, from there gently sloping to the rump and imperceptibly merging into the root of the tail. The "very slightly arched" must not degenerate to "not at all," since usually this is the consequence of too weak a back and/or too weak hindquarters. Since the back should be completely straight, a sway-back must not be allowed.

10. HINDQUARTERS: well developed, legs very muscular. Too weakly developed hindquarters disturb the whole image.

11. BELLY: Distinctly set off from the very powerful loin section, only little drawn up. When the loin section is drawn up too tightly, one sees "too much light," as the experts say. Loins must never look like those of greyhounds.

12. THE TAIL: starting broad and powerful directly from the rump, is long, very heavy, ends in a powerful tip and, in repose, hangs down straight, turning slightly upwards in the lower third only, which is not to be considered a fault. In a great many specimens the tail is carried with the end slightly bent and therefore hangs down in the shape of an f. However, it may not be carried too erect or even rolled over the back. A slight curl of the tail tip is sooner admissible. The height of the tail root established how the tail is carried. If it is too high, it will not start evenly from the rump, and then the tail will never be carried hanging down. If it is

Middle Atlantic Saint Bernard Club held in Philadelphia in December of 1953 saw Best of Breed win go to Ch. Major v. Neu-Habsburg, owned by Stanley H. Bussinger. Judge is Arthur Hesser. Jack Sheahan handled. Best of Opposite Sex went to Zilli v. Mullern, on right; Stanley Bussinger, owner-handler.

curled in addition to all the other evils, the whole image is deformed. A curling tail is to be rejected in my opinion just like too light eyes.

13. FOREARM: Very powerful and extraordinarily muscular.

14. FORELEGS: Straight, strong.

15. HINDLEGS: Hocks moderately angulated. Depending on the presence of single or double dewclaws, more or less turning outward with feet, which must not be confused with cow-hocks.

The 1957 Mid-Atlantic Saint Bernard Club Specialty show saw Powell's Little John the Best of Breed winner. Club President John C. Sheahan III poses with Herman Peabody and Laurence Powell and a bevy of trophy presenters dressed in native Swiss costume.

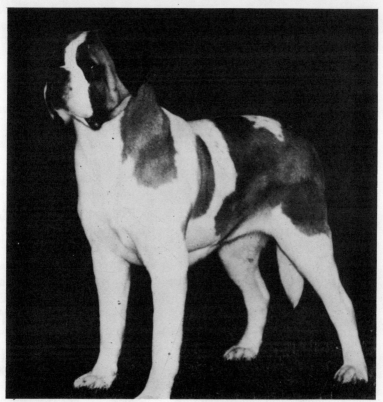

Champion Twoey von Mardonof, owned by Mary Lou and Donald Dube. Twoey was Best of Winners at the 1971 National Specialty show at 17 months of age. She was bred by Carol DiRosa.

16. FEET: Broad, moderately closed, with powerful, rather strongly arched toes. The single or double dew-claws are set low, such that they are positioned almost at the same height as the sole, whereby the pad area is increased and the dog cannot break through a snow surface as easily. Dogs exist, which carry a regularly formed fifth toe (thumb) on the hind feet. The so-called wolves' claws, which sometimes can be found on the inside of the hind feet, are incompletely developed toes and are worthless in use and do not contribute to the evaluation of the dog.

Less is said about the shape of front and hind feet. They should be nicely rounded, with powerful, well arched toes, never so-called "hare feet." Since wolves' claws do not influence judging, they are best removed already in the very young dog (shortly after birth). It is not a fault, but these dewclaws can sometimes cause quite unpleasant problems if they become ingrown. That legs with dew-claws sink less deeply into the snow should not be given in the Standard any more, since it is rather illogical.

Hind legs are "moderately angulated" at the hocks. Let us not blame a dog too quickly, if he is too straight. According to the Standard, hocks as present in German Shepherd dogs are to be rejected. "Straight" means vertical and this is a fault.

17. COAT: is very dense, shorthaired (stockhaarig), lying smooth, firm, but not feeling rough to the touch. Thighs are slightly bushy. The tail at the root has longer and denser hair, which gradually becomes shorter toward the tip. The tail appears bushy not forming a flag.

The coat is not measured with a centimeter measure, but is divided into short and long haired dogs, (rough and smooth coated). Specimens with less short hair can be among rough coated dogs. There is no middle route and when doubt exists, the judge has to ascertain the group into which the dog belongs. The sub-division of short haired dogs into "short-smooth and long-hair (Kurz-Stock und Langhaar)", as it is practiced in Germany, does not conform with the Standard, even though the word ("stock-haarig") appears in the description of "shorthair," but it is given in the same breath, which means that "stockhaar" is not intended for another variety.

18. COLOR: White with red or red with white, the red in its various shades; white with brindle patches from gray-yellowish to gray-brown or exactly these colors with white markings. The colors red or gray-yellow and brown-yellow are entirely of equal value.

Absolutely necessary markings are: white chest, feet, and tip of tail, nose band, collar; spot on the nape and blaze are very desirable. Never of one color or without white. All other colors are faulty, except the very favored dark shadings on the head (mask) and ears. One distinguishes between mantle dogs and splash-coated dogs.

As already mentioned under "general appearance", no mention exists concerning white head markings, half mask, no mask, completely white head, etc., not even in the color description. In

Champion Bryjon's Damocles von Kris, Saint Bernard owned by Dr. and Mrs. E. E. Breyfogle, is pictured winning Best in Show at the Essex County Kennel Club show on July 20, 1957.

my opinion, color is of secondary meaning, whereby the better color should win, but under the condition that the best type is given preference under all circumstances, even if the color is not completely free of fault. Let us avoid emphasis on subordinate matter and let us not spoil the work of many years to attain today's type, for which we ought to be thankful. Thus a collar is nicer than no collar, a blaze nicer than no blaze, a clean white muzzle better than one with freckles, a mask better than no mask, a good angulation better than straight hindlegs, a sound dog better than a not so sound one ("sound" to be interpreted as without fault, healthy in body and spirit). But in all these cases the good head type should be favoured. Whoever does not go along with this, should better occupy himself with another breed, where the head type is less involved, and leave St. Bernards alone.

19. THE SHOULDER HEIGHT: of the dog should be a minimum of 70 cm, the one of the bitch 65 cm. Female animals are of a more delicate and finer build throughout.

There is nothing more to be added to the shoulder height. The Standard speaks of a "minimum" of 70 cm for dogs, 65 cm for bitches. Whoever will go to the trouble to measure several St. Bernards, will determine that the prescribed height is a *minimum* height indeed, since show dogs, as a rule, far exceed this minimum.

It should be mentioned, that the Germans increased this minimum by 5 cm and that only the English do not give a minimum nor a maximum height. The English Standard says: "The taller the better, provided the symmetry is maintained."

All other countries hold exactly to the oldest data of the Swiss Standard, even America, where the heights translate to 27.56 inches (70 cm) for dogs and 25.59 inches (65 cm) for bitches. Heaven forbid, if the minimum were taken as the rule. At the moment we still have everywhere sufficient numbers of really imposing dogs, which avoids this danger. The Standard speaks clearly about a powerful, high, muscular, and imposing appearance. One cannot speak of an imposing appearance any more at a height of 70 cm. For comparison purposes some measurements of other breeds:

Newfoundland: Average height 71 cm (28 inches) desired.

Leonburger: Dogs 75–86 cm, Bitches 70–80 cm.

Great Dane: Minimum height 76 cm, 80 cm and more desirable. The taller the better, provided proportions are maintained.

German Shepherd: Dogs 60–65 cm, bitches 55–60 cm.

The St. Bernard Standard then is at the lower limit with respect to height. This is under the assumption that we might be going in the direction of an age of dwarf St. Bernards.

20. FAULTS: are all deviations from the Standard, such as swayback and disproportionately long back, hocks too much bent, and upward growing hair in the spaces between the toes.

The best method is to visit shows and kennels. You can study the very best dogs at shows and impress these on your memory. One condition should be fulfilled. The dogs must have been judged by a specialist judge, who knows his business and has many years of experience. Then you will have the best opportunity to see dogs who come closest to the ideal. Do not forget, that the Ideal is an imagined picture of something which is close to perfection, thus a model image, a dream image. Dreams even as ideals are not realities. The Ideal, however, comes rather close to reality. I only wish to say that a dog who appears to us as almost the Ideal, may yet have several faults.

The real fancier and judge will not, however, judge a dog by his faults, but by his assets, which every dog has, even one classified last in shows. A judge who exclusively counts faults is certainly not a good judge. The good qualities should also be counted in the less well placed dogs. When a dog is shown, you get a certain impression. If the overall impression is immediately good, then you will watch for faults. If the overall impression is bad, then you seek good points, which can be found even in the worst dog. We miss in the Standard a description of the "running gear." Probably less attention was paid to this in earlier days. Every breed

American and Canadian Ch. Hope's Gallant Goliath with three-year-old Deborah Hope. Goliath was bred by Robert Hope, Hopehaus Saint Bernard Kennels, Renton, Wash.

has its natural gait. A calmly walking St. Bernard will gait majestically, evenly and, in spite of its weight and size, elegantly. The "running gear" is also a component of the so-called "nobility." The dog must go somewhat faster in the ring, so that we can establish whether the good build is maintained even in motion; a bad build comes to light easier. A well-built dog, as a rule, will also have an excellent gait and vice versa. Seldom will one find a dog trot like a horse, that moves simultaneously both left and thereafter both right legs. If a dog gaits and holds his tail somewhat higher, one can neglect it, provided that he carries his tail hanging straight down when calm. A curled tail is a distinct fault and spoils the whole appearance. A curled tail cannot be improved. However, a tail which is carried somewhat too high can be improved by repeated tapping on the tail. The dog will soon notice what his master expects from him.

Lesser results can be expected during fast gait. Wrong shoulder stance and weak legs appear clearly during gaiting and fast running. Badly built hindquarters (cow-hocked-steep-overbuild, cow-hocked with hocks turned inward just as in cows) cause a plump gait; a sway-back (saddle-back) can never appear elegant and it disturbs the regularity during gaiting.

An originally shorthaired St. Bernard was the model for the establishment of the Standard. Only a few lines are added to the Standard of this shorthaired model:

The long-haired variety completely resembles the shorthaired variety except for the coat, which is not shorthaired (stockhaarig) but of medium length, plain to slightly wavy, never rolled or curly and not shaggy either. Usually on the back, especially in the region from the haunches to the rump, the hair is more wavy, which, by the way, is slightly indicated also in the shorthaired dog and even the Hospice dog. The tail is bushy with dense hair of moderate length. Rolled or curly hair on the tail is not desirable. A tail with a parting or a flag-tail is faulty. Face and ears are covered with short and soft hair; longer developed, silky hair at the base of the ear is permitted. Forelegs are only slightly feathered; strongly developed pants (bushy) at the thighs. *Faulty* are all external shapes which remind us of the crossing with the Newfoundland, such as for example a disproportionately long back, too strongly angulated hocks and upward rising hair between the toes.

# CHAPTER 4

# BUYING YOUR
# SAINT BERNARD PUPPY

There are several trails that will lead you to a litter of puppies where you can find the Saint Bernard puppy of your choice. Write to the parent club and ask for the names and addresses of members who have puppies for sale. The addresses of Saint Bernard clubs can be secured by writing the American Kennel Club, 51 Madison Avenue, New York, N.Y. 10010. They keep an accurate, up-to-date list of reputable breeders where you can seek information on obtaining a good, healthy puppy. You might also check listings in the classified ads of major newspapers. The various dog magazines also carry listings; for example, Popular Dogs magazine carries a column on the breed each and every month.

It is to your advantage to attend a few dog shows in the area where many purebred dogs of just about every breed are being exhibited in the show ring. Even if you do not wish to buy a show dog, you should be familiar with what the better specimens look like so that you may at least get a worthy specimen for your money. You will learn a lot by observing the dogs in action in the show ring, or in a public place where their personalities come to the fore. The dog show catalogue will list the dogs and their owners with local kennel names and breeders which you can visit to see the types they are breeding and winning with at the shows. Exhibitors at these shows are usually delighted to talk to people about their dogs and the specific characteristics of this particular breed.

Once you have chosen the Saint Bernard as your choice of the breeds because you admire its exceptional beauty, intelligence and personality, and because you feel the Saint Bernard will fit in with your family's way of life, it is wise to do a little research on the breed. The American Kennel Club library, your local library, bookshops, and the club can usually supply you with a list of

Mt. Moriah Mardoug and Tara are the best of friends. They are owned by Stanley and Doane Bethiel, Holbrook, L.I., N.Y.

reading matter or written material on the breed, past and present. Then once you have drenched yourself in the Saint Bernard's illustrious history and have definitely decided that this is the dog for you, it is time to start writing letters and making phone calls to set up appointments to see litters of puppies!

A word of caution here: don't let your choice of a kennel be determined by its nearness to your home, and then buy the first "cute" puppy that races up to you or licks the end of your nose! All puppies are cute, and naturally you will have a preference among those you see. But don't let preferences sway you into making a wrong decision.

If you are buying your dog as a family pet, a preference might not be a serious offense. But if you have had, say, a color preference since you first considered this breed, you would be wise to stick to it—color or coat pattern is important because you will want your dog to be pleasing to the eye as well. And if you are buying a show dog, an accepted coat or color pattern is essential, according to the Standard for the breed. In considering your purchase you must

Beau Cheval's Kelli La Mardoug, sired by Beau Cheval's Parish Mardoug, out of Ch. Beau Cheval's Tralee Mardoug. Kelli is now deceased.

Scotholme Kennels' Champion Mister Sam, owned by the Bernard Lawsons.

Ch. Bomar's Pride watches over author's baby and puppy.

think clearly, choose carefully, and make the very best possible choice. You will, of course, learn to love your Saint which ever one you finally decide upon, but a case of "love at first sight" can be disappointing and expensive later on, if a show career was your primary objective.

To get the broadest possible concept of what is for sale and the current market prices, it is recommended that you visit as many kennels and private breeders as possible. With today's reasonably safe, inexpensive and rapid flights on the major airlines, it is possible to secure dogs from far-off places at nominal additional charges, which will allow you to buy the valuable bloodline of your choice, if you have a thought toward a breeding program in the future.

While it is always safest to actually *see* the dog you are buying, there are enough reputable breeders and kennels to be found for you to buy a dog with a minimum of risk once you have made up your mind what you want, and when you have decided whether you will buy in this country or import to satisfy your concept of the breed Standard. If you are going to breed dogs, breeding Standard

Children line up with Beau Cheval puppies.

type is a moral obligation, and your concern should be with buying the very best bloodlines and individual animals obtainable, in spite of cost or distance.

It is customary for the purchaser to pay the shipping charges, and the airlines are most willing to supply flight information and prices upon request. Rental on the shipping crate, if the owner does not provide one for the dog, is nominal. While unfortunate instances have occurred on the airlines in the transporting of animals by air, the major airlines are making improvements on safety measures and have reached the point of reasonable safety and cost. Barring unforeseen circumstances, the safe arrival of a dog you might buy can pretty much be assured if both seller and purchaser adhere to and follow up on even the most minute details from both ends.

## THE PUPPY YOU BUY

Let us assume you want to enjoy all the antics of a young puppy and decide to buy a six- to eight-week-old puppy. This is about the age when a puppy is weaned, wormed and ready to go out into the world with a responsible new owner. It is better not to buy a puppy under six weeks of age, they simply are not yet ready to leave the mother. At eight to twelve weeks of age you will be able to notice much about the appearance and the behavior. Puppies, as they are remembered in our fondest childhood memories, are gay and active and bouncy, as well they should be! The normal puppy should be interested, alert, and curious, especially about a stranger. If a puppy acts a little reserved or distant, however, this need not be misconstrued as shyness or fear. It merely indicates he hasn't made up his mind if he likes you as yet! By the same token, he should not be fearful or terrified by a stranger—and especially should not show any fear of his owner!

In direct contrast, the puppy should not be ridiculously over-active either. The puppy that frantically bounds around the room and is never still is not particularly desirable. And beware of "spinners!" Spinners are the puppies or dogs that have become neurotic from being kept in cramped quarters or in crates and behave in this emotionally unstable manner when loosed in adequate space. When released they run in circles and seemingly "go wild." Puppies with this kind of traumatic background seldom ever

Happiness is . . . a Saint puppy! On the left, a smooth male at eight weeks of age, sired by Glyndon's Monsignor Von Padre; and on the right a two-week-old smooth male sired by Beau Cheval's Vicar v Chaparral. Breeder is Gretchen Hoover, Glyndon Saints, Reisterstown, Md.

Indian Mountain's Wampam, pictured at nine weeks of age, waiting for his jeep to take off. He is sired by Ch. Illo v Vogelheim Ex Indian Mountain's Shawnee. Owners are Ruthe and John Young.

Beau Cheval's Shamison, sired by Ch. Beau Cheval's Shamrock x Beau Cheval's Mystic. Owned by Jean and U. Ross, Blackwood, N.J.

Longhaired puppy, sired by Ch. Beau Cheval's Padre, enjoys rocking chair.

regain full composure or adjust to the big outside world. The puppy which has had the proper exercise and appropriate living quarters will have a normal, though spirited, outlook on life and will do his utmost to win you over without having to go into a tailspin.

If the general behavior and appearance of the dog thus far appeals to you, it is time for you to observe him more closely for additional physical requirements. First of all, you cannot expect to find in the puppy all the coat he will bear upon maturity, thanks to good food and the many wonderful grooming aids which can be found on the market today. Needless to say, the healthy puppy's coat should have a nice shine to it, and the more dense at this age, the better the coat will be when the dog reaches adulthood.

Look for clear, dark, sparkling eyes, free of discharge. Dark eye rims and lids are indications of good pigmentation which is important in a breeding program, or even for generally pleasing good looks. From the time the puppy first opens his eyes until he is about three months old, however, it must be remembered that the eyes have a slight blue-ish cast to them. The older the puppy, the darker the eye, so always ascertain the age of the puppy and the degree of darkness that should be in the eye at this particular time of its life.

Beau Cheval's Drama Mardoug, at six weeks, in training for future shows. She is now owned by the author and J. Ramirez.

All aboard! Donna Dube takes off on 10½-month-old Mardonof's the Yankee Trader. Owned by the Donald Dubes of North Attleboro, Mass.

When the time comes to select your puppy, take an experienced breeder along with you. If this is not possible, take the Standard for the breed with you. These Standards may be obtained from the local club or found in the *American Kennel Club Dog Book* which can be obtained at any library. Then try to interpret the Standard as best you can by making comparisons between the puppies you see.

Check the bite carefully. Proper bite is illustrated in detail in this book and we urge you to check it carefully. While the first set of teeth can be misleading, even the placement of teeth at this young age can be a fairly accurate indication of what the bite will be in the grown dog. The gums should be a good healthy pink in color, and the teeth should be clear, clean and white. Any brown cast to them could mean a past case of distemper, and would assuredly count against the dog in the show ring, or against the dog's general appearance at maturity.

Puppies take anything and everything into their mouths to chew on while they are teething, and a lot of infectious diseases are

Four of five roughs in a litter of seven that survived from Beau Cheval's Parish and Beau Cheval's Toffe. Left to right are Heiress, Psalms, Drama and Genesis. Bred by M. J. Anderson, Wycombe, Pa.

introduced this way. The aforementioned distemper is one, and the brown teeth as a result of this disease never clear. The puppy's breath should not be sour or even unpleasant or strong. Any acrid odor could indicate a poor mixture of food, or low quality of meat, especially if it is being fed raw. Many breeders have compared the breath of a healthy puppy to that of fresh toast, or as being vaguely like garlic. At any rate, a puppy should never be fed just table scraps, but should have a well-balanced diet containing a good dry puppy chow, and a good grade of fresh meat. Poor meat, too much cereal, or fillers, tend to make the puppy too fat. We like puppies to be in good flesh, but not fat from the wrong kind of food!

It goes without saying that we want to find clean puppies. The breeder or owner who shows you a dirty puppy is one from whom to steer away! Look closely at the skin. Rub the fur the wrong way or against the grain; make sure it is not spotted with insect bites, or red, blotchy sores or dry scales. The vent area around the tail should not show evidences of diarrhea or inflammation. By the same token, the puppy's fur should not be matted with dry excrement or smell of urine.

True enough, you can wipe dirty eyes, clean dirty ears, and give the puppy a bath when you get it home, but these are all indications of how the puppy has been cared for during the important formative first months of its life, and can vitally influence its future health and development. There are many reputable breeders raising healthy puppies that have been reared in proper places and under the proper conditions in clean establishments, so why take a chance on a series of veterinary bills and a questionable constitution?

## MALE OR FEMALE?

The choice of sex in your puppy is also something that must be given serious thought before you shop. Here again, for the pet owner, the sex that would best suit the family life you enjoy would be the paramount choice to consider. For the breeder or exhibitor, there are other considerations. If you are looking for a stud to establish a kennel, it is essential that you select a dog with both testicles evident, even at a tender age, and verified by a veterinarian before the sale is finalized.

One testicle, or a monorchid, automatically disqualifies the dog from the show ring or from a breeding program, though monorchids are capable of siring. Additionally, it must be noted that monorchids frequently sire dogs with the same deficiency, and to introduce this into a bloodline knowingly is an unwritten sin in the dog fancy. Also, a monorchid can sire cryptorchids. Cryptorchids have no testicles and are sterile.

If you desire a dog to be a member of the family, the best selection would probably be a female. You can always go out for

High Chateau's Tara, long-haired bitch, ten months old, bred by H. Vogel. Sired by Tito del Soccorso and out of Emi V. Mallen. Owned by Ann Golden and Deena Jerson, Oyster Bay Cove, L.I., N.Y.

stud service if you should decide to breed. You can choose the bloodlines doing the most winning because they should be bred true to type, and you will not have to foot the bill for the financing of a show career. You can always keep a male from your first litter that will bear your own "kennel name" if you have decided to proceed in the "kennel business."

An additional consideration in the male versus female decision for the private owner is that with males, there might be the problem of leg-lifting and with females, there is the inconvenience while they are in season. However, this need not be the problem it used to be—pet shops sell "pants" for both sexes, which help to control this situation in the home.

## THE PLANNED PARENTHOOD BEHIND YOUR PUPPY

Never be afraid to ask pertinent questions about the puppy, as well as questions about the sire and dam. Feel free to ask the breeder if you might see the dam, not only to establish her general health, but her appearance as a representative of the breed. Ask also to see the sire if they are his owners. Ask what the puppy has been fed and should be fed after weaning. Ask to see the pedigree, and inquire if the litter or the individual puppies have been registered with the American Kennel Club, how many of the temporary and/or permanent inoculations the puppy has had, when and if the puppy has been wormed, and if it has had any illness, disease or infection.

You need not ask if the puppy is housebroken . . . it won't mean much. He may have gotten the idea as to where "the place" is where he now lives, but he will need new training to learn where "the place" is in his new home! And you can't really expect too much from them at this age anyway. Housebreaking is entirely up to the new owner. We know puppies always eliminate after they eat, so it is up to you to remember to take the dog out immediately after each meal. They also eliminate when they first awaken and sometimes dribble when they get excited. If friends and relatives are coming over to see the new puppy, make sure he is walked before he greets them at the front door. This will help.

The normal time period for puppies around three months of age to eliminate is about two to three hours. So as the time draws near, either take the puppy out or indicate the newspapers for

Helen Kay, author of "Man and Mastiff," pictured in March 1967 with a Saint Bernard puppy.

the same purpose. Housebreaking is never easy, but anticipation is about 90 per cent of the problem. The schools that offer to housebreak your dog are virtually useless. Here again the puppy will learn the "place" at the schoolhouse, but coming home he will need new training for the new location.

A reputable breeder will welcome any and all questions you might ask and will voluntarily offer additional information, if only to brag about the tedious and loving care he has given his litter. He will also sell a puppy on 24 hour veterinary approval. This means you have a full day to get the puppy to a veterinarian of your choice to get his opinion on the general health of the puppy before you make a final decision. There should also be veterinary certificates and full particulars on the dates and types of inoculations the puppy has been given to date.

## PUPPIES AND WORMS

Let us give further attention to the unhappy and very unpleasant subject of worms. Generally speaking, most all puppies—even those raised in clean quarters—come into contact with worms early in life. They can be passed down from the mother before birth or picked up during their first encounters with the earth or quarters. To say that you must not buy a puppy because of the presence of worms is nonsensical. You might be passing up a fine

Indian Mountain's Tom Tom and Shawnee learn all about the keg. Owners are Ruthe and John Young of East Stroudsburg, Pa.

Benedictine and Beth Beatty, 2½ months and two years respectively, await bedtime. Benny is owned by the Robert Beattys of Philadelphia.

Bittersweet Nantuck, owned by Diane Wenstob, 1045 Canyon Blvd., N. Vancouver, B.C., Canada.

quality animal that can be freed of worms in one short treatment. True, a heavy infestation of worms of any kind in a young dog is dangerous and debilitating.

The extent of infection can be readily determined by a veterinarian and you might take his word as to whether the future health and conformation of the dog has been damaged. He can prescribe the dosage and supply the medication at the time and you will already have one of your problems solved. The kinds and varieties of worms and how to detect them is described in detail elsewhere in this book and we advise you to check the matter out further if there is any doubt in your mind as to the problems of worms in dogs.

## VETERINARY INSPECTION

While your veterinarian is going over the puppy you have selected to purchase, you might just as well ask him for his opinion of it as a breed of dog as well as facts about its general health. While few veterinarians can claim to be breed standard experts, they

Three puppy bitches, 4½ weeks old, out of Dakotas Cherry O Let, sired by Prairieaire Sweeps of Basko, owned by John Ramirez, Downey, Cal.

usually have a "good eye" for a fine specimen and can advise you where to go for further information. Perhaps they can also recommend other breeders for opinions. The vet can point out structural faults or organic problems that affect all breeds and can usually judge whether an animal has been abused or mishandled and whether it is over- or undersized.

We would like to emphasize here that it is only through this type of close cooperation between owners and veterinarians that we can expect to reap the harvest of modern research and advance. Most reputable veterinarians are more than eager to learn about various purebred dogs, and we in turn must acknowledge and apply what they have proven through experience and research in their field. We can buy and breed the best dog in the world, but when disease strikes we are only as safe as our veterinarian is capable—so let us keep them informed breed by breed and dog by dog! The veterinarian represents the difference between life and death!

# CHAPTER 5

# HOW TO SELECT A
# SAINT BERNARD PUPPY

Don't expect to find a good show puppy at the local pet shop or at your neighbors where they have just had their first or even third litter. For although this is possible, the odds are very much against it.

The breeder who has his first litter may have a good puppy to offer you, but how will he know which one it is? Unless the bitch is outstanding, according to an expert's opinion, or unless the breeding was planned by an experienced breeder familiar with the bloodlines, it is unwise to buy from this litter.

Beware of the "puppy mill" breeders who turn them out "like flies"—they usually produce flies, too. Beware of the breeder who offers what he claims to be quality for $50, because the puppies usually aren't even worth that much. Beware also of the breeder who has no background in producing fine dogs, or has never owned a good dog, and cannot give satisfactory answers to your questions about his success in his chosen "business." Breeding bad Saint Bernards can be profitable for those who do not buy decent stock, do not attend dog shows, have low overhead, do not use veterinarians, seldom worm the dogs, and feed just enough food to keep them alive. This type of "kennel operation" thrives in one of two ways: they wholesale their puppies before they are old enough to worm, inoculate, or eat a great deal; or secondly, they undersell the large, established, and well-known kennels around them.

If you have already purchased your first Saint Bernard, and it turned out to be just pet quality, don't feel badly. Pet quality is about standard procedure for most inexperienced Saint buyers. Just remember you are now out to do better this time around! If you really want a good dog, searching for it will be well worth the time you devote to it, and reputable breeders usually stand behind their stock. They want you to have the best they have to offer since you are still serious about the breed and expect to better the breed in the future. Explain this to them and they will be more than happy to have one of their better dogs well placed. The average Saint buyer usually just wants a pet to loll around the house and look cute. The really serious-minded buyers are few and far between, so breeders will be glad to assist those that wish to breed and show their Saint Bernards.

## THE SELECTION OF THE PUPPY

With the Standard fresh in your mind, look for the puppy with heavy bone, heavy frame, good muscle development, plenty of substance, and good movement. With large breeds it is almost essential that you see the litter move around in a large area, outside if possible. Then narrow your choice down to two, *if* you can find two you like, and observe these two puppies carefully as they run and play.

As we said before, don't be turned off by the sleepy puppy (if you feel he looks best of all) just because he isn't playing. He could be sleepy, from having played himself out just before you arrived! Most puppies are cute, but they do not really develop individual

This puppy illustrates poor and splayed feet, with bad spread of toes. This condition, however, was corrected later as the puppy grew up with necessary vitamins and the gravel stone run. Dog pictured at ten weeks of age is owned by Marlene Anderson.

Common Saint Bernard faults—no chest, sagging topline, straight rear, faulty hocks and lack of angulation with straight stifles.

personalities until they get away from the kennel and start getting used to their new loved ones.

Look for a wide front and a wide rearend. Watch out for bowed front legs and feet that turn out in opposite directions. Choose the prettiest puppy only if it also possesses the correct type. Do not be fooled by a long red and white coat, and the "Spaniel look." This could turn out to be the typical rough-coated Zero!

The head is very important with puppies. Does he have the all-important blocky-type head, with *broad*, *short* muzzle and *wide* dome, above a *sharp* stop? Are his lips deep and pendant now? They should be! He should look, even at this age *strong*, *noble* and *big* to you.

Long, narrow noses simply do not ever get wide. Avoid them. Tight lips never become deep and pendant, and narrow skulls do not gain necessary width either. Avoid them also. Muzzles that are snipey and run downhill will stay that way, or perhaps get worse.

Barllo v. Greta, four months old, with very low ear set. The puppy showed little promise of correcting the ear set, but is well on the way to finishing his championship with an excellent head now. Sired by Ch. Illo vom Vogelheim and out of Beau Cheval's Greta v. Tablo. Owned and bred by Mr. and Mrs. Thomas Ryan, Worcester, Pa.

If the puppy does not have bone now, it will not develop heavy bone later. Hold back the puppy's ears and view him from the top of his head. Does the skull gradually taper to a point at the tip of the nose? You should see a blocky skull, with NO tapering. Learn to look for this in young puppies, for it is easy to be fooled by an otherwise pretty head.

Chests may be undeveloped at this age and usually come down later, but if there is chest there now so much the better! Splayed or spread toes can correct themselves later, but look for the puppy with tight feet now and one that stands high on his feet. Weak pasterns are common to heavy or fat puppies, so take this into consideration.

It is very common in puppies three months old and upward to have bad toplines. High rears are frightening to look at, but usually level out later, unless one or both parents have the same problem. If they do, this is then cause for concern. Otherwise do not let it influence your final decision.

If the puppy is obviously weak in the rear end, do not buy it. Young puppies may be loose in the back, but they should still walk and stand wide. Exercise, vitamins, and maturity helps, and sometimes they will gradually widen out. However, if there is any

Barllo v. Greta of Hollow Acres, owned by Scott Ryan, Hollow Acres Farm, Worcester, Pa., showing excellent ear-set at maturity.

Beau Cheval's Atlana Mardoug at one year of age. Owned by Marcia McDonald, Putnam, Conn. Although "Lana" has good head type, she is undershot, which a trained and experienced breeder could see without opening her mouth.

doubt in your mind, do not buy this puppy no matter how good it looks otherwise. An experienced eye can detect a good rear in young puppies, from ages six to twelve weeks, but they do not always stay that way either! Sound rears at twelve weeks are your best bet and the older the puppy is, the less guesswork there is in the dog you are buying.

There is nothing uglier than a rolled-over tail on an otherwise attractive and beautiful Saint Bernard. Most puppies carry their tails high, and these we refer to as "puppy tails." They do not usually stay high for long. True tail carriage can be seen at around four months and will indicate what the tail carriage will be the rest of their lives. A "gay" tail is all right when the dog is in action, as long as it does not get higher than the back and does not roll up like a Keeshonden tail. Look for a long, thick tail that hangs low and presents a pleasing picture as the dog moves along.

In the show ring, some judges will measure the tail for length by holding the tip against the dog's hock. If the tail does not reach the hock, it is not correct in the judge's eyes. Few judges measure tails and while the tail that reaches to, or just below the hock, is more correct, a Saint with too short a tail, but with good carriage, will have a chance at championship.

The puppy you consider should be a miniature replica of what you want in the adult dog. Many a potential champion photographed in show pose at six weeks will present the same lovely picture at four years of age after he has won his title. You *can* see the potential at six weeks. If you are looking for a show dog, the older the puppy is when you buy it, the better.

Many kennels breed their inferior bitches to champions and sell the puppy entirely on the reputation, name and show record of the stud. Do not be fooled by this. Insist on seeing both parents, if they are available. Even a good stud cannot produce miracles and the litter usually resembles the dam. Do not just buy the dog's background. Study the pedigree, but study the puppy most of all!

## WHAT SHOULD A SAINT PUPPY COST?

If you are looking for a nice pet for the children, you should be able to find a well-bred, perhaps even mis-marked puppy, for about the same amount of money as any other popular breed. Remember, the show kennel's pets are usually less expensive in the

Faulty head—no type, complete lack of lip, long narrow "Collie nose," no stop, flat skull, small eyes. Notice poor markings, also.

Poor Saint Bernard head— no lip, lack of stop, long narrow muzzle, flat skull.

long run than the pet shop's pets—and they are bred from show dogs! Sometimes a breeder will sell a "whitehead" (no color on the head to speak of) for less. The price would be lower for a brown-nosed Saint puppy. You might even consider a puppy with a minor case of Hip Dysplasia. These puppies are sometimes free, or offered at a very low cost to help absorb some of the costs of breeding the litter. Runts, or the smallest puppy in the litter, are also sold at less cost at times and grow up to be just as nice and sometimes just as big as their double-size littermates.

But you should expect to pay twice as much for a better speci-men—a beautiful dog which you can show, breed and, most of all, be proud of.

## THE CONDITIONS OF SALE

While it is customary to pay for the puppy before you take it away with you, you should be able to give the breeder a deposit, if there is any doubt about the puppy's health. You might also postdate a check to cover the 24-hour veterinary approval. If you do decide to take the puppy the breeder is required to supply you with a pedigree, along with the puppy's registration paper. He is also obliged to supply you with complete information and American Kennel Club instructions on how to transfer ownership of the puppy into your name.

Some breeders will offer buyers time payment plans for con-venience, if the price on a show dog is very high, or if deferred payments are the only possible way you can purchase the dog. However, any such terms must be worked out between buyer and breeder and should be put in writing to avoid later complications.

You will find most breeders cooperative if they believe you are sincere in your love for the puppy and that you will give it the proper home and show ring career, if it is sold as a show quality specimen of the breed. Remember, when buying a show dog, it is impossible to guarantee nature. A breeder can only tell you what he *believes* will develop into a show quality dog. So be sure your breeder is an honest one.

Also, it is only fair to the breeder that if you purchase a show specimen and promise to show the dog, that you do show it! It is a waste to have a beautiful dog that deserves recognition in the show ring sitting at home as a family pet. This is especially true

Typical topline of a growing Saint—high in the rear, an awkward growing period that will improve with age. Puppy also has a stern face, which is not desirable.

if the breeder offered you a reduced price because of the advertising his kennel and bloodlines would receive by your showing the dog in the ring. If you want a pet, buy a pet. Be honest about it, and let the breeder decide on this basis which is the best dog for you. Your conscience will be clear and you'll both be doing a real service to the breed.

## BUYING AND BREEDING SHOW PUPPIES

If you plan to breed or show your puppy, make it clear that you intend to do so, so that the breeder will help you select the very best puppy. If you are dealing with a reputable breeder and an established kennel, you must rely partially if not entirely on their choice, since they know their bloodlines and what they can produce better than anyone else. He knows how his stock develops, and he would be foolish to sell you a puppy that could not stand up as a breed force or that would misrepresent his stock in the show ring.

However, you must also realize that the breeder may be keeping

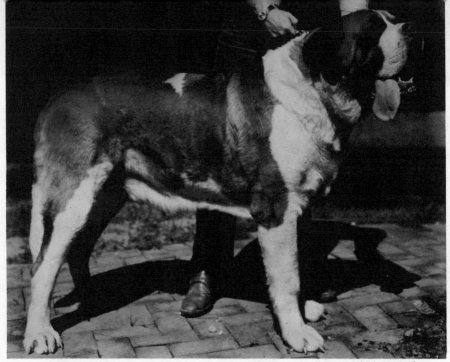

Omar, owned by J. T. Martin, Trenton, N.J., is a huge mantled smooth, sired by Ch. Illo vom Vogelheim and out of Beau Cheval's Toffe la Mardoug. He stands 32 inches high and weighs over 200 pounds. Breeder is M. J. Anderson.

the best puppy in the litter to show and breed himself. If this is the case, you might be wise to select the best puppy of the opposite sex so that the dogs will not be competing against one another in the show rings for their championship points.

Prices vary on all puppies, of course, but a good show prospect at eight weeks to six months of age will sell for several hundred dollars. If the puppy is outstanding, and the pedigree and parentage the same, it will go higher. Reputable breeders, however, stand behind their puppies and should something drastic develop, such as Hip Dysplasia, etc., their obligation to make an adjustment is usually honored.

## COST OF BUYING YOUNG ADULTS OR GROWN STOCK

Prices in this category really fluctuate. Some grown dogs are offered free of charge, or are put out with owners on breeder's terms. But do not count on obtaining a worthy dog free of charge. Good dogs are much in demand. Most of the worthy brood bitches are quite expensive. For a valuable show and breeding specimen over one year of age, of either sex, you must be prepared to pay somewhere around $1,000. Dogs of this calibre are difficult to find and do not come cheap, as many wealthy people have found out!

## WHAT TO LOOK FOR WHEN BUYING ADULT STOCK

First, take a good look at the dog. Does it strike you immediately as looking like the photographs you have seen of great Saint Bernards of the past? If it is a poor specimen, there is no need to look further into its background. Go elsewhere. If it is a quality specimen, look further into its pedigree. If you have not heard of the immediate parents, do not give up, they may be excellent, but just never were shown. Ask advice from someone on the third and fourth generations. By asking someone for advice, we do not necessarily mean an officer or a member of a Saint club who shows in obedience, or someone who owns an inferior specimen, or the woman down the street who pretends to be an expert. We mean a

Young Edward Hill II with Fitzgerald Brumus II, owned by Ed Hill of New York.

breeder or judge with experience in breeding and/or showing Saint Bernards of quality. Most reputable breeders would be flattered to be called upon for help of this kind. They might also wonder why you do not buy from them if they have something for sale, and you must be aware of professional jealousy. If you are reasonably familiar with the Standard, however, and get an expert opinion, between the two you can usually come up with the answers you want to help you make your decision.

## TEMPERAMENT—THE VERY IMPORTANT FACTOR

A vicious or untrustworthy Saint Bernard is not worth having! No matter how inexpensive, don't buy it! The background of adult dogs that are suddenly for sale is to be questioned. Have they bitten anyone? Have they lunged at anyone or attempted to bite on occasion, and if so, why? Do they dislike children? Have they been around infants or teenagers? Do they dislike one sex in humans, and if so, why? Do they particularly dislike one member of the family? Can they be trusted with strangers and around food? You

Mont D'Or After All, seven-week-old longhaired male puppy is bred and owned by Ann and Richard Golden of Oyster Bay Cove, L.I.

Ch. Beau Cheval's Padre when he was a five-week-old Saint.

Dalerie and Daria
Anderson with
puppies Classic
and Claire.
White puppy is
Bichon.

will be wise to ask these questions and any others that come to mind.

There are many sad, but true, tales about mean and/or vicious Saints, for unfortunately, they are not all angelic and sweet. Fear, mistreatment, and downright cruelty are the chief causes for a dog to turn mean, but it is also inherited in many cases. There are bloodlines that are notorious for bad behavior and unpredictable actions, from adult or early maturing dogs that were angelic before a sudden and surprise attack on someone. All these factors must be considered when buying a grown dog. You can't be too careful!

In some cases insanity is the reason. Dogs can lose their minds, also. The quicker you realize this, the more cautious you will be. Always remember you are dealing with an animal, whose instincts are different from ours. Brain tumors might also be responsible for sudden change in behavior. If your dog begins to act strange, don't waste a moment. Have it checked out by a veterinarian and take his advice even though he may recommend euthanasia.

A Saint Bernard is a large and strong animal, and a mean one is nothing to gamble with when your safety is involved. Our breed basically is well-known for its sweet and loving nature, but through popularity and indiscriminate breeding, that loving nature cannot *always* be guaranteed.

## WHEN DOES A SAINT REACH MATURITY?

Many breeders and Saint Bernard owners believe that their dogs are fully grown at one year of age, at the time the American Kennel Club no longer considers a dog a puppy. Although your dog may have reached its full height, and therefore said to be "grown," it is still far from reaching its full *maturity*.

In fact, certain bloodlines mature differently—some earlier and some later in life, just as in children. Some Saints mature earlier and are ready to enter the show ring and earn championship points at just over one year of age. Others require several years to reach their full bloom. There are those who believe that the dogs that mature earlier in life also succumb earlier as well, often victims of bone and heart ailments, living what is perhaps about a half of the normal Saint's lifespan.

Experienced breeders are inclined to say that the majority of Saints have fully developed and are mature at about the age of five. The head especially is not fully developed until approximately this age. Often the dog has not reached its full height, weight and breadth until five years of age. This should be the peak year for the Saint Bernard, when he is at his best in the show ring as well.

# CHAPTER 6

# SAINT BERNARD MARKINGS

One of the surest ways to tell an unknowledgable breeder is by the description of his latest litter, be it his first or fiftieth! Advertisements brag about "even markings," "full masks," or "monk's caps." One breeder advertises his dogs have "full monk's masks"! A Monk's cap is the dark spot that tops many a white domed puppy's head, and it is thought by many to be worth something "extra." Those who think so are wrong, and those who charge more for puppies that have this common marking are obviously misleading the buying public, and showing others how little they really know. Beagles, Coonhounds, and many mongrels have such spots on their heads, too.

Our Standard does not dote on markings and uses the word FAVORITE when covering head markings, such as the dark mask and ears. Needless to say, most puppies which don't have a full or symmetrical black mask, or have white, or partially white ears, are considered unworthy for show and breeding purposes. These are usually sold as pets with the advice never to breed or show them, or they are put down. Seldom do we see half-masks in the ring; however, dogs with white on their ears are sometimes seen. It's sad, but true, that the highest percentage of breeders cull their litters by judging on markings alone.

We will never know how many great dogs were destroyed as mis-marks! Or how great a mis-marked puppy was destined to become, or how often a white-eared Saintlet was sold as a pet, when in reality it was the best dog in its litter. If we are to judge and pick our quality dogs according to our standard of perfection, we should not consider the lack of a black mask a disqualification for breeding, or even showing. Without the mask, the dog has other qualities to be considered. If all other things measure up to our Standard, and the dog is exceptional otherwise, then it will not produce any more half-masks than its litter brother or sister, and should be bred to a dog with the "favorite" black points.

There are champions of record with half-masks, and without going into their names, there are also champions with white ears, whole and partial. There are champions with little or nearly no white blaze; some without white on the nape of the neck, and still others with nearly no white on their feet, not to mention none on their legs or chest. So, don't give up on that outstanding mis-marked puppy or adult, for it may be the foundation of your kennel, or even your next champion!

## MIS-MARKS AND MISFITS IN SAINT BERNARDS

To the Saint Bernard owner, or would-be owner, and some fanciers as well, the term "mis-mark" does not always ring a bell. We still have some breeders who have been breeding Saints for many years and claim they have never bred or housed such a dog. We see very few at matches, or shows, and rarely do we have these dogs brought in for stud service. We are supposed to be living in a modern era where it is no longer a stigma to have a retarded child, or an incurable disease. But, to own such a dog, or breed a litter with half-masks or brown-noses among them is still whispered about!

We do have a Standard of perfection which the breeder tries, or certainly should try, to uphold. In our Standard, the paragraph concerning color reads: "Necessary markings are: white chest, feet and tip of tail, nose band, collar or spot on nape; the latter and blaze are very desirable. Never of one color or without white. Faulty are all other colors except the favorite dark shadings on the head (mask) and ears. One distinguishes between mantle dogs and splash-coated dogs." Does this mean that a dog without a complete mask over both eyes is wrong? It would seem so, wouldn't it? But our Standard does leave room for doubt in this area.

Let us define the commonly used term "half-mask". It usually refers to a dog that has only one eye covered with the traditional, and favorite, black markings, or "mask." If the dog has no mask over either eye, it would probably be termed a "white head" by most breeders, although the correct term here would be "no mask," if the dog still had the correct dark ears. We have never seen a complete "white-headed" Saint and never bred one without any color on the head itself.

A half-masked Saint of quality. Beau Cheval's Ella La Mardoug was sired by Ch. Illo vom Vogelheim out of Beau Cheval's Bella Mia El 'Cid.

One of the finest dogs we have ever owned was referred to as a "white head." She whelped 13 puppies in her first litter and all were perfectly marked. One went on to become a famous champion, a Specialty winner and a sire of champions. She whelped 13 in her second litter and again all were perfectly marked. Another had a black spot around one eye, covering it entirely, like a black patch. She also had completely brown and black shaded ears. Her body structure, rear and front movement, hips, bite, eyes and lips were flawless. A beautiful, sound, typey bitch, with incorrect head markings, she was never shown, but her progeny have yet to produce a mis-marked puppy. Now, we do not conclude that these dogs would never produce mis-marks, but we do find the ratio high for well marked puppies, considering the background. In our experience with breeding mis-marked animals, I find no evidence to prove that a perfectly marked dog will produce more perfectly marked offspring than a mis-marked one, provided the mis-mark is bred with a perfectly marked dog, of course!

When we were breeding many dark mantled dogs, we never came up with a half-mask, or white head. We did have many puppies that lacked the necessary wide blaze and wide nose band,

An example of a half-masked Saint Bernard of excellent type. The left ear is mottled and body predominantly white. A bitch like this need not be discarded from a breeding program. This is Willow Point's Dontchano, owned by Donald Ashman and Bruce Chapman.

the white collar and white spot on the nape. We also termed the puppies with little or not enough white on their faces "mis-marks."

On my trip to the Hospice, in Switzerland, I noticed an oil painting of a Hospice bitch that hangs in the dining room of the hotel. It is noteworthy that this bitch was maskless and showed only a tinge of color on one ear. Her overall body color had little or no markings. We are told that the Hospice dogs were often "white heads," and that they were used to eliminate the freckles or dark spots on the face and legs. This may or may not be true. My theory is that the dogs were bred for rescue work only, without thought to physical beauty, and the breeders were right in doing this. This was not a beauty contest, and the dogs did not attend dog shows. It was strictly a matter of the human lives that were at stake. Only dogs that showed heroic and intelligent tendencies were used for lifesaving in the deep snow. If one is lost and freezing to death, the color and markings of the dogs that rescue him are of no consequence whatsoever!

The point is: Which is worse, a mis-marked Saint with a good sound working body and a beautiful head, or a crippled, incorrect, well-marked dog? We see such poor dogs and some of them even win at shows. Isn't this worse than a mis-marked dog that has the movement and body of the true working Saint? Thank goodness the judges today are broad-minded enough to put an imperfectly marked dog up—if it is the best overall dog in the ring otherwise!

## OTHER IMPERFECTIONS

### Brown Noses or Livers

When a Saint Bernard is born with the lack of black pigment, the puppy will have the coloring of a red Doberman Pinscher, or a Brittany Spaniel, with the liver-colored nose, instead of the correct black nose. These dogs mature into nice looking animals with carrot-red coloring. They have pale blue eyes as puppies, which turn into amber at maturity.

They are just as big, sweet, and every bit as healthy as their black-nosed brothers and sisters in the same litter. Unfortunately, they are sometimes more beautiful in conformation and type. These Saints are incorrect and are termed misfits. Some breeders put them down at birth. It is interesting that many breeders really do not recognize this fault in a newly born or even several-weeks-old puppy, but new breeders are not always aware of such a thing until it happens to them.

These dogs should be placed in the same category as a white German Shepherd or a white Boxer. They do not lack anything else in their physical or mental makeup except color. This is not always true with other breeds. Some owners of brown-nosed dogs have tried unsuccessfully to exhibit them. You will only embarrass yourself and the breeder. These dogs should be sold or placed without papers (this is up to the breeder's discretion) with the understanding that they are never to be shown or bred, but kept as pets only. They make excellent pets, as anyone who has ever owned one can attest.

If pedigrees carried notations of such imperfections, it would lessen the chance of producing brown-nosed Saints, since it takes "two to tango." Two dogs are responsible for this imperfection, correctly termed as the "Dudley nose." Many breeders are stumped when their bitch or dog has a brown-nosed puppy, or perhaps two or three. Sometimes entire litters are born with brown noses and lips. When it is discovered that this is a fault and the breeder knows the puppies are next to worthless, he may direct full blame on the stud dog. This is unfair and unfortunate, since the fault is the result of a combination of recessive genes. Remember, both parents must carry genes for Dudley noses! Some studs never sire a brown-nosed puppy, if they are bred only to bitches which are dominant for black points, such as noses, foot pads, lips and eye rims. The same holds true for bitches. You can breed your dog or bitch which carries this brown gene and never again come up with brown-nosed puppies, if you choose the right mate.

### Freckles

There is nothing more detracting from an otherwise beautiful Saint than a dog that has a gorgeous head covered with black or brown freckles. Some dogs even have freckles going into the blaze and down the white of the chest and front legs. It must be remembered that a good dog should not be faulted for freckling, as our Standard does not mention them. The judge is left to his personal preference. Certainly you would breed to a fine male if he had all you wanted in a stud dog, even if he were freckled.

Foreign judges have stated that our Standard left out the word

Piffy Collins and Florence Andersen hold two rough coated Beau Cheval puppies. Mrs. Andersen is a well-known fancier in Saints.

freckles, or brown/black spots, since they are not supposed to exist on our Saints. Our picture of the Standard illustrates that freckled dogs are wrong and objectionable. Anyone who prefers a heavily freckled dog to a "clean" one is a poor judge of Saint Bernards. Still, we do have buyers who want a freckled Saint, no matter what! Many breeders and judges find nothing offensive about them, and, needless to say, numerous champions and point winners are freckled.

## Blue or Blue-Speckled Eyes

A recent litter of Saint Bernard puppies was called to our attention since every puppy had one blue, marbelized, or china eye. This is a rare happening in our breed. It may never be noticed by some judges and we know that dogs with obvious blue coloring in their eyes have even become champions . . . not to mention dogs which are even partially blind with blue covering the entire eyeball, the result of serious eye damage. Some judges apparently do not look into the eyes or such dogs would not finish.

Blue in the eye or an eye that suddenly turns blue in a young puppy can also be the result of recessive genes, though it may never occur again in repeat breedings. If you do repeat a breeding, and the blue eye shows up once again, then of course you change studs for subsequent breedings.

Not all the buying public knows that one blue eye and one brown eye, or brown noses, are incorrect, and many of these puppies are also sold for top dollar. The saddest part of all is that the seller does not always know it's wrong either. Many Saint Bernard breeders have never seen the Standard!

## Blue Saint Bernards

Another rarity is grey Saints, or those which are often termed "Blues." Some are being seen in different parts of the country. They have a definite blue cast to the coat, none of the traditional brown or orange coloring, but more like a grey Newfoundland, or grey-blue Great Dane. These dogs usually have amber eyes and a lot of pink pigment on the lips and eye rims. This too is wrong, according to our Standard, but many breeders have sold these dogs to the unknowing public as "typical" for our breed—just another "color variation"—which is wrong.

In Europe, we do not see mis-marks or half-masks, brown noses, or even heavily freckled Saint Bernards. They simply do not let them live. As it was pointed out by a Saint breeder here, "They have concentrated on beauty for so long, they really have the elegance and color perfection in their dogs that we don't seem to have. We, in America, concentrate on structure and even more, on soundness."

The difference is there, when observed, and what a difference! The European breeders put down all mis-marks and misfits and even some good dogs if the litter number exceeds six, since the law forbids more than six to live. But Europe still produces as many mis-marks as we do, so they have not answered this problem of imperfections in our breed through culling.

## Dry Mouths

When buyers propose to purchase their first Saint Bernard, we often hear the question, "Do yours have dry mouths?", or "I understand there are two types of Saint Bernards, dry mouths and wet mouths." What they are referring to, we assume, is whether

A little Saint looks longingly and lovingly at Ch. Beau Cheval's Mt. Lesa Mardoug. Willow Point Saints, Milford, Mich. Bruce and Marilyn Chapman. Lesa is now deceased.

the dog drools, since there are no such terms as wet and dry mouths used by breeders. Dogs with pendulant lips do drool, and you must realize that on occasion your Saint Bernard will drool. It has nothing to do with his breeding. Many people find drooling offensive or unpleasant, but if you want a Saint, be prepared for it. Some do, however, drool a lot less than others.

## Ripples and Swirls

It sounds like the title for a song for a marching band, but here again misinformed people have come up with these terms and have even invented the cause: crosses between short- and long-haired Saints! This simply is not true. Imagine the frustration of the Saint breeder who has a buyer come to his kennel to purchase a dry-mouthed Saint with ripples and swirls and which must be BIG (because Saints are supposed to be, you know) and RED (because that's the best color.) When he is told there is no such thing, he goes on to another kennel!

With so much indiscriminate breeding going on while Saints are reaching new peaks of popularity, we can ill-afford this false advertising and misrepresentation of their qualities and characteristics, invented solely by people who will say anything to sell a puppy.

Beau Cheval's first litter of smooth (or short) haired Saints. From this litter, four became champions.

## CHAPTER 7

# THE ROUGH OR THE SMOOTH SAINT BERNARD

Breeders in Europe refer to the two coat textures in this breed as long-haired or short-haired, which will soon become the preferred term in this country as well. But to date, the dogs have been referred to as roughs and smooths and for the purposes of this chapter we will refer to them as such.

In the beginning, I housed only rough Saints. I saw smooths at the local shows and was not particularly impressed by them. In fact,

Sixteen-week-old
male Saint. Sired
by Ch. Beau
Cheval's Padre,
out of Von
Alpler's
Something
Fancy. Alpler
Kennels,
Leavenworth, Ks.

I recall remarking that they resembled Bloodhounds—a remark that is an insult to a smooth fancier. I did not realize that smooths of that particular breeding would still not impress me ten years later, for there are smooths and *there are Smooths.*

Approximately three years later, I was to see the kind of smooth that really excited me—a Saint of such size, strength, and power,

Apple-Creek's Mescha, at five weeks of age. She was bred and is owned by Mr. and Mrs. Freeman Bixler, Drums, Pa. She is out of Christy's Miss Kitty, sired by Beau Cheval's Padre La Mardoug.

Beau Cheval's Cherie at seven weeks old. She is owned by Mr. and Mrs. Paul W. Klco, of Mount Laurel, N.J. and sired by Beau Cheval's Baron Ex Beau Cheval's Cherna.

Little Jackie Costello of Chicago poses with Rufus, a three-year-old Saint Bernard, to help announce that the Saint Bernard is gaining fastest of all breeds in popularity in the United States.

that I accepted the challenge to breed dogs like this even though I had none in my kennel with which to begin. The dog that impressed me was a large linebred male puppy, which concentrated the best of Riga and Powell bloodlines.

Prior to viewing this dog, I had decided on the type of Saint I wanted to breed. A photograph of the head of a young Swiss import, Kobi v Steinernhof (then a Canadian Champion only), possessing the true majesty and nobility of expression I wanted, caused me to purchase my first smooth Saint—his granddaughter, and she was bred back to Kobi, her grandsire. It was smooth to smooth, and I was sure I was on the right track by concentrating on him.

Benedictine and Gabby, two of
Robert Beatty's Saint puppies, at
four weeks of age.

A "Poncho" puppy, with son of the
owners of Devinedale Kennels, Mr.
and Mrs. T. Devine, Chatham, N.Y.

Tapan Zee II, short-haired smooth puppy from Beau Cheval Kennels.

Best Brace in Show at the Westminster Kennel Club Show on February 12, 1963 was Rex Robert's glorious Saint Bernards, Wunderbar Von Narbenholt and Ch. Haagen Von Narbenholt. The judge was Virgil Johnson, and the handler is Miss Jessica Roberts.

Winners of the Saint Bernard classes at the December 1965 Eastern Dog Club show were Ch. Shady Lady of Barca on the left, handled by Alfred Saba, Jr. and Ch. Switzer of Shady Hollow on the right with handler Frank Ashbey. Shady Hollow Kennels are owned by Phyllis Jackson Smith of Johnston, R.I.

Rough puppies from smooth sire, Beau Cheval's Parish and rough dam,
Beau Cheval's Toffe la Mardoug.

John C. Sheahan
IV, of Media, Pa.,
pictured with his
Saint Bernard
Missy.

Thor Von Skala,
a son of Ch. Kurt
v Alpine Plateau.
Owned by Phyllis
Smith of
Johnston, R.I.

Saints of the past . . .

Handler John M. Creighton with a winning smooth-coated Saint Bernard owned by John C. Sheahan III of Pennsylvania. His name is Champion Dean of Highmont.

My husband and I owned perhaps ten Saints then, all of the rough variety, and we could plainly see we had been wasting our time breeding and housing them. The smooths we first bred out-moved and had far better type than the roughs. We were determined to develop a line from this first litter of seven. From the litter, four were shown and became champions; all went on to produce champions, which in turn produced champions.

That was 1960, and since that time, we have bred or owned 47 champions of record to date, none of which was purchased with as much as one point. Of those 47 champions, only five were not of my breeding. This does not compare with breeders like Beatrice Knight, who has bred some 80 to 100 champions in thirty years,

Ch. Sanctuary Woods Coat of Arms, age 3½, a short-haired dog owned by Beatrice Knight and R. L. Golden, Oyster Bay, L.I., N.Y.

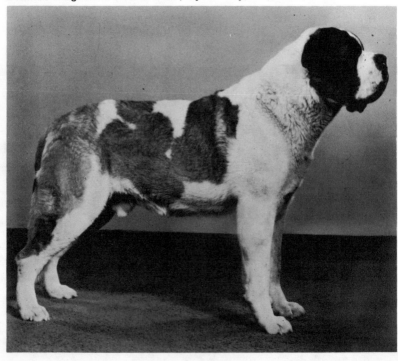

A rough puppy, son of Ch. Otto, owned and bred by Ann Mann, The Abbey Kennels, Odessa, Fla.

but the success of our breeding program cannot be denied, and the percentage of champions produced is high.

When asked what a new breeder should start with in coat type, I always reply: SMOOTH! This is my humble and honest opinion, based on experience, over a ten-year period of breeding both coats. I find that smooths produce better type, more soundness of body, and fewer problems connected with the breeding of giant dogs. I might also mention that less care and coat conditioning are required for smooths.

I seldom breed rough to rough, and when I do, the percentage of sound, typey offspring is low. I usually advise clients who have rough bitches in heat to use smooth studs—just to be safe and produce better dogs. This advice is based on a follow-up study over a two-year period of all the puppies that I produced and sold. All our smooth studs and rough studs are from a predominantly smooth background.

Six-week-old Donna Dube is enjoying guarded sleep, thanks to Champion Carmen Show Girl of Ox Yoke, owned by Mary Lou and Donald Dube of the Mardonof Kennels.

All this tells you is that I prefer smooths over roughs for my personal breeding program. However, I have no coat preference regarding individual Saints, for I am drawn to the most beautiful dog, and coat does not enter into it. I have seen dozens of near perfect smooths. I have, however, traveled in this country and Europe and I have yet to see the near perfect rough. I have never bred a dog with which I am completely satisfied, and I haven't come close to breeding a rough that has contented me.

The most magnificent rough I have seen was International Champion Anton v Hofli, owned by Dr. Antonio Morsianni of Italy, and bred and purchased from Switzerland. He is pictured in this book. Anton possessed the true nature of a Saint as well as living up to the first paragraph in our Standard, which describes a tall and upstanding dog. Too many winning roughs are feminine, small, and lack bone and substance. Too many "pretty" roughs are slab-sided, shallow in front, and hide all their flaws beneath a luxurious thick coat of lovely red mantled long hair.

Many judges are impressed with this lovely outward appearance, and do not look beneath the coat for the many faults that exist. It's like viewing the ten most beautiful girls in the pageant dressed in fur coats. How does one know what kind of framework lies beneath?

Please remember the smooth Saint was the *original*. It remains the chief factor necessary in a correct breeding program. To those who refuse to face this fact, I can only say, you are breeding dogs, but that's all! The breeder who wants to breed Standard-type Saints uses both coats in his breeding program.

The buying public needs to be educated in many areas. It's true that they perhaps can find only rough coats to view and buy in some states. But how will they ever come to know the smooth Saint if they never see one?

Baron's Tyras von Hi-Tor, 20-month-old son of the famous Alpineacres Baron von Shagg-Bark, pictured winning Best of Winners under Judge Virginia Hampton in the summer of 1971. This was a win he repeated at the Eastern Dog Club show in Boston in December of the same year. He is owned by Ann T. Tenner of Hi-Tor Farm Kennels, Wells, Maine.

Ch. Roca's Image of Zee displays beautiful head type, with disposition to match. A young smooth dog, he's owned by Mr. and Mrs. Michael Borheady of Flemington, N.J.

Beau Cheval's Royal Mardoug, owned by Lt.-Col. Paul J. and Margaret D. Phillips. Sired by Ch. Beau Cheval's Padre, and out of Ch. Beau Cheval's Contesa.

Vicar's Deacon of Glyndon, bred by Marlene Anderson and Gretchen Hoover, is owned by Mr. and Mrs. James Macaluso of Baltimore, Md. He is shown with Steven Macaluso.

Ch. Patrich's Forward Pass, shown with Tammy Aitken, is owned by Mr. and Mrs. Frank Aitken of Manhattan Beach, Calif. Snoopy is out of Ch. Charlinore's Grand Ursula, and a grandson of Ch. Kobi v. Steinernhof. The young champion, bred by Pat and Richard Wiggins, has excellent type, color and disposition and was handled to his title by his owner.

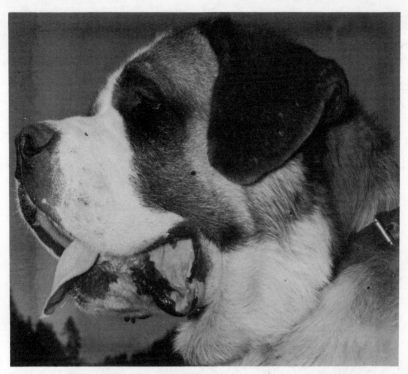

Head study of Ch. Sanctuary Woods Fantabulous, from the kennels of Beatrice Knight, taken in August, 1962.

Ch. Roca's Image of Zee, son of Beau Cheval's Tapan Zee II, plays fetch with his litter brother Sasha (left).

AKC Judge Richard Tang's Niclause Jon Triston, now deceased. Smooth son of Powell's Champion Tristan of Riga.

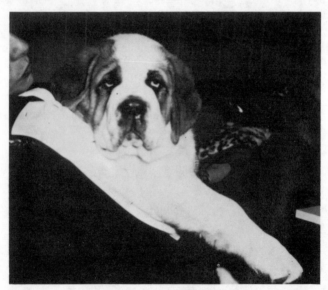

Beau Cheval's Epic la Mardoug, owned by Leslie and Shelly Golden, Bala Cynwyd, Pa. Sired by Ch. Beau Cheval's Golden Ceasar and out of Beau Cheval's Toldya Mardoug. Bred by M. J. Anderson.

Beau Cheval's Berne, longhaired puppy, poses at six weeks.

"Anchor" (Roca's Image of Zee) at seven months of age, with owner Carol Borheady of Flemington, N.J.

I often hear the argument that the novice breeder cannot sell a smooth puppy. If this same novice knew the great selling points a smooth has over a rough, and could correctly answer all and any questions on the two different coats, this problem would not exist. More important, they should, if at all possible, let the prospective buyer see both coats at maturity and then the smooth Saint will sell itself.

Try these selling points if the question comes up:

1. For the lady who hates hair all over the house . . . buy a smooth.

2. For easy flea and tick detection . . . buy a smooth rather than a rough.

3. For less grooming . . . buy a smooth.

4. For breeding purposes . . . buy a smooth.

5. For less growth and bone problems . . . buy a smooth.

Now it might be said, and somewhat truly, that roughs finish their championships more easily than smooths, and that the largest number of big winners are of the rough coat. This can only reflect on the judges. Our experience, which represents over ten years of breeding both coats, and using a greater number of smooths in our breeding program, indicates that the incidence of Hip Dysplasia is high er in roughs than in smooths.

# CHAPTER 8
# BREEDING YOUR SAINT BERNARD

Let us assume the time has come for your dog to be bred, and you have decided you are in a position to enjoy producing a litter of puppies that you hope will make a contribution to the breed. The bitch you purchased is sound, her temperament is excellent and she is a most worthy representative of the breed.

You have taken a calendar and counted off the ten days since the first day of red staining and have determined the tenth to 14th day which will more than likely be the best days for the actual mating. You have additionally counted off 59–63 days before the puppies will be born to make sure everything necessary for their arrival will be in good order by that time.

From the moment the idea of having a litter occurred to you, your thoughts should have been given to the correct selection of a proper stud. Here again the novice would do well to seek advice on analyzing pedigrees and tracing bloodlines for your best breedings. As soon as the bitch is in season and you see color (or staining) and a swelling of the vulva, it is time to notify the owner of the stud you selected and make appointments for the breedings. There are several pertinent questions you will want to ask the stud owner after having decided upon the pedigree.

## THE HEALTH OF THE BREEDING STOCK

Some of your first questions should be: Has this adult male ever sired a litter? Has his sperm count been checked? Has he been X-rayed for Hip Dysplasia and found to be clear? Does he have two normal-sized testicles? Do not be impressed with the owner's romantic tales of his "Romeo" behavior. You can hear just as many stories about the amorous male that thinks he's a stud, but has never yet made a successful tie. Ask if he needs human assistance to complete a breeding and what his score is on the number of breedings that have produced a litter. Is he a lazy or aggressive stud; in other words, does he give up easily if the bitch does not cooperate?

When considering your bitch for this mating, you must take into consideration a few important points that lead to a successful breeding. Has she had normal heat cycles? Four months may be normal for some, but six or nine months is normal for most. Has she ever been bred before and what were the results? Did she have normal puppies? Too many runts—mis-marks, brown noses, etc.? Has she ever had a vaginal infection? Did she have a normal delivery and did the pregnancy go its full term? Did she have to have one or more Cesarean sections? Was she a good mother, and did she have a lot of milk, or none at all? Did she allow assistance during delivery? Did the puppies all survive or did you lose several from the litter shortly after birth?

Don't buy a bitch that has problem heats and never a litter. And don't be afraid to buy a healthy maiden bitch, since chances are, if she is healthy and from good stock, she will be a healthy producer for you. Don't buy a monorchid male, or one with a low sperm count. Any veterinarian can give you a count and you will do well to require one, especially if it is to be the stud dog for a kennel. Older dogs that have been good producers and are for sale are usually not too hard to find at good established kennels. If they are not too old and have sired show quality puppies, they can give you some excellent litters from which to establish your breeding stock from solid bloodlines.

## THE WEDDING DATE

Now that you have decided upon the proper male and female combination to produce what you hope will be—according to the pedigrees—a fine litter of puppies, it is time to set the date. You have selected the two days (with one day lapse in between) that you feel are best for the breeding, and you call the owner of the stud. The bitch always goes to the stud, unless, of course, there are extenuating circumstances and the stud then goes to the female. You set the date and the time and arrive with the dog and the *money*.

Standard procedure is payment of a stud fee at the time of the first breeding, if there is a tie. For the stud fee, you are entitled to two breedings with ties. Contracts may be written up with specific conditions on breeding terms, of course, but this is general pro-

Rylands Brandy x Ch. Rajah v. Heidengeld litter. Puppies are eight days old. From this litter came Ch. Indian Mountain Pawnee.

cedure. Often a breeder will take the pick of a litter to protect and maintain his bloodlines. This can be especially desirable if he needs an outcross for his breeding program. He may also wish to maintain his bloodline if you have originally purchased the bitch from him and the breeding will continue his line-breeding program. This should all be worked out ahead of time and written and signed before the two dogs are bred together. Remember that the payment of the stud fee is for the services of the stud—not for a guarantee of a litter of puppies. This is why it is so important to make sure you are using a proven stud. Bear in mind, also, that the American Kennel Club will not register a litter of puppies sired by a male that is under eight months of age. In the case of the older dog, they will not register a litter sired by a dog over 12 years of age, without a witness to the breeding in the form of a veterinarian or other responsible person.

Many studs over 12 years of age are still fertile and capable of producing puppies, but if you do not witness the breeding there is always the danger of a "substitute" stud being used to produce a litter. This brings up the subject of sending your bitch away to be bred, if you cannot accompany her.

The disadvantages of sending a bitch away to be bred are numerous. First of all, she will not be herself in a strange place and may be difficult to handle. Transportation—if she goes by air—while reasonably safe, is still a traumatic experience and there is the danger of her being put off at the wrong airport, not being fed or watered properly, etc. Some bitches get so upset that they go out of season and the trip, which may prove expensive, especially on top of a substantial stud fee, will have been for nothing.

If at all possible, accompany your bitch so that the experience is as comfortable for her as it can be. In other words, make sure before setting this kind of schedule for a breeding that there is no stud in the area that might be as good for her as the one that is far away. We do not wish to have you sacrifice the proper breeding for convenience, since bloodlines are so important, but we do put the safety of the bitch above all else. There is always a risk in traveling, since dogs are considered cargo on a plane.

## HOW MUCH DOES THE STUD FEE COST?

The stud fee will vary considerably—the better the bloodlines, the more winning the dog does at shows, the higher the fee. A top winning dog could run up to $500. Here again, there may be exceptions. Some breeders will take part cash and then, say, third or fourth pick of the litter. The fee can be arranged by a private contract, rather than the traditional procedure we have described.

Many Saints not only require the aid and assistance of the owners, but breeding racks are often necessary to accomplish the mating. Following this chapter are complete instructions on how the owner of a Saint can build one of these racks himself, or where he can purchase one if he so desires.

## THE BREEDING RACK

While there are breeding racks available for sale, it is also quite possible to build your own without having any specific talent for

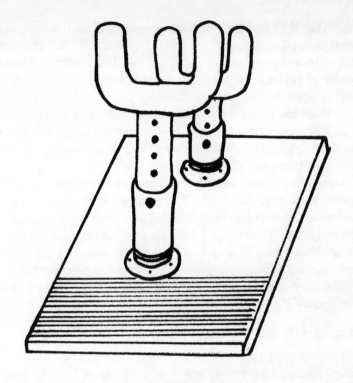

Sketch of Breeding Rack

construction. The materials needed to build a rack for a Saint Bernard are as follows:

The Platform

A piece of plywood 32 inches wide × 48 inches long and $\frac{3}{4}''$ thick

A piece of corrugated rubber matting for the end (see drawing)

2 pipe flanges—2 inches each

2 pieces of 2 inch pipe—15 inch each

2 pieces of $1\frac{3}{4}$ inch pipe—15 inches each

Sponge rubber

Masking tape

2 pins or nails $\frac{1}{4}$ inch × 3 inches long

2 pieces of flat iron $\frac{1}{4}$ inch thick, $1\frac{1}{2}$ inches wide, 22 inches long.

Take the two-inch pipe flanges, bolt the front flange 10 inches from the end of the platform board and center it. Bolt the second flange 16 inches in back of the first flange and center it. Take two pieces of two-inch pipe 15 inches long, with threads on one end only, and screw these into the flanges. The base is now complete.

From the top of the pipes, measure down one inch and drill a $\frac{1}{4}$ inch hole to allow for a pin to enter for adjusting the rack later on. Take two pipes 15 inches long by $1\frac{3}{4}$ inches and drill $\frac{1}{4}$ inch holes down the pipe one inch apart.

Next take the two pieces of flat iron metal and bend into a "U" shape, with the base of the "U" approximately 10 inches across and six inches rising on either side. Have the flat metal welded onto the end of the $1\frac{3}{4}$ inch pipe. Then cover it with the sponge rubber, using the masking tape to cover the metal well. Use the pins, or nails, for adjusting to the proper height for the breeding bitch.

Use the yellow pages for plumbing materials or welding services, if necessary.

## USING THE BREEDING RACK

This breeding rack will become one of the most useful items in your breeding program. It is practically a "must" for the breeder with stud dogs where all kinds of uncooperative bitches may be coming in for stud service. Some bitches, especially the first time, will be frightened (or vicious) from fear; others are spoiled. This positive type of assistance will be necessary if the breeding is to be a success. Also, the "wild" bitch may snap or attack the stud and, depending upon his experience, he may become discouraged from breeding.

It is always the safest procedure to "muzzle" the bitch. This can be done with a ladies stocking tied around the muzzle with a half knot, crossed under the chin and knotted at the back of the neck. There is enough "give" in the stocking for her to breathe or salivate freely and yet not open her jaws far enough to bite. Place her in the "saddle" on the rack and loosely tie her front legs with a soft leash to the pole on the front of the rack. Make sure she is comfortable in the saddle by adjusting the pins to proper height. The owner of the bitch should remain in front of the bitch to calm and reassure her as much as possible.

If the male will not mount on his own initiative, because he is disconcerted with the apparatus, it may be necessary for the owner to assist in lifting him on to the bitch. Once he gets the idea, additional assistance probably will not be necessary. Once the tie is accomplished the owner of the stud should remain close at hand to see that the stud does not try to break away before the tie has been completed. At times, a male gets bored, especially if the tie is a long one, and he attempts to run off. This could prove injurious. Once you are certain the tie has been completed, the stud can be carefully lifted off, if he seems unable to do it himself.

We cannot stress here too strongly that, while some bitches carry on physically, and vocally, there is no way the bitch can be hurt. However, a stud can be seriously or even permanently damaged by a bad breeding. Therefore, the owner of the bitch should be advised that she must try to calm, but not be alarmed by, the bitch who is behaving badly. All concentration should be devoted to the stud and a successful and properly executed service.

Many people are of the opinion that breeding dogs is simply a matter of placing a male and female in close proximity, and letting nature take its course. While sometimes this is true, you cannot count on it. In the case of Saint Bernards, it is usually a matter of hard work to accomplish a breeding. The dogs are large and it usually requires two people and a breeding rack, especially if one or both of the dogs are inexperienced. If the owners are also inexperienced, it might as well never take place at all! It is wise when planning to breed your dog to have at least one of the people on hand well experienced.

## ARTIFICIAL INSEMINATION

Breeding by means of artificial insemination is usually unsuccessful, unless under a veterinarian's supervision, and can lead to an infection for the bitch and discomfort for the dog. The American Kennel Club requires a veterinarian's certificate to register puppies from such a breeding. Although the practice has been used for over two decades, it now offers new promise since research has been conducted to make it a more feasible procedure for the future.

Great dogs may eventually look forward to reproducing themselves years after they have left this earth. There now exists a frozen semen concept that has been tested and works. The study, headed by Dr. Stephen W. J. Seager, M.V.B., and instructor at the University of Oregon Medical School, has the financial support of the American Kennel Club, indicating that organization's interest in the work. The study is being monitored by the Morris Animal Foundation, Denver, Colo.

Dr. Seager announced in 1970 he had been able to preserve dog semen and to produce litters with the stored semen. The possibilities of selective, world-wide breedings by this method are exciting. Imagine simply mailing a vial of semen to the bitch! The perfection of line-breeding by storing semen without the threat of death interrupting the breeding program is exciting, also.

As it stands today, the technique for artificial insemination requires the depositing of semen (taken directly from the dog) into the bitch's vagina, past the cervix and into the uterus by syringe. The correct temperature of the semen is vital, and there is no guarantee of success.

The storage method, if adopted, will present a new era in the field of purebred dogs.

## THE GESTATION PERIOD

Once the breeding has taken place successfully, the seemingly endless waiting period of 63 days begins. For the first ten days after the breeding, you do absolutely nothing for the bitch—just spin dreams about the delights you will share with the family when the puppies arrive.

Around the tenth day it is time to begin supplementing the diet of the bitch with vitamins and calcium. We strongly recommend that you take her to your veterinarian for a list of the proper supplements and the correct amounts for your particular bitch. Guesses, which may lead to excesses or insufficiencies, can ruin a litter. For the price of a visit to your veterinarian, you will be confident that you are feeding properly.

The bitch should be free of worms, of course, and if there is any doubt in your mind, she should be wormed now, before the third week of pregnancy. Your veterinarian will advise you on the necessity of this as well.

## PROBING FOR PUPPIES

Far too many breeders are overanxious about whether the breeding "took" and are inclined to feel for puppies or persuade a

Brandi and five-week-old puppies spend the afternoon outdoors. They are owned by the Robert Beattys of Philadelphia.

veterinarian to radiograph or X-ray their bitches to confirm it. Unless there is reason to doubt the normalcy of a pregnancy, this is risky. Certainly 63 days are not too long to wait, and why risk endangering the litter by probing with your inexperienced hands? Few bitches give no evidence of being in whelp, and there is no need to prove it for yourself by trying to count puppies.

## ALERTING YOUR VETERINARIAN

At least a week before the puppies are due, you should telephone your veterinarian and notify him that you expect the litter and give him the date. This way he can make sure that there will be someone available to help, should there be any problems during the whelping. Most veterinarians today have answering services and alternate veterinarians on call when they are not available themselves. Some vets suggest that you call them when the bitch starts labor so that they may further plan their time, should they be needed. Discuss this matter with him when you first take the bitch to him for her diet instructions, etc., and establish the method which will best fit in with his schedule.

## DO YOU NEED A VETERINARIAN IN ATTENDANCE?

Even if this is your first litter, we would advise that you go through the experience of whelping without panicking and calling desperately for the veterinarian. Most animal births are accomplished without complications, and you should call for assistance only if you run into trouble.

When having her puppies your bitch will appreciate as little interference and as few strangers around as possible. A quiet place, with her nest, a single familiar face and her own instincts are all that is necessary for nature to take its course. An audience of curious children squealing and questioning, other family pets nosing around, or strange adults should be avoided. Many a bitch who has been distracted in this way has been known to devour her young. This can be the horrible result of intrusion of the bitch's privacy. There are other ways of teaching children the miracle of birth, and there will be plenty of time later for the whole family to enjoy the puppies. Let them be born under proper and considerate circumstances.

## LABOR

Some litters—many first litters—do not run the full term of 63 days. So, at least a week before the puppies are actually due, and at the time you alert your veterinarian as to their arrival, start observing the bitch for signs of the commencement of labor. This will manifest itself in the form of ripples running down the sides of her body, which will come as a revelation to her as well. It is most noticeable when she is lying on her side—and she will be sleeping a great deal as the arrival date comes closer. If she is sitting or walking about, she will perhaps sit down quickly or squat peculiarly. When you notice this for the first time, your vigil has begun. As the ripples become more frequent, birth time is drawing near and you will be wise not to leave her. Usually within 24 hours before whelping, she will stop eating, and as much as a week before, she will begin digging a nest. The bitch should be given something resembling a whelping box with layers of newspaper (black and white only) to make her nest. She will dig more and more as birth approaches and this is the time to begin making your promise to stop interfering unless your help is specifically required. Some bitches whimper, others are silent, but whimpering does not necessarily indicate trouble.

## THE ARRIVAL OF THE PUPPIES

The sudden gush of green fluid from the bitch indicates that the water or fluid surrounding the puppies has "broken" and they are about to start down the canal and come into the world.When the water breaks, birth of the first puppy is imminent. The first puppies are usually born within minutes to a half hour of each other, but a couple of hours between the later ones is not uncommon. If you notice the bitch straining constantly without producing a puppy, or if a puppy remains partially in and partially out for too long, it is cause for concern. Breach births (puppies born feet instead of head first) can often cause delay or hold things up, and this is often a problem which requires veterinary assistance.

## FEEDING THE BITCH BETWEEN BIRTHS

Usually the bitch will not be interested in food for about 24 hours before the arrival of the puppies, and perhaps as long as two or three days after their arrival. The placenta which she cleans up after each puppy is high in food value and will be more than ample to sustain her. This is nature's way of allowing the mother to feed herself and her babies without having to leave the nest and hunt for food during the first crucial days. The mother always cleans up all traces of birth in the wilds so as not to attract other animals to her newborn babies.

However, there are those of us who believe in making food available, should the mother feel the need to restore her strength during or after delivery—especially if she whelps a large litter. Raw chopmeat, beef bouillon, and milk are all acceptable and may be placed near the whelping box during the first two or three days. After that, the mother will begin to put the babies on a sort of schedule. She will leave the whelping box at frequent intervals, take longer exercise periods, and begin to take interest in other things. This is where the fun begins for you. Now the babies are no longer soggy, little, pinkish blobs. They begin to crawl around and squeal and hum and grow before your very eyes!

It is at this time, if all has gone normally, that the family can be introduced gradually and great praise and affection given to the mother.

"Dupe" at 21 days.

"Dupe" at ten months.

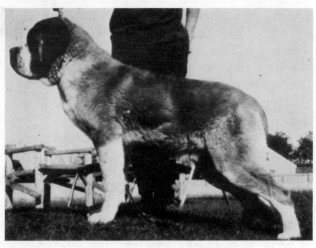

A Saint Bernard puppy grows up. Champion Mardonof's Duplicate of Image is the son of two Specialty—winning show dog parents—American and Bermuda Champion Mardonof's Image of Figaro and Champion Mardonof's Duchess Melina.

## BREACH BIRTHS

Puppies normally are delivered head first. However, some are presented feet first and this is referred to as a "breach birth." Assistance is often necessary to get the puppy out of the canal, and great care must be taken not to injure the puppy or the dam.

Aid can be given by grasping the puppy with a piece of turkish toweling and pulling gently during the dam's contractions. Be

159

Like father, like son . . . at the Hospice in Switzerland.

careful not to squeeze the puppy too hard, merely try to ease it out by moving it gently back and forth. Because even this much delay in delivery may mean the puppy is drowning, do not wait for the bitch to remove the sac. Do it yourself by tearing the sac open to expose the face and head. Then cut the cord anywhere from one-half to three-quarters of an inch away from the navel. If the cord bleeds excessively, pinch the end of it with your fingers and count five. Repeat if necessary. Then pry open the mouth with your finger and hold the puppy upsidedown for a moment to drain any fluids from the lungs. Next, rub the puppy briskly with turkish or paper toweling. You should get wriggling and whimpering by this time.

If the litter is large, this assistance will help conserve the strength of the bitch and will probably be welcomed by her. However, it is best to allow her to take care of at least the first few herself to preserve the natural instinct, and to provide the nutritive values obtained by her consumption of the afterbirths.

## DRY BIRTHS

Occasionally, the sac will break before the delivery of a puppy and will be expelled while the puppy remains inside, thereby depriving the dam of the necessary lubrication to expel the puppy normally. Inserting vaseline or mineral oil via your finger will help the puppy pass down the birth canal. This is why it is essential that you be present during the whelping so that you can count puppies and afterbirths and determine when and if assistance is needed.

## THE TWENTY-FOUR-HOUR CHECKUP

It is smart to have a veterinarian check the mother and her puppies within 24 hours after the last puppy is born. The veterinarian can check for a cleft palate or umbilical hernia and may wish to give the dam—particularly if she is a show dog—an injection of Pituitin to make sure of the expulsion of all afterbirths and to tighten up the uterus. This can prevent a sagging belly after the puppies are weaned and the bitch is being readied for the show ring.

## FALSE PREGNANCY

The disappointment of a false pregnancy is almost as bad for the owner as it is for the bitch. She goes through the entire 63 days with all the symptoms—swollen stomach, increased appetite, swollen nipples—even makes a nest when the time comes. You may even take an oath that you noticed the ripples on her body from the labor pains. Then, just as suddenly as you made up your mind that she was definitely going to have puppies, you will know that she definitely is not! She may walk around carrying a toy as if it were a puppy for a few days, but she will soon be back to normal and acting just as if nothing happened—and nothing did!

## CAESAREAN SECTION

Should the whelping reach the point where there is a complication, such as the bitch not being capable of whelping the puppies herself, the "moment of truth" is upon you and a Caesarean section may be necessary. The bitch may be too small or too immature to expel the puppies herself; or her cervix may fail to dilate enough to

Gretchen Hoover and one of her Glyndon Saint Bernard puppies at two weeks of age, sitting in a trophy won by one of his ancestors.

Babies together . . . Karin Thorne, daughter of Cam and Richard Thorne, Pinckney, Mich., with her Saint Bernard puppy.

allow the young to come down the birth canal; or there may be torsion of the uterus, a dead or monster puppy, a sideways puppy blocking the canal, or perhaps toxemia. A Caesarean section will be the only solution. No matter what the cause, get the bitch to the veterinarian immediately to insure your chances of saving the mother and/or the puppies.

The Caesarean section operation (the name derived from the legend that Julius Caesar was delivered into the world by this method) involves the removal of the unborn young from the uterus of the dam by surgical incision into the walls through the abdomen. The operation is performed when it has been determined that for some reason the puppies cannot be delivered normally. While modern surgical methods have made the operation itself reasonably safe, with the dam being perfectly capable of nursing the puppies shortly after the completion of the surgery, the chief danger lies in the ability to spark life into the puppies immediately upon their removal from the womb. If the mother dies, the time element is even more important in saving the young, since the oxygen supply

Indian Mountain's Pocohontas with "Troubles," at the kennels in East Stroudsburg, Pa., owned by Ruthe and John Young.

ceases upon the death of the dam, and the difference between life and death is measured in seconds.

After surgery when the bitch is home in her whelping box with the babies, she will probably nurse the young without distress. You must be sure that the sutures are kept clean and that no redness or swelling or ooze appears in the wound. Healing will take place naturally and no salves or ointments should be applied unless prescribed by the veterinarian, for fear the puppies will get it into their systems. Check the bitch for fever if there is any doubt, restlessness, (other than the natural concern for her young) or a lack of appetite, but do not anticipate trouble.

## EPISIOTOMY

Even though the large breeds of dogs, such as the Saint Bernard, are generally easy whelpers, any number of reasons might occur to cause the bitch to have a difficult birth. Before automatically resorting to Caesarean section, many veterinarians are now trying the technique known as episiotomy.

Used rather frequently in human deliveries, episiot‑
nounced A-PEASE-E-OTT-O-ME) is the cutting of the n
between the rear opening of the vagina back almost to the

of the anus. After delivery it is stitched together, and barring complications, heals easily, presenting no problem in future births.

## ORPHAN PUPPIES

Should you experience the misfortune of having a litter of orphaned puppies, either because the dam has died, or is for some reason unwilling or unable to take care of the puppies herself, there is still a good possibility of saving them. With today's substitutes for mother's milk, and with a lot of perseverance on your part, it can be done.

The first step is to take the puppies far enough away from the mother so that their odor and crying does not make her restless or remind her that she is not doing the job herself. The next step is to see that they are kept warm and dry and out of drafts. This can be accomplished by placing them in a deep box on a heating pad in a quiet, secluded spot in the house where there is no bright light to injure their sensitive eyes when they begin to open at anywhere from one to two weeks of age.

Caution! The most important point regarding the heating pad is that you must be absolutely sure it is not too hot. There have been enough reports of "cooked" puppies to turn us into vegetarians! Put the heating pad on its very lowest temperature, cover it with several thicknesses of newspaper and a small baby blanket on top of that. Test it by holding your wrist and inner arm on it steadily for a few minutes to see if the heat is too intense. If it is, more newspaper must be added. There should be barely more than a discernible warmth—not heat. Also make sure that at least a third of the bottom of the box is not covered with the heating pad so that if the heat builds up, the puppy's natural instinct might help them escape to a section of the box which is not heated—just as they would crawl away from the dam if they were too warm or snuggle up to her if they felt the need for warmth. Too much heat also tends to dehydrate the puppies. Make sure, also, the heating pad is well secured so that the puppies do not suffocate under it while moving around in the box.

Now that you have the puppies bedded down properly in a substitute environment comparable to one they would share with their natural mother, you provide the survival diet! Your substitute formula must be precisely prepared, always served heated to body

164

Head study of Beau Cheval's Texan la Mardoug, owned by Thomas and Regina Keiter of Pennsylvania. Sired by Beau Cheval's Tapan Zee II and out of Ch. Beau Cheval's Della la Mardoug, Texan is the perfect gentleman.

temperature and refrigerated when not being fed. Esbilac, a vacuum-packed powder, with complete feeding instructions on the can, is excellent and about as close to mother's milk as you can get. If you can't get Esbilac, or until you do get Esbilac, there are two alternative formulas that you might use.

Mix one part boiled water with five parts of evaporated milk and add one teaspoonful of di-calcium phosphate per quart of formula. Di-calcium phosphate can be secured at any drug store. If they have it in tablet form only, you can powder the tablets with the back part of a tablespoon. The other formula for newborn puppies is a combination of eight ounces of homogenized milk mixed well with two egg yolks.

You will need baby bottles with the three-hole nipples. Sometimes doll bottles can be used for the newborn puppies, which should be fed at six-hour intervals. If they are consuming sufficient amounts, their stomachs should look full, or slightly enlarged, though never distended. Amount of formula to be fed is proportionate to size and age, and growth and weight of puppy, and is indicated on the can of Esbilac or on the advice of your veterinarian. Many breeders like to keep a baby scale nearby to check the weight of the puppies to be sure they are thriving on the formula.

At two to three weeks you can start adding Pablum or some other high protein baby cereal to the formula. Also, baby beef can be licked from your finger at this age, or added to the formula. At four weeks the surviving puppies should be taken off the diet of Esbilac and put on a more substantial diet, such as wet puppy meal or cereals with chopped beef. However, Esbilac powder can still be mixed in with the food for additional nutrition.

## HOW TO FEED THE NEWBORN PUPPIES

When the puppy is a newborn, remember that it is vitally important to keep the feeding procedure as close to the natural mother's routine as possible. The newborn puppy should be held in your hand in an almost upright position with the bottle at an angle to allow the entire nipple area to be full of the formula. Do not hold the bottle upright so the puppy's head has to reach straight up toward the ceiling. Do not let the puppy nurse too quickly or take in too much air and possibly get colic. Once in a while, take the bottle away and let him rest for a moment and swallow several

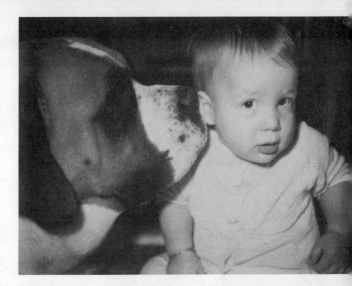

Beau Cheval's ZEE ZEE Rider shares a secret with his buddy, Joe Collins. Beau is sired by Beau Cheval's Tapan Zee II out of Indian Mountain's Honey Bear. The twosome lives in Springfield, Pa.

times. Before feeding, always test the nipple to see that the fluid does not come out too quickly, or by the same token, too slowly so that the puppy gets tired of feeding before he has had enough to eat.

When the puppy is a little older, you can place him on his stomach on a towel to eat, and even allow him to hold on to the bottle or to "come and get it" on his own. Most puppies enjoy eating and this will be a good indication of how strong an appetite he has and his ability to consume the contents of the bottle.

It will be necessary to "burp" the puppy. Place a towel on your shoulder and hold the puppy on your shoulder as if it were a human baby, patting and rubbing it gently. This will also encourage the puppy to defecate. At this time, you should observe for diarrhea or other intestinal disorders. The puppy should eliminate after each feeding with occasional eliminations between times as well. If the puppies do not eliminate on their own after each meal, massage their stomachs and under their tails until they do.

You must be sure to keep the puppies clean. If there is diarrhea the puppy should be washed and dried off. Under no circumstances should fecal matter be allowed to collect on their skin or fur.

All this—plus your determination and perseverance—might save an entire litter of puppies that would otherwise have died without their real mother.

Beau Cheval's Vicar v Chaparral prefers his outdoor quarters to being inside—especially when it snows! "Gus" is co-owned by his breeder, Marlene J. Anderson, and Gretchen Hoover of Glyndon Saints, Reisterstown, Md.

Longhaired puppy, Beau Cheval's Zurich, is set-up at six weeks.

## WEANING THE PUPPIES

There are many diets today for young puppies, including all sorts of products on the market for feeding the newborn, for supplementing feeding the young and for adding this or that to diets, depending on what is lacking in the way of complete diet.

When weaning puppies, it is necessary to put them on four meals a day, even while you are tapering off with the mother's milk. Six in the morning, twelve noon, six in the evening and midnight is about the best schedule since it fits in with most human eating plans. Meals for the puppies can be prepared immediately before or after your own meals, without too much of a change in your schedule.

### 6 A.M.

Two meat and two milk meals serve best and should be served alternately, of course. Assuming the 6 a.m. feeding is a milk meal the contents should be as follows: Goat's milk is the very best milk to feed puppies, but is expensive and usually available only at drug stores, unless you live in farm country where it could be inexpensive. If goat's milk is not available, use evaporated milk (which can be changed to powdered milk later on) diluted to two parts evaporated milk and one part water, along with raw egg yoke, honey or Karo syrup, sprinkled with a high-protein baby cereal and some wheat germ. As the puppies mature cottage cheese may be added or, at one of the two milk meals, it can be substituted for the cereal.

## NOON

A puppy chow which has been soaked according to the time specified on the wrapper should be mixed with raw or simmered chop meat in equal proportions with a vitamin powder added.

## 6 P.M.

Repeat the milk meal.

## MIDNIGHT

Repeat the meat meal.

Please note that specific proportions of the suggested diet are not given. Each serving will depend entirely upon the size of the litter and will increase proportionately with their rate of growth. However, it is safe to say that the most important ingredients are the milk and cereal, and the meat and puppy chow which forms the basis of the diet. Your veterinarian can advise on the proportions if there is any doubt in your mind as to how much to use.

We would like to point out that there are some basic concepts in a successful feeding program. Remember, that if there is any doubt in your mind about an ingredient, ask yourself, "Would I give it to my own baby?" If the answer is no, then don't give it to your puppies. At this age, the comparison between puppies and human babies can be a good guide.

If you notice that the puppies are "cleaning their plates" you are perhaps not feeding enough to keep up with their rate of growth. Increase the amount at the next feeding. Observe them closely; puppies should each "have their fill" because their rate of growth is so rapid at this age. If they have not satisfied themselves, increase your proportions for the next feeding. You will find that if given all they can handle, they will not overeat. When they know they do not have to fight for the last morsel, they will eat to their natural capacity.

While it is not the most pleasant subject to discuss, many

puppies will regurgitate their food, perhaps a couple of times, before they manage to retain it. If they do bring up their food, allow them to eat it again, rather than clean it away. Sometimes additional saliva is necessary for them to digest it, and you do not want them to skip a meal because it is an unpleasant sight for you to observe.

This same regurgitation process holds true sometimes with the bitch, who will bring up her own food for her puppies every now and then. This is a natural instinct on her part which stems from the days when dogs were giving birth in the wilds. The only food the mother could provide at weaning time was too rough and indigestible for her puppies. Therefore, she took it upon herself to pre-digest the food until it could be retained by her young. Bitches today will sometimes resort to this instinct, especially bitches which love having litters and have a strong maternal instinct. Some help you wean their litters, others give up feeding entirely once they see you are taking over.

Beau Cheval's Bergen, smooth male owned by Mr. and Mrs. Ainslie Perrault Jr. of Tulsa, Okla. Bergen was sired by Beau Cheval's Vicar and is out of Beau Cheval's Tallihatche.

Two Saints are better than one . . . Darin and Wendy Beyer with their show and pet Saint Bernards romping in the snow. The Beyers own the Ad-Astra Kennels.

When weaning the mother is kept away from the puppies for longer and longer periods of time. This is done over a period of several days. Then she is eventually separated from them all day, leaving her with them only at night for comfort and warmth. This gradual separation aids in helping the mother's milk disappear gradually and her suffering less distress after feeding a large litter.

If the mother continues to carry a great deal of milk with no signs of it tapering off, consult your veterinarian before she gets too uncomfortable. She may cut the puppies off from her supply of milk too abruptly, before they are completely on their own.

There are many opinions on the proper age to start weaning puppies. If you plan to start selling them between six and eight weeks, weaning should begin between two and three weeks of age. Here again, each bitch will pose a different problem. The size and weight of the litter should help determine this age and your veterinarian will have an opinion as he determines the burden the bitch is carrying by the size of the litter and her general condition. If she is being pulled down by feeding a large litter, he may suggest that you start at two weeks. If she is glorying in her motherhood without any apparent taxing of her strength he may suggest three to four weeks. You and he will be the best judges. But remember, there is no substitute that is as perfect as mother's milk—and the longer the puppies benefit from it, the better. Other food yes, but mother's milk first and foremost for the best puppies!

## SOCIALIZING YOUR PUPPY

The need for puppies to get out among people and other animals cannot be stressed enough. Kennel-reared dogs are subject to all sorts of idiosyncrasies and seldom make good house dogs or normal members of the world around them when they grow up.

The crucial age, which determines the personality and general behavior patterns which will predominate the rest of the dog's life are formed between the ages of three to ten weeks. This is particularly true during the 21st to 28th day. It is essential that the puppy be socialized during this time by bringing him into the family life as much as possible. Floor surfaces, indoor and outdoor, should be experienced; handling by all members of the family and visitors is important, preliminary grooming (use a toothbrush gently on small breeds) gets him used to a lifelong necessity; light training, such as setting him up on tables and cleaning teeth and ears and cutting nails, etc., has to be started early if he is to become a show dog. The puppy should be exposed to car riding, shopping tours, a leash around its neck, children—your own and others, and in all possible ways develop relationships with humans.

It is up to the breeder, of course, to protect the puppy from harm or injury during this initiation into the wide world. The benefits reaped from proper attention will pay off in the long run with a well-behaved, well-adjusted grown dog capable of becoming an integral part of a happy family.

# CHAPTER 9

# GENETICS

No one can guarantee nature! But, with facts and theories at your command you can at least, on paper, plan a litter of puppies that should fulfill your fondest expectations. Since the ultimate purpose of breeding is to try to improve the breed, this planning, no matter how uncertain, should be earnestly attempted.

There are a few terms you should be familiar with to help you understand the breeding procedure and the structure of genetics. The first thing that comes to mind is the Mendelian Law—or The Laws of Mendelian Inheritance. Who was Mendel? Gregor Mendel was an Austrian clergyman and botanist born in Brunn, Moravia. He developed his basic theories on heredity while working with peas. Not realizing the full import of his work, he published a paper on his experiments in a scientific journal in the year 1866. That paper went unnoticed for many years, but the laws and theories put forth in it have been tried and proven. Today they are accepted by scientists as well as dog breeders.

To help understand the Mendelian law as it applies to breeding dogs, we must acquaint ourselves with certain scientific terms and procedures. First of all, dogs possess glands of reproduction which are called gonads. The gonads of the male are in the testicles which produce sperm, or spermatozoa. The gonads of the female are the ovaries and produce eggs. The bitch is born with these eggs and, when she is old enough to reproduce, she comes into heat. The eggs descend from the ovaries via the Fallopian tubes to the two horns of the uterus. There they either pass on out during the heat cycle or are fertilized by the male sperm in the semen deposited during a mating.

In dog mating, there is what we refer to as a tie, which is a time period during which the male pumps about 600 million spermatozoa into the female to fertilize the ripened eggs. When the sperm and the ripe eggs meet, zygotes are created and the little one-celled

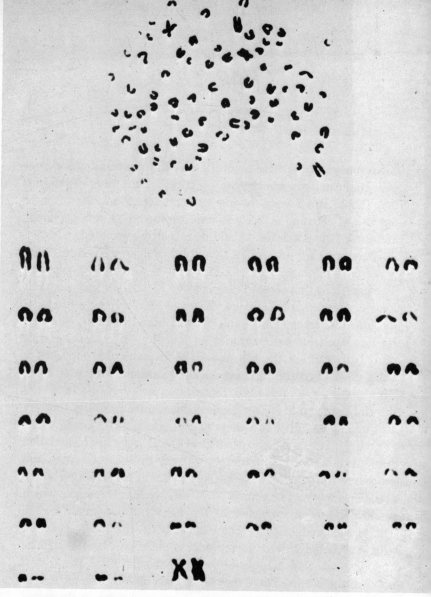

The dog has 78 chromosomes while man has 46 and the cat has 38. The two members of each pair of chromosomes look alike except for the sex chromosomes. A female has two large X chromosomes (see lower right in the illustration). The male has one X chromosome and a small Y chromosome which is the determinant for maleness. The preparation pictured above was made from a white blood cell of a female Keeshond. The chromosomes have been paired according to size.

Bittersweet Noah Ross, Shagg Bark's Bunty Bumper x Shagg Bark's Tollyanna. Owned by Diane Wenstob, North Vancouver, B.C., Canada.

future puppies descend from the Fallopian tubes into the uterus where they attach themselves to the walls of the uterus and begin to develop. With all inherited characteristics determined as the zygote was formed, the dam now must only assume her role as incubator for her babies, which are now organisms in their own right. The bitch has been bred and is now in whelp!

Let us take a closer look at what is happening during the breeding phenomenon. We know that while the male deposits as many as 600 million sperm into the female, the number of ripe eggs she releases will determine the number of puppies in the litter. Therefore, those breeders who advertise their stud as "producer of large litters" do not know the facts. The bitch determines the size of the litter; the male the sex of the puppies. It takes only one sperm of the 600 million to produce a puppy.

Each dog and bitch possesses 39 pairs of chromosomes in each reproductive germ cell. The chromosomes carry the genes, like peas in a pod, and there are approximately 150,000 genes in each

A puppy dog poses with friend Can. Ch. Beau Cheval's Mocca la Mar-doug, at the home of Mr. and Mrs. Bruce Chapman, Milford, Mich.

Champion Switzer of Shady Hollow takes time out from the show ring to give pal James Lynch, Jr. a ride. Switzer's owner is Phyllis Jackson Smith of Rhode Island and Jimmy's owner is Mrs. Lynch.

Willow Point's Ezekiel v. Padre, 16-month-old long-haired son of Ch. Beau Cheval's Padre la Mardoug, owned by the Allens of Michigan.

Ch. Beau Cheval's Tilde and Beau Cheval's Vicount Drambuie photographed on the New England circuit picking up points toward championship. Rodney Parker handled Tilde and pro-handler Alan Levine handled Drambuie to a title in Canada as well. Drambuie is owned by Randy Parker of Brownsville, Pa., and is the sire of Ch. Beau Cheval's Contesa Mardoug, a Group winner.

177

chromosome. These chromosomes split apart and unite with half the chromosomes from the other parent and the puppy's looks and temperament are created.

To understand the procedure more thoroughly, we must understand that there are two kinds of genes—dominant and recessive. A dominant gene is one of a pair whose influence is expressed to the exclusion of the effects of the other. A recessive gene is one of a pair whose influence is subdued by the effects of the other. Most of the important qualities we wish to perpetuate in our breeding programs are carried on by the dominant genes. It is the successful breeder who becomes expert at eliminating recessive or undesirable genes and building up the dominant or desirable genes. This principle holds true in every phase of breeding—inside and outside the dog!

There are many excellent books available which will take you deeper into the fascinating subject of canine genetics. You can learn about your chances of getting so many black, so many white, and so many black and white puppies, etc. Avail yourself of this information before your next—or hopefully, first—breeding. We have merely touched upon genetics here to point out the importance of planned parenthood. Any librarian can help you find further information, or books may be purchased offering the very latest findings in canine genetics. It is a fascinating and rewarding program toward creating better dogs.

At a Saint Bernard Club of Southern California meeting in Woody's Alpine Inn, Monterey Park, back in 1964, H. Carlton Doe made up a Saint Bernard-sized hamburger, which he fed to "Red," a champion Saint owned by Mrs. Lillian Hershey of Huntington Park, the club's vice president.

# CHAPTER 10

# NUTRITION

### FEEDING THE ADULT DOG

The puppies' schedule of four meals a day should drop to three and then to two, so that by the time the dog reaches one year of age, it is eating one meal a day.

A willing
assistant in a
skier's paradise
in Andermatt,
Switzerland.

The time when you feed him each day can be a matter of the dog's preference or your convenience, so long as once in every 24 hours the dog receives a meal that provides him with a complete, balanced diet. In addition, of course, fresh clean water should be available at all times.

There are many brands of dry food, kibbles and biscuits on the market which are all of good quality. There are also many varieties of canned dog food which are of good quality and provide a balanced diet for your dog. But, for those breeders and exhibitors who show their dogs, additional care is given to providing a few "extras" which enhance the good health and good appearance of show dogs.

A good meal or kibble mixed with water or beef broth and raw meat is perhaps the best ration to provide. In cold weather many breeders add suet or corn oil (or even olive or cooking oil) to the

"Grizzly Bear," a gentle Saint Bernard dog from Denali, Alaska, was winner of the Ken-L Ration gold medal as 1970 America's Dog Hero of the Year. He is owned by Mr. and Mrs. David Gratias, and won his medal for fighting off a real grizzly bear that attacked Mrs. Gratias on her front porch. The Saint crashed into the bear, fighting it off, and when Mrs. Gratias regained consciousness after having been scratched and bitten, she found "Grizzly" licking her face. Her baby inside the house was safe.

mixture and others make use of the bacon fat after breakfast by pouring it over the food.

Salting a dog's food in the summer helps replace the salt he "pants away" in the heat. Many breeders sprinkle the food with garlic powder to sweeten the dog's breath and prevent gas, especially in breeds that gulp or wolf their food and swallow a lot of air. We prefer garlic powder, the salt is too weak and the clove is too strong.

There are those, of course, who cook very elaborately for their dogs, which is not necessary if a good meal and meat mixture is provided. Many prefer to add vegetables, rice, tomatoes, etc., in with everything else they feed. As long as the extras do not throw the nutritional balance off, there is little harm, but no one thing should be fed to excess. Occasionally liver is given, as a treat at home. Fish, which most veterinarians no longer recommend even for cats, is fed to puppies, but should not be given in excess of once a week. Always remember: No one thing should be given as a total diet. Balance is most important; steak or 100 per cent meat can kill a dog.

In March of 1971, the National Research Council investigated a great stir in the dog fancy about the all-meat dog-feeding controversy. It was established that meat and meat by-products constitute a complete balanced diet for dogs only when it is further fortified with vitamins and minerals.

Therefore, a good dog chow or meal mixed with meat provides the perfect combination for a dog's diet. While the dry food is a complete diet in itself, the fresh meat additionally satisfies the dog's anatomically and physiologically meat-oriented appetite. While dogs are actually carnivores, it must be remembered that when they were feeding themselves in the wilds they ate almost the entire animal they captured, including its stomach contents. This provided some of the vitamins and minerals we must now add to the diet.

The standards for diets which claim to be "complete and balanced" are set by the Subcommittee on Canine Nutrition of the National Research Council (NRC) of the National Academy of Sciences. This is the official agency for establishing the nutritional requirements of dog foods. Most all foods sold for dogs and cats meet these requirements and manufacturers are proud to say so on

Beau Cheval's Tempest Mardoug nurses a sore paw. She's owned by Hope and Muhrlein of Washington.

their labels, so look for this when you buy. Pet food labels must be approved by the Association of American Feed Control Officials, Pet Foods Committee. Both the Food and Drug Administration and the Federal Trade Commission of the AAFCO define the word "balanced" when referring to dog food as:

"Balanced is a term which may be applied to pet food having all known, required nutrients in a proper amount and proportion based upon the recommendations of a recognized authority (The National Research Council is one) in the field of animal nutrition, for a given set of physiological animal requirements."

With this much care given to your dog's diet, there can be little reason for not having happy well-fed dogs in proper weight and proportions for the show ring.

## OBESITY

As we mentioned above, there are many "perfect" diets for your dogs on the market today, that when fed in proper proportions should keep your dogs in "full bloom." However, there are those owners who, more often than not, indulge their own appetites and are inclined to overfeed their dogs as well. A study in Great Britain in the early 1970's found a major percentage of obese people also had obese dogs. The entire family was overfed and all suffered from the same condition.

Charlie Brown of Stouffville, Ontario, was installed in Purina's Animal Hall of Fame in recognition of his finding David Martell who was lost in heavy snow. The Saint remained with David in the heavily wooded area, supplying the warmth of his body until rescuers, led by the dog's master, Lorne Rose, were able to locate the boy and bring him out by snowmobile. Charlie Brown is shown with Mrs. Rose.

Obesity in dogs is a direct result of the animal's being fed more food than he can properly "burn up" over a period of time, so it is stored as fat or fatty tissue in the body. Pet dogs are more inclined to become obese than show dogs or working dogs, but obesity also is a factor to be considered with the older dog since his exercise is curtailed.

A lack of "tuck up" on a dog, or not being able to feel the ribs, or great folds of fat which hang from the underside of the dog can all be considered as obesity. Genetic factors may enter into the picture, but usually the owner is at fault.

The life span of the obese dog is decreased on several counts. Excess weight puts undue stress on the heart as well as the joints. The dog becomes a poor anesthetic risk and has less resistance to viral or bacterial infections. Treatment is seldom easy or completely effective, so emphasis should be placed on not letting your dog get FAT in the first place!

# CHAPTER 11

# BATHING AND GROOMING YOUR SAINT BERNARD

If you can wash a car, you can wash a Saint Bernard! For those of you who have never done either, here is how you bathe a Saint.

The process requires no special skill—just lots of muscle, endurance and determination. A few tips and time-savers will get you through it without too much trouble. Bathing a Saint is difficult only if you are a little old lady, a little old man, or a little child. However, even if you are a big man or woman, you may still need someone to hang onto the dog while you scrub away the dirt. Begin by putting on your oldest sneakers, sweat shirt and blue jeans, or perhaps a bathing suit. For no matter how big the dog is, when the bath is over you will be soaked, your bathroom or basement will be a splattered mess, and you will be ready for a bath of your own!

## BATHING THE FULL GROWN DOG

Any of the following receptacles are suitable for a full-grown Saint: Your own bathtub, a double-sink (two legs in each side) in the basement, a galvanized tub, the children's plastic pool (if you can get the kids out of it), the old mill pond, a clean creek, a lake, or the ocean. If you use a stall shower be sure the dog doesn't exit through the glass! You will need an ordinary garden hose, if you are using tubs, and a big bucket. It will take five to ten pails of warm soapy water to suds the dog and the same amount or more of cool clean water to rinse him.

If you can get the dog to step into the tub by himself, good for you. But more than likely you will have to lift him into the tub yourself. If your dog has been shedding a lot, you will do well to brush out as much of the loose fur as possible before bathing him. Eye cream or mineral oil will prevent soap from burning eyes.

Ch. Baldur of Sunny Slopes, CD, owned by Mr. and Mrs. Howard Parker of Stamford, Conn.

Soak down the dog, and then soap him. You should have the pails of water at arm's reach and plenty of towels—including one for yourself! Use good protein shampoo, created for dogs and available at pet shops and grooming stores. Creme rinses, beer rinses, lemon or egg rinses are not necessary, but make the dog smell wonderful, and certainly do them no harm. So if your dog insists on sleeping with you, you may wish to indulge him in these extras.

The entire body is wetted down and soaped. Cool water is all right, even if you are washing him outdoors; however, it could invite a cold. Warm water is best, since the shampoo will lather better. Be sure to lather well, especially under the tail where the coat may be discolored and carry an odor. Save the head until last so that if you do get soap in his eyes, you will be ready to rinse all shampoo away anyway.

Be sure that all the shampoo is thoroughly rinsed out of the coat. You will probably have to straddle him to keep him in the tub and he will be most anxious to get away so he can shake all over the place. Hold him in the tub until the first towel is thrown over him and he is partially drip-dried. The first inclination will be for the dog to roll in the grass, your carpet, or your bed! Therefore, be sure that he stays in one place until he is almost completely dry so that he doesn't get dirty all over again. Towel him dry as much as possible and then tie him in the sunshine or place him in a cage near a heater, or on a grooming table where you can blow him dry with a dog-dryer.

Making friends, a particular talent of the Saint.

Beau Cheval's Rommel Mardoug, a large smooth-mantled male, owned by M. J. Anderson and Thomas Finney, was sired by the German import Ch. Illo vom Vogelheim, and out of Beau Cheval's Toffe la Mardoug, also bred by M. J. Anderson. Rommel's show career was interrupted by a car accident that almost killed his former co-owner and injured Rommel. However, he is expected to become a champion of record.

Large heavy-coated Saints can take many hours to dry, some take a full day, especially in winter or if they have a profuse coat. Be sure the dog is in no danger of catching cold because of extreme changes in temperature.

## HOW OFTEN DO YOU BATHE A SAINT?

It is not necessary to bathe the average Saint if it is just a pet and a house dog unless, of course, he rolls around in the yard and gets to smelling a bit, or unless he has tangled with a skunk. The normal Saint can be cleaned with a "dry" bath. Corn starch is the best thing to use. Sprinkle it liberally into the coat and then brush it out with a bristle brush. If you do this inside the house, you should stand the dog on newspapers in the basement or garage. Once all the corn starch is out of the coat, spray the dog with any of the better coat conditioners and he will be smelling like a rose! For the skunk odor (and it seems that every country dog tangles with a skunk at least once in his life) the best remedy is tomato juice. It will take a case of it, perhaps, for that bath, but it will do the trick.

## BATHING PUPPIES

We do not recommend that you bathe puppies, unless they have come from a smelly kennel. Even then, if possible, give the dry corn starch or baby powder bath. If water is necessary, try bathing the necessary parts, such as the feet, head, and hindquarters. Use a bucket of sudsy water, clear clean rinse water, and a wash cloth or sponge with which to rub and towel dry immediately. Never leave a puppy to dry itself. Be sure and keep the puppy in a warm place, until he is completely dry, especially if he has been entirely immersed. He will have been frightened by the first bath and will need warmth and confidence after his experience. In winter months, baths for puppies are quite risky. Chill leaves them vulnerable to pneumonia and other diseases that might be around. The safest way is to bathe your puppy and keep him in the warm house or kennel for at least 24 hours until every hair is dry and the shock of the bath is over.

## EVERYDAY GROOMING FOR A PUPPY

A soft brush, a little scrub brush, or even a ladies' hair brush is acceptable for grooming an eight-week-old puppy up until the time he is a four-month-old Saintlet. Wire brushes at this age are too severe, although they are best for clearing mats that might appear and foreign bodies that may become imbedded in the coat. Smooth Saints require little grooming, but the roughs look nicer if they are brushed daily. They may also be sprayed with coat conditioner.

## PREPARING YOUR SAINT FOR THE SHOW RING

Every judge should be presented with a clean and well groomed dog; it could be the difference between winning and losing! Grooming your dog for the show ring is necessary for all exhibitors who expect to win. In Europe this is not always the case since the fanciers put more emphasis on showing dogs in their natural state. But, in America it is entirely different. Many hours of grooming show pride of ownership and contribute to the dog's appearance and good health. Grooming has become an art and it must be perfected if your dog is to compete successfully in the show ring.

Once your dog is bathed, additional show ring preparations are relatively easy for both the rough and the smooth. The day before the show, you dampen the coat slightly with a wet towel and go over the legs, head, chest, and other white parts of the dog, especially those that will need whitening. Then apply corn starch or white chalk liberally. Before entering the ring, brush it all out thoroughly. You may be suspended from showing and asked to leave the ring if the judge notices any whitening agent on the dog whatsoever. So be on your guard.

## GROOMING THE HEAD

The head is the most important part of your Saint's body, for it is the first part of the dog that the judge observes when the dog is standing for examination, or as he enters the ring. Eyebrows and whiskers should be trimmed off. There are rounded scissors especially made for this that are available at all pet shops. Eyes should be cleaned, making sure all matter is removed from the deep folds around the eyes. A clean wet wash cloth is best for this, just prior to entering the ring, especially if your dog has a problem with his eyes. There are also eye creams that your veterinarian can recommend. His muzzle as well as the blaze should be packed in corn starch and here again we must emphasize that all whitening

Julie Howard practices setting up Ch. Beau Cheval's Padre, looking to see what needs to be corrected in front.

Julie then leans over Padre to set front and rear legs on the judge's side.

Dog's front should be in correct position at all times, while judge is examining him.

Owner Harold Rader sets up Alpler's Fun 'N Fancy Free, sired by Beau Cheval's Padre la Mardoug and out of Von Alpler's Something Fancy.

Fancy wins! At the Saint Bernard Club's National Specialty Show in Edwardsville, Ill., 1971, Alpler's Fun 'N Fancy Free has just taken first prize in bitch puppy class at six months of age. Harold Rader is overjoyed.

Beau Cheval's
Epic La Mardoug,
smooth teenage
puppy dog,
owned by Shelly
Golden of Bala
Cynwyd, Pa. Epic
is sired by Ch.
Beau Cheval's
Golden Ceasar
out of Beau
Cheval's Toldya
Mardoug.

agents must be completely brushed out before you enter the ring. If you do not have time to wet the coat first, apply the powder and brush it out immediately. If your dog has a dry nose from panting with white "salt" lines around the edge, apply a little vaseline and rub it off. It will give the black leather a lustrous "wet look." You may also rub the excess vaseline together in your palms and apply the residue to the ears to make them "sharper." Here again, the trick is to do it very lightly.

## TAKING CARE OF THE EARS

Smelly, dirty ears where wax has been allowed to accumulate are a great dishonor to the pet or show dog. All hair should be removed from the ears either by pinching it out with your fingers or cutting it out with little rounded scissors. Clean the ear gently with alcohol soaked cotton and use cotton tips for the corners and crevices. If he shakes his head and/or scratches his ears, chances are he has ear mites or infection, both of which are a matter of immediate concern and indicate a trip to the veterinarian.

## KEEPING TOE NAILS TRIMMED

Long toe nails can ruin your dog's gait and can actually make his feet hurt. There is further discomfort and danger if they are so long they grow back into the dog's leg or foot. Heavy duty clippers are needed for Saints. You may need the veterinarian to cut the very thick ones, and if you are sensitive to the bleeding when they are cut too short, a trip to the veterinarian is best. Look at the underside of the nail, and cut to the "quick" or where the pink begins as you would on your own nails. If bleeding persists a surgical powder made especially for this to clot the blood is helpful. A little smear of vaseline spread over the end of the nail and held against your finger tightly for a few minutes will also stop the bleeding.

# CHAPTER 12

# TRAINING YOUR SAINT BERNARD

There are few things in the world a dog would rather do than please his master. Therefore, obedience training, or even the initial basic training, will be a pleasure for your dog, if taught correctly, and will make him a much nicer animal to live with for the rest of his life.

## WHEN TO START TRAINING

The most frequently asked question by those who consider training their dog is, naturally, "What is the best age to begin training?" The answer is, "not before six months." A dog simply cannot be sufficiently or permanently trained before this age and be expected to retain all he has been taught. If too much is expected of him, he can become frustrated and it may ruin him completely for any serious training later on, or even jeopardize his disposition. Most things a puppy learns and repeats before he is six months of age should be considered habit rather than training.

## THE REWARD METHOD

The only proper and acceptable kind of training is the kindness and reward method which will build a strong bond between dog and owner. A dog must have confidence in and respect for his teacher. The most important thing to remember in training any dog is that the quickest way to teach, especially the young dog, is through repetition. Praise him when he does well, and scold him when he does wrong. This will suffice. There is no need or excuse for swinging at a dog with rolled up newspapers, or flailing hands which will only tend to make the dog hand shy the rest of his life. Also, make every word count. Do not give a command unless you intend to see it through. Pronounce distinctly with the fewest possible words, and use the same words for the same command every time.

Making friends in the snow

Lineup of Saint bitches in summer outdoor dog show. Center bitch is Ch. Beau Cheval's Contesa, owned by Whayne Head and M. J. Anderson. Handler is D. J. Anderson.

Include the dog's name every time to make sure you have his undivided attention at the beginning of each command. Do not go on to another command until he has successfully completed the previous one and is praised for it. Of course, you should not mix play with the serious training time. Make sure the dog knows the difference between the two.

In the beginning, it is best to train without any distractions whatsoever. After he has learned to concentrate and is older and more proficient, be should perform the exercises with interference, so that the dog learns absolute obedience in the face of all distractions. Needless to say, whatever the distractions, you never lose control. You must be in command at all times to earn the respect and attention of your dog.

## HOW LONG SHOULD THE LESSONS BE?

The lessons should be brief with a young dog, starting at five minutes, and as the dog ages and becomes adept in the first lessons,

One of the first dog training schools in the Pennsylvania area, the Delaware County Dog Training class graduation, features Jack Sheahan and his Ch. Beau of Highmont, CD.

Colt Forty Five v Real Gusto, CDX, bred by T. and J. Bakas. Owner and handler was Camilla Thorne. Colt was her first Saint and the first dog she ever trained. He was highest scoring Saint in Michigan in 1967 and second highest in the USA the same year. From Mar-Wol Kennel, Pinckney, Mich.

increase the time all the way up to one-half hour. Public training classes are usually set for one hour, and this is acceptable since the full hour of concentration is not placed on your dog alone. Working under these conditions with other dogs, you will find that he will not be as intent as he would be with a private lesson where the commands are directed to him alone for the entire thirty minutes.

Saint puppy Shadow of Edelweiss v.d. Hutte, owned by Mrs. Di Rosa.

Champion and well-known Specialty winner Traci La Mardoug, from the famous Mardoug line of Beau Cheval Saints. Traci has won under specialists from this country and in Europe.

If you should notice that your dog is not doing well, or not keeping up with the class, consider putting off training for awhile. Animals, like children, are not always ready for schooling at exactly the same age. It would be a shame to ruin a good obedience dog because you insist on starting his training at six months rather than at, say, nine months, when he would be more apt to be receptive both physically and mentally. If he has particular difficulty in learning one exercise, you might do well to skip to a different one and come back to it again at another session. There are no set rules in this basic training, except, "don't push"!

## WHAT YOU NEED TO START TRAINING

From three to six months of age, use the soft nylon show leads, which are the best and safest. When you get ready for the basic training at six months of age, you will require one of the special metal-link choke chains sold for exactly this purpose. Do not let the word "choke" scare you. It is a soft, smooth chain and should be held slack whenever you are not actually using it to correct the dog. This chain should be put over the dog's head so that the lead can be attached over the dog's neck rather than underneath against his throat. It is wise when you buy your choke collar to ask the sales person to show you how it is to be put on. Those of you who will be taking your dog to a training class will have an instructor who can show you.

To avoid undue stress on the dog, use both hands on the lead. The dog will be taught to obey commands at your left side, and therefore, your left hand will guide the dog close to this collar on a six-foot training lead. The balance of the lead will be held in your right hand. Learn at the very beginning to handle your choke collar and lead correctly. It is as important in training a dog as is the proper equipment for riding a horse.

## WHAT TO TEACH FIRST

The first training actually should be to teach the dog to know his name. This, of course, he can learn at an earlier age than six months, just as he can learn to walk nicely on a leash or lead. Many puppies will at first probably want to walk around with the leash in their mouths. There is no objection to this if the dog will walk while doing it. Rather than cultivating this as a habit, you will find that if you don't make an issue of it, the dog will soon realize that carrying the lead in his mouth is not rewarding and he'll let it fall to his side where it belongs.

We also let the puppy walk around by himself for a while with the lead around his neck. If he wishes to chew on it a little, that's all right too. In other words, let it be something he recognizes and associates with at first. Do not let the lead start out being a harness.

If the dog is at all bright, chances are he has learned to come on command when you call him by name. This is relatively simple with sweet talk and a reward. On lead, without a reward, and on command without a lead is something else again. If there has been, or is now, a problem, the best way to correct it is to put on the choke collar and the six-foot lead. Then walk away from the dog, and call him, "Pirate, come!" and gently start reeling him in until the dog is in front of you. Give him a pat on the head and/or a reward.

Walking, or heeling, next to you is also one of the first and most important things for him to learn. With the soft lead training starting very early, he should soon take up your pace at your left side. At the command to "heel" he should start off with you and continue alongside until you stop. Give the command, "Pirate, sit!"

Beau Cheval's Dorie La Mardoug, shorthaired bitch, owned by the Johnsons of Philadelphia. Sire is Ch. Illo v Vogelheim and Ch. Beau Cheval's Alisia is dam.

Ch. X Illo vom Vogelheim, a smooth short-coated mantled male, imported from Germany. Illo is a large male, weighing about 200 pounds, a sire of champions and producer of size, substance and bone. He is owned by M. J. Anderson.

Ch. Alpler's Fancy Dandy, 1½-year-old dog, shown finishing under Kay Wesser, at Topeka Kennel Club in October, 1971. From Alpler Kennels, Leavenworth, Kansas.

This is taught by leaning over and pushing down on his hindquarters until he sits next to you, while pulling up gently on the collar. When you have this down pat on the straight away, then start practicing it in circles, with turns and figure eights. When he is an advanced student, you can look forward to the heels and sits being done neatly, spontaneously, and off lead as well.

## THE "DOWN" COMMAND

One of the most valuable lessons or commands you can teach your dog is to lie down on command. Some day it may save his life, and is invaluable when traveling with a dog or visiting, if behavior and manners are required even beyond obedience. While repeating the words, "Pirate, down!" lower the dog from a sitting position in front of you by gently pulling his front legs out in front of him. Place your full hand on him while repeating the command, "Pirate, down!" and hold him down to let him know you want him to *stay* down. After he gets the general idea, this can be done from a short distance away on lead along with the command, by pulling the lead down to the floor. Or perhaps, you can slip the lead under your shoe (between the heel and the sole) and pull it directly to the floor. As the dog progresses in training, a hand signal with or without verbal command, or with or without lead, can be given from a considerable distance by raising your arm and extending the hand palm down.

A novice class graduation ceremony for John Creighton's Dog Training Class. The Saint Bernard's master deserted him momentarily to take the class picture. The photographer, Jack Sheahan; the graduate, Ch. Beau of Highmont.

Thrasher's Choo Choo v Whiz is pictured going Best of Winners at the Orange Empire Dog Show in January, 1972, under Judge Mrs. Ben McCourt. He is co-owned by his breeder, Mrs. Dianna L. Thrasher and Bob Ohs, of Brea, Cal.

## THE "STAY" COMMAND

The stay command eventually can be taught from both a sit and a down position. Start with the sit. With your dog on your left side in the sitting position give the command, "Pirate, stay!" Reach down with the left hand open and palm side to the dog and sweep it in close to his nose. Then walk a short distance away and face him. He will at first, having learned to heel immediately as you start off, more than likely start off with you. The trick in teaching this is to make sure he hears "stay" before you start off. It will take practice.

Willow Point's Ezra V Padre, ten months old, owned by Mr. Lee of Chugiak, Alaska. Bred by Bruce Chapman, Ezra is sired by Ch. Beau Cheval's Padre la Mardoug.

American and Canadian Champion Alpineacres Baron v Shagg-Bark, owned by Ann and Tom Renner, Wells, Maine, and handled by Bruce Crabb. Baron is pictured here winning the Breed at the 1971 Brookhaven Kennel Club Show under Judge Earl Adair.

If he breaks, sit him down again, stand next to him, and give the command all over again. As he masters the command, let the distance between you and your dog increase while the dog remains seated. Once the command is learned, advance to the stay command from the down position.

## THE STAND FOR EXAMINATION

If you have any intention of going on to advanced training in obedience with your dog, or if you have a show dog which you feel you will enjoy showing yourself, a most important command which should be mastered at six months of age, is the stand command. This is essential for a show dog since it is the position used when the show judge goes over your dog. This is taught in the same manner as the stay command, but this time with the dog remaining up on all four feet. He should learn to stand still, without moving his feet and without flinching or breaking when approached by either you or strangers. The hand with palm open wide and facing him

"Heel" to some dogs means obedience training, but to this Saint Bernard it means his master is in the shoe products business. The Goodyear Public Relations department sent out this charming photograph of the dog trying to retrieve a biscuit from behind a barricade of Neolite sheeting out of which heels have been stamped.

Carol DiRosa and her obedience-trained dog, Edel·
weiss, CD. Ms. DiRosa is from Fallsington, Pa.

should be firmly placed in front of his nose with the command,
"Pirate, stand!" After he learns the basic rules and knows the
difference between stand and stay, ask friends, relatives, and
strangers to assist you with this exercise by walking up to the dog
and going over him. He should not react physically to their touch.
A dog posing in this stance should show all the beauty and pride of
being a sterling example of his breed.

## FORMAL SCHOOL TRAINING

We mentioned previously about the various training schools and
classes given for dogs. Your local kennel club, newspaper, or the
yellow pages of the telephone book will put you in touch with
organizations in your area where this service is performed. You and
your dog will learn a great deal from these classes. Not only do they
offer formal training, but the experience for you and your dog in
public, with other dogs of approximately the same age and with the

Beau Cheval's Peer Mardoug, a teenage puppy of rough coat variety, owned by Julie Howard of Woodbridge, Va.

American and Canadian Champion Noel Von Kris is pictured winning Group Second under Judge Robert Waters at Vancouver, B.C., after finishing for a championship from the classes, and winning the breed over many American and Canadian champions. Noel is always handled by her owner, Duane J. Holiday of Sacramento, Calif.

On guard at the top of the stairs is Ch. Beau of Highmont, CD, watching over the Sheahan household . . . and it looks as if he means business!

same purpose in mind is invaluable. If you intend to show your dog, this training is valuable ring experience for later on. If you are having difficulty with the training, remember, it is either too soon to start—or YOU are doing something wrong!

## ADVANCED TRAINING AND OBEDIENCE TRIALS

The A.K.C. obedience trials are divided into three classes: Novice, Open and Utility.

In the Novice Class, the dog will be judged on the following basis:

| TEST | MAXIMUM SCORE |
|---|---|
| Heel on lead . . . . . . . . . | 35 |
| Stand for examination . . . . . | 30 |
| Heel free—on lead . . . . . . | 45 |
| Recall (come on command) . . . | 30 |
| One-minute sit (handler in ring) . . . | 30 |
| Three-minute down (handler in ring) . . | 30 |
| Maximum total score . . . . . | 200 |

If the dog "qualifies" in three shows by earning at least 50% of the points for each test, with a total of at least 170 for the trial, he has earned the Companion Dog degree and the letters C.D. (Companion Dog) are entered after his name in the A.K.C. records.

After the dog has qualified as a C.D., he is eligible to enter the Open Class competition, where he will be judged on this basis:

| TEST | MAXIMUM SCORE |
|---|---|
| Heel free | 40 |
| Drop on Recall | 30 |
| Retrieve (wooden dumbbell) on flat | 25 |
| Retrieve over obstacle (hurdle) | 35 |
| Broad jump | 20 |
| Three-minute sit (handler out of ring) | 25 |
| Five-minute down (handler out of ring) | 25 |
| Maximum total score | 200 |

Again he must qualify in three shows for the C.D.X. (Companion Dog Excellent) title and then is eligible for the Utility Class, where he can earn the Utility Dog (U.D.) degree in these rugged tests:

| TEST | MAXIMUM SCORE |
|---|---|
| Scent discrimination (picking up article handled by master from group) Article 1 | 20 |
| Scent discrimination Article 2 | 20 |
| Scent discrimination Article 3 | 20 |
| Seek back (picking up an article dropped by handler) | 30 |
| Signal exercise (heeling, etc., on hand signal) | 35 |
| Directed jumping (over hurdle and bar jump) | 40 |
| Group examination | 35 |
| Maximum total score | 200 |

For more complete information about these obedience trials, write for the American Kennel Club's *Regulations and Standards for Obedience Trials*. Dogs that are disqualified from breed shows because of alteration or physical defects are eligible to compete in these trials.

Beau Cheval's Snowbound, long-haired daughter of Ch. Beau Cheval's Padre. Owned by Julie Howard, Woodbridge, Va.

Beau Cheval's Psalmes, long-haired puppy owned by Eleanor Wichie of West Virginia. He is sired by Beau Cheval's Parish out of Toffe.

# CHAPTER 13
# SHOWING YOUR SAINT BERNARD

Let us assume that after a few months of tender loving care, you realize your dog is developing beyond your wildest expectations and that the dog you selected is very definitely a show dog! Of course, every owner is prejudiced. But if you are sincerely interested in going to dog shows with your dog and making a champion of him, now is the time to start casting a critical eye on him from a judge's point of view.

There is no such thing as a perfect dog. Every dog has some faults perhaps even a few serious ones. The best way to appraise your dog's degree of perfection is to compare him with the Standard for the breed, or before a judge in a show ring.

## MATCH SHOWS

For the beginner there are "mock" dog shows, called Match Shows, where you and your dog go through many of the procedures of a regular dog show, but do not gain points toward championship. These shows are usually held by kennel clubs, annually or semi-annually, and much ring poise and experience can be gained there. The age limit is reduced to two months at match shows to give puppies four months of training before they compete at the regular shows when they reach six months of age. Classes range from two to four months; four to six months; six to nine months; and nine to twelve months. Puppies compete with others of their own age for comparative purposes. Many breeders evaluate their litters in this manner, choosing which is the most outgoing, which is the most poised, the best showman, etc.

For those seriously interested in showing their dog to full championship, these match shows provide important experience for both the dog and the owner. Class categories may vary slightly, according to number of entries, but basically include all the classes that are included at a regular point show. There is a nominal entry fee and, of course, ribbons and usually trophies are given for your efforts as well. Unlike the point shows, entries can be made on the day of the show right on the show grounds. They are unbenched and provide an informal, usually congenial atmosphere for the amateur, which helps to make the ordeal of one's first adventures in the show ring a little less nerve-wracking.

## THE POINT SHOWS

It is not possible to show a puppy at an American Kennel Club sanctioned point show before the age of six months. When your dog reaches this eligible age, your local kennel club can provide you with the names and addresses of the show-giving superintendents in your area who will be staging the club's dog show for them, and where you must write for an entry form. A sample entry form is included in this book.

The forms are mailed in a pamphlet called a premium list. This also includes the names of the judges for each breed, a list of the prizes and trophies, the name and address of the show-giving club and where the show will be held, as well as rules and regulations set up by the American Kennel Club which must be abided by if you are to enter.

A booklet containing the complete set of show rules and regulations may be obtained by writing to the American Kennel Club, Inc., 51 Madison Avenue, New York, N.Y., 10010.

When you write to the Dog Show Superintendent, request not only your premium list for this particular show, but ask that your name be added to their mailing list so that you will automatically receive all premium lists in the future. List your breed or breeds and they will see to it that you receive premium lists for Specialty shows as well.

Unlike the match shows where your dog will be judged on ring behavior, at the point shows he will be judged on conformation to the breed Standard. In addition to being at least six months of age (on the day of the show) he must be a thoroughbred for a point show. This means both of his parents and he are registered with the American Kennel Club. There must be no alterations or falsifications regarding his appearance. Females cannot have been spayed and males must have both testicles in evidence. No dyes or

Bayard and Barry, from a painting in Cassell's Illustrated Book of the Dog.

Abbess, painted by C. Burton Barker.

powders may be used to enhance the appearance, and any lameness or deformity or major deviation from the Standard for the breed constitutes a disqualification.

With all these things in mind, groom your dog to the best of your ability in the specified area for this purpose in the show hall and walk into the show ring with great pride of ownership and ready for an appraisal of your dog by the judge.

The presiding judge on that day will allow each and every dog a certain amount of time and consideration before making his

At the Southern California Specialty Show held in Santa Barbara in conjunction with the Santa Barbara Kennel Club Show in 1971, American and Canadian Champion Noel Von Kris is pictured winning Best of Opposite Sex under the renowned judge from Holland, Martin Zwerts. This was a back-to-back win for her since she also won at the Pacific Coast Specialty show. Mrs. Holiday handling here for owner Duane J. Holiday of Sacramento, Calif.

Eleven-year-old Melissa Wiggins handles her 11-month-old Tea and Crumpets, an early winner of many match shows. Puppy is sired by Ch. Patrich's Flaming Ember and owned by the Richard Wiggins.

decisions. It is never permissible to consult the judge regarding either your dog or his decision while you are in the ring. An exhibitor never speaks unless spoken to, and then only to answer such questions as the judge may ask—the age of the dog, the dog's bite, or to ask you to move your dog around the ring once again.

However, before you reach the point where you are actually in the ring awaiting the final decisions of the judge, you will have had to decide on which of the five classes in each sex your dog should compete.

Beau Cheval's
St. Croix
Mardoug, with
handler Julie
Howard.

# Point Show Classes

The regular classes of the AKC are: Puppy, Novice, Bred-by-Exhibitor, American-Bred, Open; if your dog is undefeated in any of the regular classes (divided by sex) in which it is entered, he or she is **required** to enter the Winners Class. If your dog is placed second in the class to the dog which won Winners Dog or Winners Bitch, hold the dog or bitch in readiness as the judge must consider it for Reserve Winners.

**Puppy Classes** shall be for dogs which are six months of age and over but under twelve months, which were whelped in the U.S.A. or Canada, and which are not champions. Classes are often divided 6 and (under) 9, and 9 and (under) 12 months. The age of a dog shall be calculated up to and inclusive of the first day of a show. For example, a dog whelped on Jan. 1st is eligible to compete in a puppy class on July 1st, and may continue to compete up to and including Dec. 31st of the same year, but is not eligible to compete Jan. 1st of the following year.

**The Novice Class** shall be for dogs six months of age or over, whelped in the U.S.A. or Canada which have not, prior to the closing of entries, won three first prizes in the Novice Class, a first prize in Bred-by-Exhibitor, American-Bred or Open Class, nor one or more points toward a championship title.

**The Bred-by-Exhibitor Class** shall be for dogs whelped in the U.S.A. which are six months of age and over, which are not champions, and which are owned wholly or in part by the person or by the spouse of the person who was the breeder or one of the breeders of record. Dogs entered in the BBE Class must be handled by an owner or by a member of the immediate family of an owner, i.e., the husband, wife, father, mother, son, daughter, brother or sister.

**The American-Bred Class** shall be for all dogs (except champions) six months of age or over, whelped in the U.S.A. by reason of a mating that took place in the U.S.A.

**The Open Class** is for any dog six months of age or over, except in a member specialty club show held for only American-Bred dogs, in which case the class is for American-Bred dogs only.

**Winners Dogs** and **Winners Bitches:** After the above male classes have been judged, the first-place winners are then **required**

to compete in the ring. The dog judged "Winners Dog" is awarded the points toward his championship title.

**Reserve Winners** are selected immediately after the Winners Dog. In case of a disqualification of a win by the AKC, the Reserve Dog moves up to "Winners" and receives the points. After all male classes are judged, the bitch classes are called.

**Best of Breed or Best of Variety Competition** is limited to Champions of Record or dogs (with newly acquired points, for a 90-day period prior to AKC confirmation) which have completed championship requirements, and Winners Dog and Winners Bitch (or the dog awarded Winners if only one Winners prize has been awarded), together with any undefeated dogs which have been shown only in non-regular classes, all compete for Best of Breed or Best of Variety (if the breed is divided by size, color, texture or length of coat hair, etc.).

**Best of Winners:** If the WD or WB earns BOB or BOV, it automatically becomes BOW; otherwise they will be judged together for BOW (following BOB or BOV judging).

**Best of Opposite Sex** is selected from the remaining dogs of the opposite sex to Best of Breed or Best of Variety.

**Other Classes** may be approved by the AKC: **Stud Dogs, Brood Bitches, Brace Class, Team Class;** classes consisting of local dogs and bitches may also be included in a show if approved by the AKC (special rules are included in the AKC Rule Book).

The **Miscellaneous Class** shall be for purebred dogs of such breeds as may be designated by the AKC. No dog shall be eligible for entry in this class unless the owner has been granted an Indefinite Listing Privilege (ILP) and unless the ILP number is given on the entry form. Application for an ILP shall be made on a form provided by the AKC and when submitted must be accompanied by a fee set by the Board of Directors.

All Miscellaneous Breeds shall be shown together in a single class except that the class may be divided by sex if so specified in the premium list. There shall be **no** further competition for dogs entered in this class. Ribbons for 1st, 2nd, 3rd and 4th shall be Rose, Brown, Light Green and Gray, respectively. This class is open to the following Miscellaneous Breeds: Akitas, Australian Cattle Dogs, Australian Kelpies, Border Collies, Cavalier King Charles Spaniels, Ibizan Hounds, Miniature Bull Terriers,

# Chart Showing Successive Classes

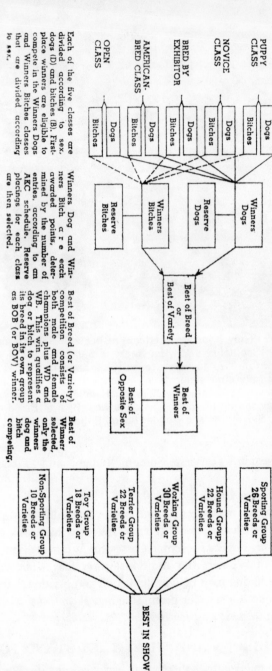

PUPPY CLASS

NOVICE CLASS

BRED BY EXHIBITOR

AMERICAN-BRED CLASS

OPEN CLASS

Dogs | Bitches (for each class)

Winners Dogs

Reserve Dogs

Winners Bitches

Reserve Bitches

Best of Breed or Best of Variety

Best of Winners

Best of Opposite Sex

Sporting Group 26 Breeds or Varieties

Hound Group 22 Breeds or Varieties

Working Group 30 Breeds or Varieties

Terrier Group 22 Breeds or Varieties

Toy Group 18 Breeds or Varieties

Non-Sporting Group 10 Breeds or Varieties

BEST IN SHOW

Each of the five classes are divided according to sex. dogs (D) and bitches (B). First-place winners are eligible to compete in the Winners Dogs and Winners Bitches classes that are divided according to sex.

Winners Dog and Winners Bitch are each awarded points, determined by the number of entries, according to an AKC schedule. Reserve placings for each class are then selected.

Best of Breed (or Variety) competition consists of both male and female champions plus WD and WB. This win qualifies a dog or bitch to represent its breed in its own group as BOB (or BOV) winner.

Best of Winner selected, only the winners dog and bitch competing.

What's in a name? Plenty, if you are a perfectly respectable Saint Bernard named Champion Scotholme's Mr. Hot Socks v. Sam. Hot Socks was Best of Winners at the Westminster Kennel Club show in 1969. He is pictured here with his litter sister, Sam's Grootly Dorg v Scotholme, bred and owned by the Scotholme Kennels. Handlers Jane Forsyth, left, and Maria Lawson on the right. The dogs went Best of Breed and Best of Opposite Sex at this show under Judge Robert Moseley.

Soft-coated Wheaten Terriers, Spinoni Italiani and Tibetan Terriers.

**If Your Dog Wins a Class . . .**

Study the classes to make certain your dog is entered in a proper class for his or her qualifications. If your dog wins his class, the rule states: *You are required* to enter classes for Winners, Best of Breed and Best of Winners (no additional entry fees). The rule states, "No eligible dog may be withheld from competition." It is not mandatory that you stay for group judging. If *your dog wins a group*, however, *you must stay for Best-in-Show competition.*

## THE PRIZE RIBBONS AND WHAT THEY STAND FOR

No matter how many entries there are in each class at a dog show, if you place first through fourth position you will receive a ribbon.

These ribbons commemorate your win and can be impressive when collected and displayed to prospective buyers when and if you have puppies for sale, or if you intend to use your dog at public stud.

All ribbons from the American Kennel Club licensed dog shows will bear the American Kennel Club seal, the name of the show, the date and the placement. In the classes the colors are blue for first, red for second, yellow for third, and white for fourth. Winners Dog or Winners Bitch ribbons are purple, while Reserve Dog and Reserve Bitch ribbons are purple and white. Best of Winners ribbons are blue and white; Best of Breed, purple and gold; and Best of Opposite Sex ribbons are red and white.

In the six groups, first prize is a blue rosette or ribbon, second placement is red, third yellow, and fourth white. The Best In Show rosette is either red, white and blue, or incorporates the colors used in the show-giving club's emblem.

Jumblena of Shady Hollow wins puppy bitch class at the 1963 Northern New Jersey Saint Bernard Club. Judge James Trullinger with Frank W. Smith, her handler and manager of Phyllis Jackson Smith's Shady Hollow Kennels.

# OFFICIAL AMERICAN KENNEL CLUB ENTRY FORM

--- INSERT BELOW — NAME OF CLUB and DATE OF SHOW ---

**CLUB** ...............................................................................................

**DATE** ...............................................................................................

**ENTRY FORM MUST BE SIGNED** on the bottom line ● by the owner or the owner's duly authorized agent, otherwise entry cannot be accepted.

**MAKE CHECKS** payable to Foley Dog Show Organization, Inc.

**MAIL ENTRIES** with FEES to Alan P. Winks, Superintendent, 2009 Ranstead Street, Philadelphia, PA 19103.

**JUNIOR SHOWMANSHIP ENTRANTS** must complete both sides of this entry form.

PLEASE TYPEWRITE OR PRINT CLEARLY

**I ENCLOSE $**..........................**for entry fees.**

● IMPORTANT—Read Carefully Instructions on Reverse Side Before Filling Out

| Breed | Variety See Instruction #1, reverse side (if any) | | Sex |
|---|---|---|---|
| **DOG Show Class** See Instruction #2, reverse side (Give age, color or weight if class divided) | | **Obedience Trial Class** | |
| If dog is entered for Best of Breed (Variety) Competition—see Instruction #3 reverse side — CHECK THIS BOX | | **Additional Classes** | |

If entry of dog is to be made in Jr. Showmanship as well as in one of the above competitions, check this box, and fill in data on reverse side.

If for Jr. Showmanship only then check THIS box, and fill in data on reverse side.

| Name of Actual Owner(s) | See Instruction #4, reverse side |
|---|---|

Name of Licensed Handler (if any) [ handler ]

Full Name of Dog

| Insert one of the following: AKC Reg. # AKC Litter # I.L.P. # Foreign Reg. # & Country | Date of Birth | Place of Birth □ U.S.A. □ Canada □ Foreign Do not print the above in catalog |
|---|---|---|
| | | **Breeder,** |

Sire

Dam

Owner's Name _____
(Please print)

Owner's Address _____

City _____ State _____ Zip Code _____

I CERTIFY that I am the actual owner of this dog, or that I am the duly authorized agent of the actual owner whose name I have entered above. In consideration of the acceptance of this entry, I (we) agree to abide by the rules and regulations of The American Kennel Club in effect at the time of this show or obedience trial, and by any additional rules and regulations appearing in the premium list for this show or obedience trial or both, and further agree to be bound by the "Agreement" printed on the reverse side of this entry form. I (we) certify and represent that the dog entered is not a hazard to persons or other dogs. This entry is submitted for acceptance on the foregoing representation and agreement.

**SIGNATURE** of owner or his agent ●
duly authorized to make this entry _____

Single copies of the latest editions of the "Rules Applying to Registration and Dog Shows" and "Obedience Regulations" may be obtained WITHOUT CHARGE from any Superintendent or from THE AMERICAN KENNEL CLUB, 51 MADISON AVENUE, NEW YORK, N. Y. 10010.

## AGREEMENT

I (we) acknowledge that the "Rules Applying to Registration and Dog Shows" and, if this entry is for an obedience trial, the "Obedience Regulations," have been made available to me (us), and that I am (we are) familiar with their contents. I (we) agree that the club holding this show or obedience trial has the right to refuse this entry for cause which the club shall deem to be sufficient. In consideration of the acceptance of this entry and of the holding of the show or obedience trial and of the opportunity to have the dog judged and to win prize money, ribbons, or trophies, I (we) agree to hold this club, its members, directors, governors, officers, agents, superintendents or show secretary, and any employees of the aforementioned parties, harmless from any claim for loss or injury which may be alleged to have been caused directly or indirectly to any person or thing by the act of this dog while in or upon the show or obedience trial premises or grounds or near any entrance thereto, and I (we) personally assume all responsibility and liability for any such claim; and I (we) further agree to hold the aforementioned parties harmless from any claim for loss of this dog by disappearance, theft, death or otherwise, and from any claim for damage or injury to the dog, whether such loss, disappearance, theft, damage, or injury, be caused or alleged to be caused by the negligence of the club or any of the parties aforementioned, or by the negligence of any other person, or any other cause or causes.

## INSTRUCTIONS

1. (Variety) If you are entering a dog of a breed in which there are varieties for show purposes, please designate the particular variety you are entering, i. e., Cocker Spaniel (solid color black, ASCOB, parti-color), Beagles (not exceeding 13 in.; over 13 in. but not exceeding 15 in.), Dachshunds (longhaired, smooth, wirehaired), Collies (rough, smooth), Bull Terriers (colored, white), Fox Terriers (smooth, wire), Manchester Terriers (standard, toy), Chihuahuas (smooth coat, long coat), English Toy Spaniels (King Charles and Ruby, Blenheim and Prince Charles), Poodles (toy, miniature, standard).

2. (Dog Show Class) Consult the classification in this premium list. If the dog show class in which you are entering your dog is divided, then, in addition to designating the class, specify the particular division of the class in which you are entering your dog, i. e., age division, color division, weight division.

3. The following categories of dogs may be entered and shown in Best of Breed competition: Dogs that are Champions of Record and dogs which, according to their owners' records, have completed the requirements for a championship, but whose championships are unconfirmed. The showing of unconfirmed Champions in Best of Breed competition is limited to a period of 90 days from the date of the show where the dog completed the requirements for a championship.

4. A dog must be entered in the name of the person who actually owned it at the time entries for a show closed. If a registered dog has been acquired by a new owner it must be entered in the name of its new owner in any show for which entries closed after the date of acquirement, regardless of whether the new owner has received the registration certificate indicating that the dog is recorded in his name. State on entry form whether transfer application has been mailed to A.K.C. (For complete rule refer to Chapter 16, Section 3.)

*JUNIOR SHOWMANSHIP* — If the dog identified on the front of this entry form is entered in Junior Showmanship, please give the following information:

CLASS SEE DESCRIPTION OF JUNIOR SHOWMANSHIP CLASSES IN THIS PREMIUM LIST.

| NAME OF JUNIOR HANDLER | | DATE OF BIRTH |
|---|---|---|

ADDRESS

| CITY | STATE | ZIP CODE |
|---|---|---|

If Junior Handler is not the owner of the dog identified on the face of this form, what is the relationship of the Junior Handler to the owner?

# QUALIFYING FOR CHAMPIONSHIP

Championship points are given for Winners Dog and Winners Bitch in accordance with a scale of points established by the American Kennel Club based on the popularity of the breed in entries, and the number of dogs competing in the classes. This scale of points varies in different sections of the country, but the scale is published in the front of each dog show catalog. These points may differ between the dogs and the bitches at the same show. You may, however, win additional points by winning Best of Winners, if there are fewer dogs than bitches entered, or vice versa. Points never exceed five at any one show, and a total of fifteen points must be won to constitute a championship. These fifteen points must be

Puppies at Beau Cheval Kennels looking forward to the glamour and excitement of a career in the show ring.

Ch. Cambo v Sauliamt, sensational Swiss import, takes Best of Breed from the classes over champion competition. Shown here winning under Judge Anthony Hodges, Cambo takes another Best of Breed, this time at the Somerset Hills Kennel Club show. Cambo is co-owned by Theresa Betty and Janet Levine, Gorham, Maine. The handler and agent is Alan Levine.

won under at least three different judges, and you must acquire at least two major wins. Anything from a three to five point win is a major, while one and two point wins are minor wins. Two major wins must be won under two different judges to meet championship requirements.

## OBEDIENCE TRIALS

Some shows also offer Obedience Trials which are considered as separate events. They give the dogs a chance to compete and score on performing a prescribed set of exercises intended to display their training in doing useful work.

There are three obedience titles for which they may compete. First, the Companion Dog or CD title; second, the Companion Dog Excellent or CDX; and third, the Utility Dog or UD. Detailed information on these degrees is contained in a booklet entitled Official Obedience Regulations and may be obtained by writing to the American Kennel Club.

## JUNIOR SHOWMANSHIP COMPETITION

Junior Showmanship Competition is for boys and girls in different age groups handling their own dog or one owned by their immediate family. There are four divisions: Novice A, for the ten to 12 year olds; Novice B, for those 13 to 16 years of age, with no previous junior showmanship wins; Open C, for ten to 12 year olds; and Open D, for 13 to 16 year olds who have earned one or more JS awards.

As Junior Showmanship at the dog shows increased in popularity, certain changes and improvements had to be made. As of April 1, 1971, the American Kennel Club issued a new booklet containing the Regulations for Junior Showmanship which may be obtained by writing to the A.K.C. at 51 Madison Avenue, New York, N.Y. 10010.

## DOG SHOW PHOTOGRAPHERS

Every show has at least one official photographer who will be more than happy to take a photograph of your dog with the judge, ribbons and trophies, along with you or your handler. These make marvelous remembrances of your top show wins and are frequently framed along with the ribbons for display purposes. Photographers can be paged at the show over the public address system, if you wish to obtain this service. Prices vary, but you will probably find it costs little to capture these happy moments, and the photos can always be used in the various dog magazines to advertise your dog's wins.

"On the Bench" at Westminster, February, 1971. Robin Young shares her lunch with Ch. Indian Mountain's Winona.

A Mid-Atlantic Saint Bernard Specialty show in the mid-fifties saw Best of Breed win go to Champion Faust v Melina, dog owned and handled by S. H. Bussinger. On the right, Best of Opposite Sex to Finette of Melina, here handled by John C. Sheahan III and owned by S. H. Bussinger. Center is Judge Dr. Henry E. Edig.

## TWO TYPES OF DOG SHOWS

There are two types of dog shows licensed by the American Kennel Club. One is the all-breed show which includes classes for all the recognized breeds, and groups of breeds; i.e., all terriers, all toys, etc. Then there are the Specialty shows for one particular breed which also offer championship points.

## BENCHED OR UNBENCHED DOG SHOWS

The show-giving clubs determine, usually on the basis of what facilities are offered by their chosen show site, whether their show will be benched or unbenched. A benched show is one where the dog show superintendent supplies benches (cages for toy dogs). Each bench is numbered and its corresponding number appears on your entry identification slip which is sent to you prior to the show date. The number also appears in the show catalog. Upon entering the show you should take your dog to the bench where he should remain until it is time to groom him before entering the ring to be judged. After judging, he must be returned to the bench until the official time of dismissal from the show. At an unbenched show the club makes no provision whatsoever for your dog other than an enormous tent (if an outdoor show) or an area in a show hall where all crates and grooming equipment must be kept.

Benched or unbenched, the moment you enter the show grounds you are expected to look after your dog and have it under complete control at all times. This means short leads in crowded aisles or getting out of cars. In the case of a benched show, a "bench chain" is needed. It should allow the dog to move around, but not get

Ch. Rajah von Heidengeld, finishing for his title under Judge Alva Rosenberg, at Camden, N.J. Rajah, an excellent producer of quality, was bred by Joseph Rose, sired by Ch. Morgan's Echo of Hillcrest, and out of Ch. Mascha von Heidengeld. Owned by M. J. Anderson, Rajah was poisoned early in his adult life by persons unknown.

down off the bench. It is also not considered "cute" to have small tots leading enormous dogs around a dog show where the child might be dragged into the middle of a dog fight.

## PROFESSIONAL HANDLERS

If you are new in the fancy and do not know how to handle your dog to his best advantage, or if you are too nervous or physically

Champion Bonnie-Jo of Shady Hollow, bred by Phyllis Jackson Smith, is shown here winning at the Foot Guard Kennel Club show with Alfred Saba, Jr. handling for owner, Olive Saba, at their February, 1964, show.

Ch. Apollo L'ours Alpine. Brutus is owned by Alan Crumbaker of Steck Road, Brookville, Ohio. Sired by Ch. Little Brutus L'ours Alpin and out of Windy L'ours Alpine, he is a smooth-mantled Saint.

unable to show your dog, you can hire a licensed professional handler who will do it for you for a specified fee. The more successful or well-known handlers charge slightly higher rates, but generally speaking there is a pretty uniform charge for this service. As the dog progresses with his wins in the show ring, the fee increases proportionately. Included in this service is professional advice on when and where to show your dog, grooming, a statement of your wins at each show, and all trophies and ribbons that the dog accumulates. Any cash award is kept by the handler as a sort of "bonus."

When engaging a handler, it is advisable to select one that does not take more dogs to a show than he can properly and comfortably

The coveted Jacob Ruppert Trophy offered by the Saint Bernard Club of America at its National Specialty show each year for the Saint placing Best of Opposite Sex.

Patrich's Flaming
Ember taking
Best of Winners
at Sahuaro State
Kennel Club,
Phoenix, Ariz.,
in October, 1970.
Judge is Nicholas
Kay; handler
Gary Zayac.

Ch. Gretal of Shady Hollow is pictured here winning at a show in July of 1966. Gretal is owned by Mrs. Bernard Heyward Lawson.

Sanctuary Woods If Only, sired by Ch. Sanctuary Woods You Lucky Boy x Sanctuary Woods Quota v. Mark. Shown taking Best of Winners in 1969 under Judge Robert Waters. Handler is D. J. Anderson. Owned by Zayes and Golden.

Champion Ramby's Bernard v Shady Hollow, bred by Alfred Saba, Jr. and handled by Jane Kamp Forsyth is pictured winning at a National Capital Kennel Club show. Ramby is co-owned by Richard Boch, Jr. and Phyllis Jackson Smith.

American and Canadian Champion Red Jacket's Bunthore winning Best of Breed at the Westchester Kennel Club show in 1970 under Judge Lorna Demidoff. Handled by Bruce Crabb of the Cavajone Kennels, N.H., for owner Paul T. Shannon of Lyme, N.H.

Ch. Ursula von Mallen, three-year-old short-haired bitch, owned by Ann and Richard Golden, Oyster Bay Cove, L.I. Breeder, David Forrest. Judge Gail Devine.

Judging at Westminster Kennel Club. Mr. Arthur Hesser compares Howard Parker's Hansel of Sunnyslope (Mrs. Parker handling) with John C. Sheahan II's Ch. Beau of Highmont, CD, before making decision.

handle. You want your dog to receive his individual attention and not be rushed into the ring at the last moment, because the handler has been busy with too many other dogs in other rings. Some handlers require that you deliver the dog to their establishment a few days ahead of the show so they have ample time to groom and train him. Others will accept well-behaved and previously trained and groomed dogs at ringside, if they are familiar with the dog and the owner. This should be determined well in advance of the show date. NEVER expect a handler to accept a dog at ringside that is not groomed to perfection!

There are several sources for locating a professional handler. Dog magazines carry their classified advertising; a note or telephone call to the American Kennel Club will put you in touch with several in your area. Usually, you will be billed after the day of the show.

## DO YOU REALLY NEED A HANDLER?

The answer to the above question is sometimes yes! However, the answer most exhibitors give is, "But I can't *afford* a professional handler!" or, "I want to show my dog myself. Does that mean my dog will never do any big winning?"

Do you *really* need a handler to win? If you are mishandling a good dog that should be winning and isn't, because it is made to

Sampson's Sambo v Shagg-Bark, owned by Ron and Nancy Bryan of Phoenix, Ariz., is pictured taking a three-point major win as Best of Winners under Judge Ted Wurmser at Phoenix dog show. The Bryans are owners of the Ronan's Desert Alps Kennels.

look simply terrible in the ring by its owner, the answer is yes. If you don't know how to handle a dog properly, why make your dog look bad when a handler could show it to its best advantage?

Some owners simply cannot handle a dog well and still wonder why their dogs aren't winning in the ring, no matter how hard they try. Others are nervous and this nervousness travels down the leash to the dog and the dog behaves accordingly. Some people are extroverts by nature, and these are the people who usually make excellent handlers. Of course, the biggest winning dogs at the shows usually have a lot of "show off" in their nature, too, and this helps a great deal.

The Gilleys' glorious Ch. Sanctuary Woods Better Times winning a Best in Show under Judge Mrs. Nathan Allan.

Ch. Indian Mountain's Winona

Ann and Tom Renner's popular American and Canadian Champion Alpineacres Baron von Shagg-Bark winning at the Elm City Kennel Club show in 1971 under Judge John Honig. Baron's handler-agent is Bruce Crabb, Cavajone Kennels, Merrimack, N.H.

## THE COST OF CAMPAIGNING A DOG
## WITH A HANDLER

Many Saint champions are shown an average of 25 times before completing a championship. In entry fees at today's prices, that adds up to about $200. This does not include motel bills, traveling expenses, or food. There have been Saint champions finished in less shows, say five to ten shows, but this is the exception rather than the rule. When and where to show should be thought out carefully so that you can perhaps save money on entries. Here is one of the services a professional handler provides that can mean a considerable saving. Hiring a handler can save money in the long run if you just wish to make a champion. If your dog has been winning

Well-known Saint Bernard fancier Harold Deitch is shown winning at a show (of the past) with a Dolomount Kennels dog.

Julie Howard gives lesson in standing still.

Dawrob's Pride, owned and bred by Fred S. Andersen, Dawrob Kennels, Woodbury, N.J., was sired by Ch. Stanridge's Hugo v. Hapsburg.

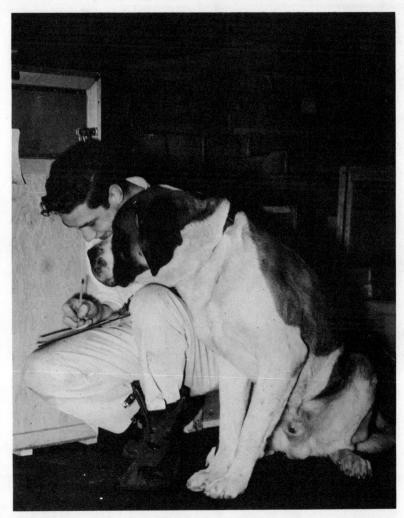

How's that again, Mac? Gerd Von Der Luege answers all questions and checks if his name is spelled correctly as Joe Bartnicki, United Air Lines' cargo handler at Chicago Municipal Airport, checks him aboard a San Francisco-bound airliner. The king-size Saint (140 pounds), a native of Switzerland, was off to appear in a show.

A Shady Hollow Kennel Saint Bernard winning under Judge William Kendrick at the 1962 Worcester, Mass. show. He is owned by Phyllis Jackson Smith of Johnston, R.I.

Beau Cheval As Ever Roma Sumit winning points towards championship at the Old Dominion Kennel Club of N. Virginia under Dr. Richard Greathouse. Douglas Anderson handling at the April 1970 show, for owners Ann and Richard Golden.

Champion Beau Cheval's Tralee Mardoug, daughter of Ch. Powell's Tristan of Riga, and granddaughter of Ch. Beau Cheval's Tablo la Mardoug. She finished with four majors, including Winners Bitch, Best of Winners, and Best of Opposite Sex at the Middle Atlantic Club's Specialty Show in 1967. This proven matron and excellent example of the smooth-haired Saint was bred and is owned by Marlene Anderson of Wycombe, Pa.

reserves and not taking the points and a handler can finish him in five to ten shows, you would be ahead financially. If your dog is not really top quality, the length of time it takes even a handler to finish it (depending upon competition in the area) could add up to a large amount of money.

Campaigning a show specimen that not only captures the wins in his breed but wins group and Best in Show awards gets up into the big money. To cover the nation's major shows and rack up a record as one of the top dogs in the nation usually costs an owner between ten and fifteen thousand dollars a year. This includes not only the professional handler's fees for taking the dog into the ring, but the cost of conditioning and grooming, board, advertising in the dog magazines, photographs, etc.

There is great satisfaction in winning with your own dog, especially if you have trained and cared for it yourself. With today's enormous entries at the dog shows and so many worthy dogs competing for top wins, many owners who said, "I'd rather do it myself!" and meant it, became discouraged and eventually hired a handler anyway.

However, if you really are in it just for the sport, you can and should handle your own dog if you want to. You can learn the tricks by attending training classes, and you can learn a lot by carefully observing the more successful professional handlers as they perform in the ring. Model yourself after the ones that command respect as being the leaders in their profession. But, if you find you'd really rather be at ringside looking on, then do get a handler so that your worthy dog gets his deserved recognition in the ring. To own a good dog and win with it is a thrill, so good luck, no matter how you do it.

Champion Scotholme Judy v Shady Hollow, Saint Bernard bitch owned by Mr. and Mrs. Bernard H. Lawson of the Scotholme Kennels in Chester Springs, Pa.

# CHAPTER 14

## GENERAL CARE AND MANAGEMENT OF YOUR SAINT BERNARD

### TATTOOING

Ninety per cent success has been reported on the return of stolen or lost dogs that have been tattooed. More and more this simple, painless, inexpensive method of positive identification for dogs is being reported all over the United States. Long popular in Canada, along with nose prints, the idea gained interest in this country when dognapping started to soar as unscrupulous people began stealing dogs for resale to research laboratories. Pet dogs that wander off and lost hunting dogs have always been a problem. The success of tattooing has been significant.

Tattooing can be done by the veterinarian for a minor fee. There are several dog "registries" that will record your dog's number and help you locate it should it be lost or stolen. The number of the dog's American Kennel Club registration is most often used on thoroughbred dogs, or the owner's Social Security number in the case of mixed breeds. The best place for the tattoo is the groin. Some prefer the inside of an ear, and the American Kennel Club has ruled that the judges officiating at the AKC dog shows not penalize the dog for the tattoo mark.

The tattoo mark serves not only to identify your dog should it be lost or stolen, but offers positive identification in large kennels where several litters of the same approximate age are on the premises. It is a safety measure against unscrupulous breeders "switching" puppies. Any age is a proper age to tattoo, but for safety's sake, the sooner the better.

The buzz of the needle might cause your dog to be apprehensive, but the pricking of the needle is virtually painless. The risk of infection is negligible when done properly, and the return of your beloved pet may be the reward for taking the time to insure positive identification for your dog. Your local Kennel Club will know of a dog registry in your area.

## OUTDOOR HOUSEBREAKING

If you are particular about your dog's behavior in the house, where you expect him to be clean and respectful of the carpets and furniture, you should also want him to have proper manners outdoors. Just because the property belongs to you doesn't necessarily mean he should be allowed to empty himself any place he chooses. Before long the entire yard will be fouled and odorous and the dog will be completely irresponsible on other people's property as well. Dogs seldom recognize property lines.

If your dog does not have his own yard fenced in, he should be walked on leash before being allowed to run free and before being

Sign says "beware of dog," but Barllo v. Greta of Hollow Acres loves everyone. He is a large short-haired male owned by Tom and Betsy Ryan, Worcester, Pa.

Ch. Little Miss No Name of Ad Astra, bred and owned by Toni Beyer, Denville, N.J.

Ch. Beau Cheval's Padre meets a
cat for the first time. "Smells good,
but can you eat it?"

"You look too nice to eat . . . just
let me smell you some more."

"Don't go away! I want to be friends . . . I won't hurt you."

"Oh boy! There she goes, and I'll never get another chance like that . . . darn it!"

259

Wory v Sauliamt, a Swiss import, owned by the Mardonof Kennels of Mr. and Mrs. Donald Dube, North Attleboro, Mass.

penned up in his own yard. He will appreciate his own run being kept clean. You will find that if he has learned his manners outside, his manners inside will be better. Good manners in "toilet training" are especially important with big dogs!

## OTHER IMPORTANT OUTDOOR MANNERS

Excessive barking is perhaps the most objectionable habit a dog indulges in out of doors. It annoys neighbors and makes for a noisy dog in the house as well. A sharp jerk on the leash will stop a dog from excessive barking while walking; trees and shrubs around a dog run will cut down on barking if a dog is in his own run. However, it is unfair to block off his view entirely. Give him some view— preferably of his own home—to keep his interest. Needless to say, do not leave a dog that barks excessively out all night.

You will want your dog to bark at strangers, so allow him this privilege. Then after a few "alerting" barks tell the dog to be quiet (with the same word command each time). If he doesn't get the idea, put him on leash and let him greet callers with you at the door until he does get the idea.

Do not let your dog jump on visitors either. Leash training may be necessary to break this habit as well. As the dog jumps in the

A Saint Bernard in full harness with cart. Don Pearson of Muncie, Ind., makes these harnesses and illustrates the proper gear.

The famous Ch. Switzer of Shady Hollow calls attention to the damage done to the crate from which he escaped on the plane coming back from the 1964 National in California. He is owned by Phyllis Jackson Smith of Johnston, R.I.

air, pull back on the lead so that the dog is returned to the floor abruptly. If he attempts to jump up on you, carefully raise your knee and push him away by leaning against his chest.

Do not let your dog roam free in the neighborhood no matter how well he knows his way home. Especially do not let your dog roam free to empty himself on the neighbor's property or gardens!

A positive invitation to danger is to allow your dog to chase cars or bicycles. Throwing tin cans or chains out of car windows at them has been suggested as a cure, but can also be dangerous if they hit the dog instead of the street. Streams of water from a

Ch. Kobi von Steinernhof II, runt of a litter of 13, was sired by Ch. Beau Cheval's Tablo la Mardoug, and out of Beau Cheval's Heidi II. Co-owned by Arthur Lewis and M. J. Anderson, Kobi was shown to his title by the Andersons, and became a Specialty Best of Breed winner. Seldom used at stud, he is the sire of Ch. Hulda von Arli, and now deceased. Bred by Marlene Anderson, Beau Cheval Farms, Wycombe, Pa.

Beau Cheval's Peer la Mardoug with his little friend, Tabatha Smith. Peer is owned by Julie Howard, Woodbridge, Va.

garden hose or water pistol are the least dangerous, but leash control is still the most scientific and most effective.

If neighbors report that your dog barks or howls or runs from window to window while you are away, crate training or room training for short periods of time may be indicated. If you expect to be away for longer periods of time, put the dog in the basement or a single room where he can do the least damage. The best solution of all is to buy him another dog or cat for companionship. Let them enjoy each other while you are away and have them both welcome you home!

## GERIATRICS

If you originally purchased good healthy stock and cared for your dog throughout his life, there is no reason why you cannot expect your dog to live to a ripe old age. With research and the remarkable foods produced for dogs, especially this past decade or so, his chances of longevity have increased considerably. If you have cared for him well, your dog will be a sheer delight in his old age, just as he was while in his prime.

We can assume you have fed him properly, if he is not too fat. Have you ever noticed how fat people usually have fat dogs because they indulge their dogs' appetite as they do their own? If there has been no great illness, then you will find that very little additional care and attention are needed to keep him well. Exercise is still essential, as is proper food, booster shots, and tender loving care.

Even if a heart condition develops, there is still no reason to believe your dog cannot live to an old age. A diet may be necessary,

Another Ken-L Ration National Dog Hero. This Saint Bernard named Beggar was 1962 winner and is shown at presentation ceremonies with his young master.

A working dog at work...the Parkers' Ch. Dass of Sunny Slopes, CD.

along with medication, and limited exercise, to keep the condition under control. In the case of deafness, or partial blindness, additional care must be taken to protect the dog, but neither infirmity will in any way shorten his life. Prolonged exposure to temperature variances, overeating, excessive exercise, lack of sleep, or being housed with younger, more active dogs may take an unnecessary toll on the dog's energies and introduce serious trouble. Good judgment, periodic veterinary checkups and individual attention will keep your dog with you for many added years.

When discussing geriatrics, the question of when a dog becomes old or aged usually is asked. We have all heard the old saying that one year of a dog's life is equal to seven years in a human. This theory is strictly a matter of opinion, and must remain so, since so many outside factors enter into how quickly each individual dog "ages." Recently, a new chart was devised which is more realistically equivalent:

| DOG | MAN |
|---|---|
| 6 months | 10 years |
| 1 year | 15 years |
| 2 years | 24 years |
| 3 years | 28 years |
| 4 years | 32 years |
| 5 years | 36 years |
| 6 years | 40 years |
| 7 years | 44 years |
| 8 years | 48 years |
| 9 years | 52 years |
| 10 years | 56 years |
| 15 years | 76 years |
| 21 years | 100 years |

It must be remembered that such things as serious illnesses, poor food and housing, general neglect and poor beginnings as puppies will all take their toll on a dog's general health and age him more quickly than a dog that has led a normal, healthy life. Let your veterinarian help you determine an age bracket for your dog in his later years.

While good care should prolong your dog's life, there are several "old age" disorders to be on the lookout for no matter how well he may be doing. The tendency toward obesity is the most common, but constipation is another. Aging teeth and a slowing down of the digestive processes may hinder digestion and cause constipation, just as any major change in diet can bring on diarrhea. There is also the possibility of loss or impairment of hearing or eyesight which will also tend to make the dog wary and distrustful. Other behavioral changes may result as well, such as crankiness, loss of patience and lack of interest, these are the most obvious changes. Other ailments may manifest themselves in the form of rheumatism, arthritis, tumors and warts, heart disease, kidney infections, male prostatism and female disorders. Of course, all of these require a veterinarian's checking the degree of seriousness and proper treatment.

Take care to avoid infectious diseases. When these hit the older dog, they can debilitate him to an alarming degree, leaving them open to more serious complications and a shorter life.

## DOG INSURANCE

Much has been said for and against canine insurance, and much more will be said before this kind of protection for a dog becomes universal and/or practical. There has been talk of establishing a Blue Cross-type plan similar to that now existing for humans. However, the best insurance for your dog is You! Nothing compensates for tender, loving care. Like the insurance policies for humans, there will be a lot of fine print in the contracts revealing that the dog is not covered after all. These limited conditions usually make the acquisition of dog insurance expensive and virtually worthless.

Blanket coverage policies for kennels or establishments which board or groom dogs can be an advantage, especially in transporting dogs to and from their premises. For the one dog owner, however,

Ch. Sanctuary Woods Trademark, 2½ years old, a short-haired dog owned by Ann and Richard Golden, Oyster Bay Cove, Long Island, N.Y. Breeder is Beatrice Knight.

Ch. Sanctuary Woods Nita Nanette is pictured finishing for her championship title at the Riverside Kennel Club in Hemet, Calif., November 1962. Nanette was handled by Lee Capodice.

whose dog is a constant companion, the cost for limited coverage is not necessary.

## THE HIGH COST OF BURIAL

Pet cemeteries are mushrooming across the nation. Here, as with humans, the sky can be the limit for those who wish to bury their pets ceremoniously. The costs of satin-lined caskets, grave stones, flowers, etc. run the gamut of prices to match the emotions and means of the owner. This is strictly a matter of what the bereaved owner wishes to do.

# IN THE EVENT OF YOUR DEATH . . .

This is a morbid thought perhaps, but ask yourself the question, "If death were to strike at this moment, what would become of my beloved dogs?"

Perhaps you are fortunate enough to have a relative, friend or spouse who could take over immediately, if only on a temporary basis. Perhaps you have already left instructions in your last will and testament for your pet's dispensation, as well as a stipend for their perpetual care.

Robert Paul, Olympic gold medal winner in pair figure skating, gives Saint Bernard Champion Zippity a grateful squeeze for helping to raise funds to send the United States team to the 1968 Winter Olympic Games.

Provide definite instructions before a disaster occurs and your dogs are carted off to the pound, or stolen by commercially minded neighbors with "resale" in mind. It is a simple thing to instruct your lawyer about your wishes in the event of sickness or death. Leave instructions as to feeding, etc., posted on your kennel room or kitchen bulletin board, or wherever your kennel records are kept. Also, tell several people what you are doing and why. If you prefer to keep such instructions private, merely place them in sealed envelopes in a known place with directions that they are to be opened only in the event of your demise. Eliminate the danger of your animals suffering in the event of an emergency that prevents your personal care of them.

## KEEPING RECORDS

Whether or not you have one dog, or a kennel full of them, it is wise to keep written records. It takes only a few moments to record dates of inoculations, trips to the vet, tests for worms, etc. It can avoid confusion or mistakes, or having your dog not covered with immunization if too much time elapses between shots because you have to guess at the last shot.

Make the effort to keep all dates in writing rather than trying to commit them to memory. A rabies injection date can be a problem if you have to recall that "Fido had the shot the day Aunt Mary got back from her trip abroad, and, let's see, I guess that was around the end of June."

In an emergency, these records may prove their value if your veterinarian cannot be reached and you have to use another, or if you move and have no case history on your dog for the new veterinarian. In emergencies, you do not always think clearly or accurately, and if dates, and types of serums used, etc., are a matter of record, the veterinarian can act more quickly and with more confidence.

# CHAPTER 15

# YOUR DOG, YOUR VETERINARIAN, AND YOU

The purpose of this chapter is to explain why you should never attempt to be your own veterinarian. Quite the contrary, we urge emphatically that you establish good liaison with a reputable veterinarian who will help you maintain happy, healthy dogs, Our purpose is to bring you up to date on the discoveries made in modern canine medicine and to help you work with your veterinarian by applying these new developments to your own animals.

We have provided here "thumbnail" histories of many of the most common types of diseases your dog is apt to come in contact with during his lifetime. We feel that if you know a little something about the diseases and how to recognize their symptoms, your chances of catching them in the preliminary stages will help you and your veterinarian effect a cure before a serious condition develops.

Today's dog owner is a realistic, intelligent person who learns more and more about his dog—inside and out—so that he can care for and enjoy the animal to the fullest. He uses technical terms for parts of the anatomy, has a fleeting knowledge of the miracles of surgery and is fully prepared to administer clinical care for his animals at home. This chapter is designed for study and/or reference and we hope you will use it to full advantage.

We repeat, we do *not* advocate your playing "doctor." This includes administering medication without veterinary supervision, or even doing your own inoculations. General knowledge of diseases, their symptoms and side effects will assist you in diagnosing diseases for your veterinarian. He does not expect you to be an expert, but will appreciate your efforts in getting a sick dog to him before it is too late and he cannot save its life.

S.W. Juri Von Fidor with young Warren Winter.

## ASPIRIN: NO PANACEA

There is a common joke about doctors telling their patients, when they telephone with a complaint, to take an aspirin, go to bed and let him know how things are in the morning! Unfortunately, that is exactly the way it turns out with a lot of dog owners who think aspirins are curealls and give them to their dogs indiscriminately. Then they call the veterinarian when the dog has an unfavorable reaction.

Aspirins are not panaceas for everything—certainly not for every dog. In an experiment, fatalities in cats treated with aspirin in one laboratory alone numbered ten out of 13 within a two-week period. Dogs' tolerance was somewhat better, as far as actual fatalities, but there was considerable evidence of ulceration in varying degrees on the stomach linings when necropsy was performed.

Aspirin has been held in the past to be almost as effective for dogs as for people when given for many of the everyday aches and pains. The fact remains, however, that medication of any kind should be administered only after veterinary consultation and a specific dosage suitable to the condition is recommended.

While aspirin is chiefly effective in reducing fever, relieving minor pains and cutting down on inflammation, the acid has been proven harmful to the stomach when given in strong doses. Only your veterinarian is qualified to determine what that dosage is, or whether it should be administered to your particular dog at all.

## WHAT THE THERMOMETER CAN TELL YOU

You will notice in reading this chapter dealing with the diseases of dogs, that practically everything a dog might contract in the way of sickness has basically the same set of symptoms. Loss of appetite, diarrhea, dull eyes, dull coat, warm and/or runny nose, and FEVER!

Therefore, it is most advisable to have a thermometer on hand for checking temperature. There are several inexpensive metal rectal-type thermometers that are accurate and safer than the glass variety which can be broken. This may happen either by dropping, or perhaps even breaking off in the dog because of improper insertion or an aggravated condition with the dog that makes him violently resist the injection of the thermometer. Either kind should be lubricated with vaseline to make the insertion as easy as possible, after it has been sterilized with alcohol.

The normal temperature for a dog is 101.5° Farenheit, as compared to the human 98.6°. Excitement, as well as illness can cause this to vary a degree or two, but any sudden or extensive rise in body temperature must be considered as cause for alarm. Your first indication will be that your dog feels unduly "warm" and this is the time to take the temperature, not when the dog becomes very ill or manifests additional serious symptoms. With a thermometer on hand, you can check temperatures quickly and perhaps prevent some illness from becoming serious.

# COPROPHAGY

Perhaps the most unpleasant of all phases of dog breeding is to come up with a dog that takes to eating stool. This practice, which is referred to politely as coprophagy, is one of the unsolved mysteries in the dog world. There simply is no explanation to why some dogs do it.

However, there are several logical theories, all or any of which may be the cause. Some say nutritional deficiencies; another says that dogs inclined to gulp their food (which passes through them not entirely digested) find it still partially palatable. There is another theory that the preservatives used in some meat are responsible for an appealing odor that remains through the digestive process. Then again poor quality meat can be so tough and unchewable, the dog swallows it whole and it passes through them in large undigested chunks.

There are others who believe the habit is strictly psychological, the result of a nervous condition or insecurity. Others believe the dog cleans up after itself, because it is afraid of being punished as it was when it made a mistake on the carpet as a puppy. Others claim boredom is the reason, or even spite. Others will tell you a dog does not want its personal odor on the premises for fear of attracting other hostile animals to itself or its home.

The most logical of all explanations and the one most veterinarians are inclined to accept is that it is a deficiency of dietary enzymes. Too much dry food can be bad and many veterinarians suggest trying meat tenderizers, monosodium glutamate, or garlic powder which gives the stool a bad odor and discourages the dog. Yeast or certain vitamins, or a complete change of diet are even more often suggested. By the time you try each of the above you will probably discover that the dog has outgrown the habit anyway. However, the condition cannot be ignored if you are to enjoy your dog to the fullest.

There is no set length of time that the problem persists, and the only real cure is to walk the dog on leash, morning and night and after every meal. In other words, set up a definite eating and exercising schedule before coprophagy is an established pattern.

"We're innocent!" say Ch. Hulda von Arli and puppy, co-owned by M. J. Anderson and Bruce Chapman. Hulda is daughter of Ch. Kobi v. Steinernhoff II and out of Beau Cheval's Tiffaney.

Mescha, at five weeks of age. She is out of Christy's Miss Kitty and Beau Cheval's Padre La Mardoug. Bred and owned by Mr. and Mrs. Freeman Bixler, Drums, Pa.

## MASTURBATION

A source of embarrassment to many dog owners, masturbation can be eliminated with a minimum of training.

The dog which is constantly breeding anything and everything, including the leg of the piano or perhaps the leg of your favorite guest, can be broken of the habit by stopping its cause.

The over-sexed dog—if truly that is what he is—which will never be used for breeding can be castrated. The kennel stud dog can be broken of the habit by removing any furniture from his quarters or keeping him on leash and on verbal command when he is around people, or in the house where he might be tempted to breed pillows, people, etc.

Hormone imbalance may be another cause and your veterinarian may advise injections. Exercise can be of tremendous help. Keeping the dog's mind occupied by physical play when he is around people will also help relieve the situation.

Females might indulge in sexual abnormalities like masturbation during their heat cycle, or again, because of a hormone imbalance. But if they behave this way because of a more serious problem, a hysterectomy may be indicated.

A sharp "no!" command when you can anticipate the act, or

a sharp "no!" when caught in the act will deter most dogs if you are consistent in your correction. Hitting or other physical abuse will only confuse a dog.

## RABIES

The greatest fear in the dog fancy today is still the great fear it has always been—rabies!

What has always held true about this dreadful disease still holds true today. The only way rabies can be contracted is through the saliva of a rabid dog entering the bloodstream of another animal or person. There is, of course, the Pasteur treatment for rabies which is very effective. There was of late the incident of a little boy bitten by a rabid bat having survived the disease. However, the Pasteur treatment is administered immediately, if there is any question of

Dog photographer William P. Gilbert caught this informal shot of a class of Saints being set up for judging at the International Kennel Club show in Chicago. Saint entries at the dog shows are steadily increasing.

exposure. Even more than dogs being found to be rabid, we now know that the biggest carriers are bats, skunks, foxes, rabbits and other warm-blooded animals, which pass it from one to another, since they do not have the benefit of inoculation. Dogs that run free should be inoculated for protection against these animals. For city or house dogs that never leave their owner's side, it may not be as necessary.

For many years, Great Britain, because it is an island and because of the country's strictly enforced six-month quarantine, was entirely free of rabies. But in 1969, a British officer brought back his dog from foreign duty and the dog was found to have the disease soon after being released from quarantine. There was a great uproar about it, with Britain killing off wild and domestic animals in a great scare campaign, but the quarantine is once again down to six months and things seem to have returned to a normal, sensible attitude.

Health departments in rural towns usually provide rabies inoculations free of charge. If your dog is outdoors a great deal, or exposed to other animals that are, you might wish to call the town hall and get information on the program in your area. One cannot be too cautious about this dread disease. While the number of cases diminishes each year, there are still thousands being reported and there is still the constant threat of an outbreak where animals roam free. And never forget, there is no cure.

Rabies is caused by a neurotropic virus which can be found in the saliva, brain and sometimes the blood of the warm-blooded animal afflicted. The incubation period is usually two weeks or as long as six months, which means you can be exposed to it without any visible symptoms. As we have said, while there is still no known cure, it can be controlled. It is up to every individual to help effect this control by reporting animal bites, educating the public to the dangers and symptoms and prevention of it, so that we may reduce the fatalities.

There are two kinds of rabies, one form is called "furious," and the other is referred to as "dumb." The mad dog goes through several stages of the disease. His disposition and behavior change radically and suddenly; he becomes irritable and vicious; the eating habits alter, and he rejects food for things like stones and sticks; he becomes exhausted and drools saliva out of his mouth almost

Francis X. Lohmann, columnist for *Popular Dogs* magazine and West Coast broadcaster, and his assistant, Margaret Wells, discuss dogs with Betty White and Allan Ludden of motion picture and television fame. Betty was chairman for National Dog week in 1971. Mr. Lohmann originated and presents his Annual Dog Parade on Hollywood Boulevard each year.

constantly. He may hide in corners, look glassy eyed and suspicious, bite at the air as he races around snarling and attacking with his tongue hanging out. At this point paralysis sets in, starting at the throat so that he can no longer drink water though he desires it desperately; hence, the term hydrophobia is given. He begins to stagger and eventually convulse and death is imminent.

In "dumb" rabies paralysis is swift, the dog seeks dark, sheltered places and is abnormally quiet. Paralysis starts with the jaws, spreads down the body and death is quick. Contact by humans or other animals with the drool from either of these types of rabies on open skin can produce the fatal disease, so extreme haste and proper diagnosis is essential. In other words, you

Champion Major v Neu-Habsburg, owned by Stanley Bussinger.

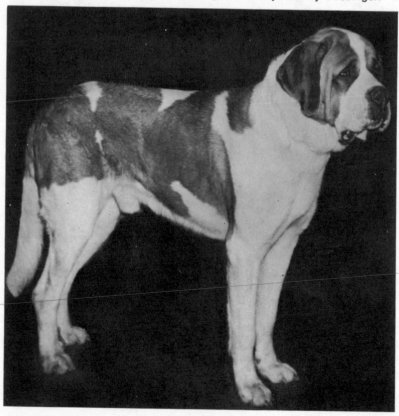

Carmen President John Ox Yoke, the dog which played an important role in breeding programs on the Northeast coast. Shady Hollow Kennels, Johnston, R.I.

do not have to be bitten by a rabid dog to have the virus enter your system. An open wound or cut that comes in touch with the saliva is all that is needed.

The incubation and degree of infection can vary. You usually contract the disease faster if the wound is near the head, since the virus travels to the brain through the spinal cord. The deeper the wound, the more saliva is injected into the body, the more serious the infection. So, if bitten by a dog under any circumstances—or any warm-blooded animal for that matter—immediately wash out the wound with soap and water, bleed it profusely, and see your doctor as soon as possible.

Also, be sure to keep track of the animal that bit, if at all possible. When rabies is suspected the public health officer will need to send the animal's head away to be analyzed. If it is found to be rabies free, you will not need to undergo treatment. Otherwise, your doctor may advise that you have the Pasteur treatment, which is extremely painful. It is rather simple, however, to have the veterinarian examine a dog for rabies without having the dog sent away for positive diagnosis of the disease. A ten-day quarantine is usually all that is necessary for everyone's peace of mind.

Rabies is no respecter of age, sex or geographical location. It is found all over the world from North pole to South pole, and has nothing to do with the old wives' tale of dogs going mad in the hot summer months. True, there is an increase in reported cases during summer, but only because that is the time of the year for animals to roam free in good weather and during the mating season when the battle of the sexes is taking place. Inoculation and a keen eye for symptoms and bites on our dogs and other pets will help control the disease until the cure is found.

## VACCINATIONS

If you are to raise a puppy, or a litter of puppies, successfully, you must adhere to a realistic and strict schedule of vaccination. Many puppyhood diseases can be fatal—all of them are debilitating. According to the latest statistics, 98 per cent of all puppies are being inoculated after 12 weeks of age against the dread distemper, hepatitis, and leptospirosis and manage to escape these horrible infections. Orphaned puppies should be vaccinated every two weeks until the age of 12 weeks. Distemper and hepatitis live-virus vaccine should be used, since they are not protected with the colostrum normally supplied to them through the mother's milk. Puppies weaned at six to seven weeks should also be inoculated repeatedly because they will no longer be receiving mother's milk. While not all will receive protection from the serum at this early age, it should be given and they should be vaccinated once again at both nine and 12 weeks of age.

Leptospirosis vaccination should be given at four months of age with thought given to booster shots if the disease is known in the area, or in the case of show dogs which are exposed on a regular basis to many dogs from far and wide. While annual boosters are in order for distemper and hepatitis, every two or three years is sufficient for leptospirosis, unless there is an outbreak in your immediate area. The one exception should be the pregnant bitch since there is reason to believe that inoculation might cause damage to the fetus.

Strict observance of such a vaccination schedule will not only keep your dog free of these debilitating diseases, but will prevent an

Champion Tommy Tucker of Shady Hollow gets the ribbon from Judge Henry Stoecker at the Great Barrington Kennel Club show in August of 1964. Bred by Phyllis Jackson Smith, he is handled by Alfred Saba, Jr., for owner Martha Willard.

epidemic in your kennel, or in your locality, or to the dogs which are competing at the shows.

## GASTRIC TORSION

Gastric torsion, or bloat, sometimes referred to simply as "twisted stomach" has become more and more prevalent. Many dogs that in the past had been thought to die of blockage of the stomach or intestines because they had swallowed toys or other foreign objects are now suspected of having been the victims of gastric torsion and the bloat that followed.

Though life can be saved by immediate surgery to untwist the organ, the rate of fatality is high. Symptoms of gastric torsion are unusual restlessness, excessive salivation, attempts to vomit, rapid respiration, pain and the eventual bloating of the abdominal region.

The cause of gastric torsion can be attributed to overeating, excess gas formation in the stomach, poor function of the stomach or intestine, blockage to entrances or exits of the stomach or intestine, or general lack of exercise. As the food ferments in the stomach, gases form which may twist the stomach in a clockwise direction so that the gas is unable to escape. Surgery, where the stomach is untwisted counter-clockwise, is the safest and most successful way to correct the situation.

The condition itself is not limited to size or breed of dog, so to avoid the threat of gastric torsion, it is wise to keep your dog well exercised to be sure the body is functioning normally. Make sure that food and water are available for the dog at all times, thereby reducing the tendency to overeat. With self-service, dry feeding, where the dog is able to eat intermittently during the day, there is not the urge to "stuff" at one time.

If you notice any of the symptoms of gastric torsion, call your veterinarian immediately!

## SNAKEBITE

As field trials and hunts and the like become more and more popular with dog enthusiasts, the incident of snakebite becomes more of a likelihood. Dogs that are kept outdoors in runs or dogs that work the fields and roam on large estates are also likely victims.

Most veterinarians carry snakebite serum, and snakebite kits are sold to dog owners for just such purpose. To catch a snakebite in time might mean the difference between life and death, and whether your area is populated with snakes or not, it behooves you to know what to do in case it happens to you or your dog.

Your primary concern should be to get to a doctor or veterinarian immediately. The victim should be kept as quiet as possible (excitement or activity spreads the venom through the body more quickly) and if possible the wound should be bled enough to clean it out before applying a tourniquet, if the bite is severe.

First of all, it must be determined if the bite is from a poisonous or non-poisonous snake. If the bite carries two horseshoe shaped pinpoints of a double row of teeth, the bite can be assumed to be non-poisonous. If the bite leaves two punctures or holes—the result of the two fangs carrying venom—the bite is very definitely poisonous and time is of the essence.

Recently, physicians have come up with an added help in the case of snakebite. A first aid treatment referred to as Hypothermia, which is the application of ice to the wound to lower body tempera-

American and Canadian Champion Beau Cheval's Babee Cyd Mardoug, long-haired female shown to her title by Bruce and Marilyn Chapman, Willow Point Saints, Milford, Mich.

ture to a point where the venom spreads less quickly, minimizes swelling, helps prevent infection and has some influence on numbing the pain. If fresh water ice is not readily available, the bite may be soaked in ice cold water. But even more urgent is the need to get the victim to a hospital or a veterinarian for additional treatment.

## EMERGENCIES

No matter how well you run your kennel or keep an eye on an individual dog, there will almost invariably be some emergency at some time that will require quick treatment until you get the animal to the veterinarian. The first and most important thing to remember is to keep calm! You will think more clearly and your animal will need to know he can depend on you to take care of him. However, he will be frightened and you must beware of fear biting. Therefore, do not shower him with kisses and endearments at this time, no matter how sympathetic you feel. Comfort him reassuringly, but keep your wits about you. Before getting him to the veterinarian try to alleviate the pain and shock.

If you can take even a minor step in this direction it will be a help toward the final cure. Listed here are a few of the emergencies which might occur and what you can do AFTER you have called the vet and told him you are coming.

### Burns

If you have been so foolish as not to turn your pot handles toward the back of the stove—for your children's sake as well as your dog's—and the dog is burned, apply vaseline or butter and treat for shock. The covering will help prevent secondary infection if the burns are severe. Electrical or chemical burns are treated the same; but with an acid or alkali burn, use, respectively, a bicarbonate of soda or vinegar solution. Then apply vaseline. Check this with the veterinarian when you call him.

### Drowning

Most animals love the water, but sometimes get in "over their heads." Should your dog take in too much water, hold him upside down and open his mouth so that water can empty from the lungs, then apply artificial respiration, or mouth-to-mouth resuscitation. Then treat for shock by covering him with a blanket, administering a stimulant such as coffee with sugar, and soothing him with voice and hand.

A winner of days gone by in both the show and obedience ring—Ch. Beau of Highmont, CD, owned by Jack Sheahan of Pennsylvania.

### Fits and Convulsions

Prevent the dog from thrashing about and injuring himself. cover with a blanket and hold down until you can get him to the veterinarian.

### Frostbite

There is no excuse for an animal getting frostbite if you are on your toes and care for the animal. However, should frostbite set in, thaw out the affected area slowly with a circulatory motion and stimulation. Use vaseline to help keep the skin from peeling off and/or drying out.

## Heart Attack

Be sure the animal keeps breathing by applying artificial respiration. A mild stimulant may be used and give him plenty of air. Treat for shock as well, and get to the veterinarian quickly.

## Suffocation

Artificial respiration and treat for shock with plenty of air.

## Sun Stroke

Cooling the dog off immediately is essential. Ice packs, submersion in ice water, and plenty of cool air are needed.

## Wounds

Open wounds or cuts which produce bleeding must be treated with hydrogen peroxide and tourniquets should be used if bleeding is excessive. Also, shock treatment must be given and keep him warm.

# THE FIRST AID KIT

It would be sheer folly to try to operate a kennel or to keep a dog without providing for certain emergencies that are bound to crop up when there are active dogs around. Just as you would provide a first aid kit for people you should also provide a first aid kit for the animals on the premises.

The first aid kit should contain the following items:

BFI or other medicated powder
jar of vaseline
Q-tips
bandage—1 inch gauze
adhesive tape
bandaids
cotton
boric acid powder

A trip to your veterinarian is always safest, but there are certain preliminaries for cuts and bruises of a minor nature that you can care for yourself.

Cuts, for instance, should be washed out and medicated powder or vaseline applied with a bandage. The lighter the bandage the better so that the most air possible can reach the wound. Q-tips can be used for removing debris from the eyes after which a mild

Ch. Beau Cheval's Duet La Mardoug, owned by Marlene J. Anderson, her breeder. Handler is co-owner Thomas Finney of River Raisin Kennels-Farm, Monroe, Mich. Duet is a short-haired female with faultless movement. Sired by Beau Cheval's Tapan Zee II out of Beau Cheval's Premier Brandee.

solution of boric acid wash can be applied. Burns can be assuaged by an application of vaseline. As for sores, use dry powder on wet sores, and vaseline on dry sores. Use cotton for washing out wounds and drying them.

A particular caution must be given here on bandaging. Make sure that the bandage is not too tight to hamper the dog's circulation.

Also, make sure the bandage is made correctly so that the dog does not bite at it trying to get it off. A great deal of damage can be done to a wound by a dog tearing at a bandage to get it off. If you notice the dog is starting to bite at it, do it over or put something on the bandage that smells and tastes bad to him. Make sure, however, that the solution does not soak through the bandage and enter the wound. Sometimes, if it is a leg wound, a sock or stocking slipped on the dog's leg will cover the bandage edges and will also keep it clean.

## HOW NOT TO POISON YOUR DOG

Ever since the appearance of Rachel Carson's book, *Silent Spring*, people have been asking, "Just how dangerous are chemicals?" In the animal world where disinfectants, room deodorants, parasitic sprays, solutions and aerosols are so widely used, the question has taken on even more meaning. Veterinarians are beginning to ask, "What kind of disinfectant do you use?" or "Have you any fruit trees that have been sprayed recently?" when animals are brought in to their offices in a toxic condition, or for unexplained death, or when entire litters of puppies die mysteriously, there is good reason to ask such questions.

The popular practice of protecting animals against parasites has given way to their being exposed to an alarming number of commercial products, some of which are dangerous to their very lives. Even flea collars can be dangerous, especially if they get wet or somehow touch the genital regions or eyes. While some products are a great deal more poisonous than others, great care must be taken that they be applied in proportion to the size of the dog and the area to be covered. Many a dog has been taken to the vet with an unusual skin problem that was a direct result of having been bathed with a detergent rather than a proper shampoo. Certain products that are safe for dogs can be fatal for cats. Extreme care must be taken to read all ingredients and instructions carefully before use on any animal.

The same caution must be given to outdoor chemicals. Dog owners must question the use of fertilizers on their lawns. Lime, for instance, can be harmful to a dog's feet. The unleashed dog that covers the neighborhood on his daily rounds is open to all sorts of tree and lawn sprays and insecticides that may prove harmful to

Ch. Bowser Waller, Best in Show at the Greater Lowell Kennel Club in August, 1967, under Judge Phil Marsh. Robert Forsyth is handler for owner Mrs. Elisabeth Roberts. Mrs. Arthur Dullinger, show chairman ,is shown presenting the Trophy. Mr. Marsh, handler Forsyth, and Edward J. Lyons, Jr. President of the Club complete the picture.

him, if not as a poison, as a producer of an allergy. Many puppy fatalities are reported when they consume mothballs.

There are various products found around the house which can be lethal, such as rat poison, boric acid, hand soap, detergents, and insecticides. The garage too may provide dangers: Antifreeze for the car, lawn, garden and tree sprays, paints, etc., are all available for tipping over and consuming. All poisons should be placed on high shelves for the sake of your children as well as your animals.

Perhaps the most readily available of all household poisons are plants. Household plants are almost all poisonous, even if taken in small quantities. Some of the most dangerous are the Elephant Ear, the Narcissus bulb, any kind of ivy leaves, Burning Bush leaves, the Jimson weed, the Dumb Cane weed, mock orange fruit, Castor Beans, Scotch Broom seeds, the root or seed of the plant called Four O'Clock, Cyclamen, Pimpernel, Lily of the Valley, the stem of the Sweet Pea, Rhododendrons of any kind, Spider Lily bulbs, Bayonet root, Foxglove leaves, Tulip bulbs, Monkshood roots, Azalea, Wisteria, Poinsettia leaves, Mistletoe, Hemlock, Locoweed and Arrowglove. In all, there are over 500 poisonous plants in the United States. Peach, elderberry and cherry trees can cause cyanide poisoning if the bark is consumed. Rhubarb leaves either raw or cooked can cause death or violent convulsions. Check out your closets, fields and grounds around your home to see what might be of danger to your pets.

## SYMPTOMS OF POISONING

Be on the lookout for vomiting, hard or labored breathing, whimpering, stomach cramps, and trembling as a prelude to the convulsions. Any delay in a visit to your veterinarian can mean death. Take along the bottle or package or a sample of the plant you suspect to be the cause to help the veterinarian determine the correct antidote.

The most common type of poisoning which accounts for nearly one-fourth of all animal victims is staphylococcic-infected food. Salmonella ranks third. These can be avoided by serving fresh food and not letting it lie around in hot weather.

There are also many insect poisonings caused by animals eating cockroaches, spiders, flys, butterflies, etc. Toads and some frogs give off a fluid which can make a dog foam at the mouth—and even kill him—if he bites just a little too hard!

Some misguided dog owners think it is "cute" to let their dogs enjoy a cocktail with them before dinner. There can be serious effects resulting from encouraging a dog to drink—sneezing fits, injuries as a result of intoxication, and heart stoppage are just a few. Whiskey for medicinal purposes, or beer for brood bitches should be administered only on the advice of your veterinarian.

There have been cases of severe damage and death when dogs

emptied ash trays and consumed cigarettes, resulting in nicotine poisoning. Leaving a dog alone all day in a house where there are cigarettes available on a coffee table is asking for trouble. Needless to say, the same applies to marijuana. The narcotic addict who takes his dog along with him on "a trip" does not deserve to have a dog. All the ghastly side effects are as possible for the dog as for the addict, and for a person to submit an animal to this indignity is indeed despicable. Don't think it doesn't happen. Ask the veterinarians that practice near some of your major hippie havens! Unfortunately, in all our major cities the practice is becoming more and more a problem for the veterinarian.

Be on the alert and remember that in the case of any type of poisoning, the best treatment is prevention.

## THE CURSE OF ALLERGY

The heartbreak of a child being forced to give up a beloved pet because he is suddenly found to be allergic to it is a sad but true story. Many families claim to be unable to have dogs at all; others seem to be able only to enjoy them on a restricted basis. Many children know animals only through occasional visits to a friend's house or the zoo.

While modern veterinary science has produced some brilliant allergists, such as Dr. Edward Baker of New Jersey, the field is still working on a solution for those who suffer from exposure to their pets. There is no permanent cure as yet.

Over the last quarter of a century there have been many attempts at a permanent cure, but none has proven successful, because the treatment was needed too frequently, or was too expensive to maintain over extended periods of time.

However, we find that most people who are allergic to their animals are also allergic to a variety of other things as well. By eliminating the other irritants, and by taking medication given for the control of allergies in general, many are able to keep pets on a restricted basis. This may necessitate the dog's living outside the house, being groomed at a professional grooming parlor instead of by the owner, or merely being kept out of the bedroom at night. A discussion of this "balance" factor with your medical and veterinary doctors may give new hope to those willing to try.

A paper presented by Mathilde M. Gould, M.D., a New York

Grand Saint Bernard and its dogs.

allergist, before the American Academy of Allergists in the 1960's, and reported in the September-October 1964 issue of the National Humane Review magazine, offered new hope to those who are allergic by a method referred to as hyposensitization. You may wish to write to the magazine and request the article for discussion with your medical and veterinary doctors on your individual problem.

## DO ALL DOGS CHEW?

All young dogs chew! Chewing is the best possible method of cutting teeth and exercising gums. Every puppy goes through this teething process. True, it can be destructive if not watched carefully, and it is really the responsibility of every owner to prevent the damage before it occurs.

When you see a puppy pick up an object to chew, immediately remove it from his mouth with a sharp "No!" and replace the object with a toy or a rawhide bone which should be provided for him to do his serious chewing. Puppies take anything and everything into their mouths so they should be provided with proper toys which they cannot chew up and swallow.

Indian Mountain's Pocohontas thinks things over. She is owned by the Indian Mountain Kennels of East Stroudsburg, Pa.

## BONES

There are many opinions on the kind of bones a dog should have. Anyone who has lost a puppy or dog because of a bone chip puncturing the stomach or intestinal wall will say "no bones" except for the processed or rawhide kind you buy in pet shops. There are those who say shank or knuckle bones are permissible. Use your own judgment, but when there are adequate processed bones which you know to be safe, why risk a valuable animal? Cooked bones, soft enough to be pulverized and put in the food can be fed if they are reduced almost to a powder. If you have the patience for this sort of thing, okay. Otherwise, stick to the commercial products.

As for dogs and puppies chewing furniture, shoes, etc., replace the object with something allowable and safe and put yourself on record as remembering to close closet doors. Keep the puppy in the same room with you so you can stand guard over the furniture.

Electrical cords and sockets, or wires of any kind, present a dangerous threat to chewers. Glass dishes which can be broken are hazardous if not picked up right after feeding.

Chewing can also be a form of frustration or nervousness. Dogs sometimes chew for spite, if owners leave them alone too long or too often. Bitches will sometimes chew if their puppies are taken away from them too soon; insecure puppies often chew thinking they're nursing. Puppies which chew wool or blankets or carpet corners or certain types of materials may have a nutritional deficiency or something lacking in their diet, such as craving the starch that might be left in material after washing. Perhaps the articles have been near something that tastes good and they retain the odor.

The act of chewing has no connection with particular breeds or ages, any more than there is a logical reason for dogs to dig holes outdoors or dig on wooden floors indoors.

So we repeat, it is up to you to be on guard at all times until the need—or habit—passes.

## HIP DYSPLASIA

Hip Dysplasia, or HD, is one of the most widely discussed of all animal afflictions, since it has appeared in varying degrees, in just about every breed of dog. True, the larger breeds seem most

Willow Point's Ezra V Padre, a ten-month-old smooth, owned by Mr. Lee of Chugiak, Alaska. Bred by Bruce Chapman, Ezra is sired by Ch. Beau Cheval's Padre la Mardoug.

susceptible, but it has hit the small breeds and is beginning to be recognized in cats as well.

While HD in man has been recorded as far back as 370 B.C., HD in dogs was more than likely referred to as rheumatism until veterinary research came into the picture. In 1935, Dr. Otto Schales, at Angell Memorial Hospital in Boston, wrote a paper on

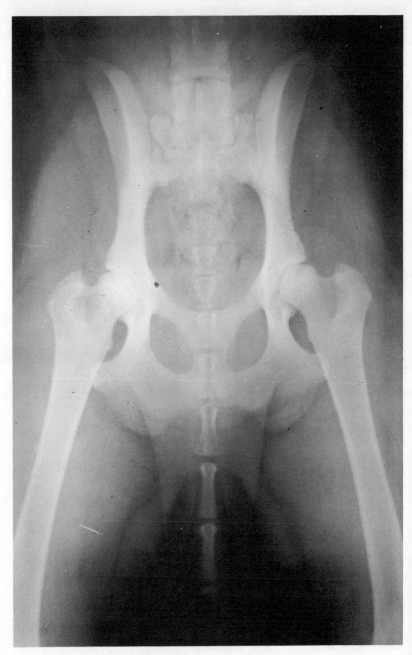

X-ray showing normal hip formation.

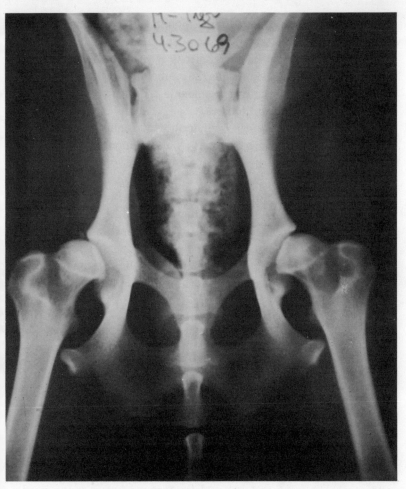

Dysplastic hips—incurable and hereditary.

Hip Dysplasia and classified the four degrees of dysplasia of the hip joint as follows:

Grade 1—slight (poor fit between ball and socket)

Grade 2—moderate (moderate but obvious shallowness of the socket)

Grade 3—severe (socket quite flat)

Grade 4—very severe (complete displacement of head of femur at early age)

HD is an incurable, hereditary, though not congenital disease of the hip sockets. It is transmitted as a dominant trait with irregular manifestations. Puppies appear normal at birth but the constant wearing away of the socket means the animal moves more and more on muscle, thereby presenting a lameness, a difficulty in getting up and severe pain in advanced cases.

The degree of severity can be determined around six months of age, but its presence can be noticed from two months of age. The problem is determined by X-ray, and if pain is present it can be relieved temporarily by medication. Exercise should be avoided since motion encourages the wearing away of the bone surfaces.

Dogs with HD should not be shown or bred, if quality in the breed is to be maintained. It is essential to check a pedigree for dogs known to be dysplastic before breeding, since this disease can be dormant for many generations. It has been estimated that 90 per cent of all Saints are affected to some degree.

## ELBOW DYSPLASIA

The same condition can also affect the elbow joints and is known as Elbow Dysplasia. This also causes lameness, and dogs so affected should not be used for breeding.

## PATELLAR DYSPLASIA

Some of the smaller breeds of dogs also suffer from Patella Dysplasia, or dislocation of the knee. This can be treated surgically, but the surgery by no means abolishes the hereditary factor. Therefore, these dogs should not be used for breeding.

All dogs—in any breed—should be X-rayed before being used for breeding. The X-ray should be read by a competent veterinarian, and the dog declared free and clear.

## HD PROGRAM IN GREAT BRITAIN

The British Veterinary Association (BVA) has made an attempt to control the spread of HD by appointing a panel of members of their profession who have made a special study of the disease, to read X-rays. Dogs over one year of age may be X-rayed and certified as free. Forms are completed in triplicate to verify the tests. One copy remains with the panel, one copy is for the owner's veterinarian, and one for the owner. A record is also sent to the

British Kennel Club for those wishing to check on a particular dog for breeding purposes.

## THE UNITED STATES REGISTRY

In the United States we have a central Hip Dysplasia Foundation, known as the OFA (Orthopedic Foundation for Animals). This HD control registry was formed in 1966. X-rays are sent for expert evaluation by qualified radiologists.

All you need do for complete information on getting an X-ray for your dog is to write to the Orthopedic Foundation for Animals

Ch. Beau Cheval's Traci La Mardoug and Beau Cheval's Shamrock Mardoug, shown at Heart of America Kennel Club Show, March, 1971. Judge was Swiss authority Albert de la Rie. Ch. Traci was Best of Opposite Sex and her half brother, Shamrock, was Winners Dog, Best of Winners and Best of Breed over champions. Traci is handled by Douglas J. Anderson, and Shamrock by Urban Ross of Blackwood, N.J., his owner. Both dogs were bred by M. J. Anderson, and sired by Ch. Magus von Echo.

at 817 Virginia Ave., Columbia, Mo., 65201, and request their Dysplasia packet. There is no charge for this kit. It contains an envelope large enough to hold your X-ray film (which you will have taken by your own veterinarian), and a drawing showing how to position the dog properly for X-ray. There is also an application card for proper identification of the dog. Then, hopefully, your dog will be certified "normal." You will be given a registry number which you can put on his pedigree, use in your advertising, and rest assured your breeding program is in good order.

All X-rays should be sent to the address above. Any other information you might wish to have may be requested from Mrs. Robert Bower, OFA, Route 1, Constantine, Mo., 49042.

We cannot urge strongly enough the importance of doing this. While it involves time and effort, the reward in the long run will more than pay for your trouble. To see the heartbreak of parents and children when their beloved dog has to be put to sleep because of severe Hip Dysplasia as the result of bad breeding is a sad experience. Don't let this happen to you or to those who will purchase your puppies!

Additionally, we should mention that there is a method of palpation to determine the extent of affliction. This can be painful if the animal is not properly prepared for the examination. There have also been attempts to replace the animal's femur and socket. This is not only expensive, but the percentage of success is small.

For those who refuse to put their dog down, there is a new surgical technique which can relieve pain, but in no way constitutes a cure. This technique involves the severing of the pectinius muscle which, for some unknown reason brings relief from pain over a period of many months—even up to two years. Two veterinary colleges in the United States are performing this operation at the present time. However, the owner must also give permission to "de-sex" the dogs at the time of the muscle severance. This is a safety measure to help stamp out Hip Dysplasia, since obviously the condition itself remains and can be passed on.

## HOT SPOTS

Many Saint Bernards will itch and scratch and almost overnight break out with a "hot spot." It is a common and bothersome problem in Saints, and is often mistakenly diagnosed as wet

Ch. Ryland's Thundercloud, at ten months of age. Now ten years old, Thunder is an active stud in excellent health. He's owned by Marian Sharp of Flanders, N.J.

eczema, dry eczema, mange, or perhaps something even worse! A hot spot is a place where the skin is raw, red and oozing with blood or pus. Veterinarians will sometimes prescribe cortisone, but cortisone can produce other problems and must be given with extreme caution. There is a simple "home remedy" which is very inexpensive and most convenient, and almost always works:

Take one fourth cup of laundry bleach to one full cup of water, and pour it over the affected area twice daily. Dust with corn starch in between times. If the area is raw and bloody, try to dry it up with corn starch first . . . but the bleach is necessary to effect a cure. Another treatment used by some of the old time breeders is tincture of green soap which can be purchased in any drug store. Others have achieved results with B.F.I. powder, or antibiotic wound powders or dressing powders also available at drug stores.

Diligent care is required to halt soreness and, of course, never shave the area. The dog can be ready for the show ring once again in a matter of days if treatment is begun before there is too great a loss of hair.

## SWOLLEN JOINTS

Many Saints suffer with swollen elbows and a condition similar to a ballplayer's "water on the knee" or "water on the elbow." The joints are usually affected because many dogs drop to the ground with their full weight when lying down. The weight of the dog hitting the hard floor surface bruises these joint areas and causes them to swell and become painful. Sometimes they require surgery or other relief from a veterinarian. Relieving the problem by draining off the fluids with a needle is not the answer. Too often the condition reoccurs. An experienced veterinarian who has treated this condition before will use the successful method of injection of Morgument salve into the swollen joints and daily rubbing it into the affected area. The salve treatment does work, if done often and without interruption.

## INCURVED EYELIDS OR ENTROPION

This is a common condition in Saint Bernards, where the eyelids of the dog turn inward and the eyelashes of the dog rub and irritate the eyeballs. Surgery is usually required, but here again the expert veterinarian is essential for success. Many of the operations do not cure the condition and are, in fact, no help at all. Eye cream and medication can be used on dogs that are seriously affected, but relying on the advice of the veterinarian who is experienced in this condition in Saints is the best idea of all.

# CHAPTER 16
# THE BLIGHT OF PARASITES

Dogs can be afflicted by both internal and external parasites. The external parasites are known as fleas, ticks and lice. All of these, while bothersome, can be treated with sprays and bath dips and a lot of fortitude. However, the internal parasites, or worms of various kinds, are usually well-infested before discovery and require more substantial means of ridding the dog of them completely.

The most common of all is the round worm. This, like many other parasitic worms, is excreted in egg or larvae form and passed on to other dogs in this manner.

Worm medicine should be prescribed by a veterinarian, and dogs should be checked for worms at least twice a year, or every three months if there is a known epidemic in your area, and during the summer months when fleas (tapeworm carriers) are plentiful.

Other types of worms are hookworms, whipworms, tapeworms, heartworms, kidney and lung worms. Each can be peculiar to a part of the country or may be carried by a dog from one area to another. Symptoms for worms might be vomiting intermittently, eating grass, lack of pep, bloated stomach, rubbing tail along the ground, loss of weight, dull coat, anemia and pale gums, eye discharge, or unexplained nervousness and irritability.

Never worm a sick dog, or a pregnant bitch after the first two weeks, or a constipated dog which will retain the strong medicine within his body for too long a time. The best, safest way to determine the presence of worms is to test for them before they do excessive damage.

## HOW TO TEST YOUR DOG FOR WORMS

Worms can kill your dog if the infestation is severe enough. Even light infestations of worms can debilitate a dog to the point where he is more susceptible to other serious diseases that can kill, if the worms do not.

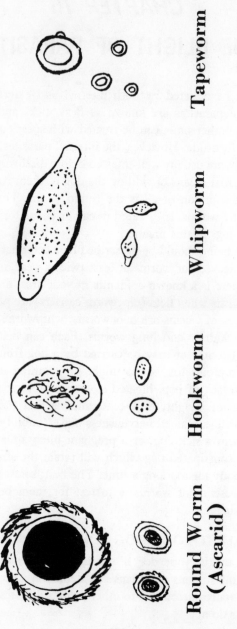

Round Worm (Ascarid)    Hookworm    Whipworm    Tapeworm

Eggs of certain parasites (enlarged 100 or 400 times) commonly seen in dogs.

Ch. Sanctuary Woods Four Winds, owned by O. M. and Lee Capodice, Norwalk, Calif., is pictured winning under Judge Frances O. Holland at the Portland Kennel Club show. Handler is Johnnie Long.

Today's medication for worming is relatively safe and mild, and worming is no longer the traumatic experience for either dog or owner that it used to be. Great care must be given, however, to the proper administration of the drugs. Correct dosage is a "must" and clean quarters are essential to rid your kennel of these parasites. It is almost impossible to find an animal that is completely free of parasites, so we must consider worming as a necessary evil.

However mild today's medicines may be, it is inadvisable to worm a dog unnecessarily. There are simple tests to determine the presence of worms and this chapter is designed to help you make these tests yourself. Veterinarians charge a nominal fee for this service, if it is not part of their regular office visit examination. It is a simple matter to prepare fecal slides that you can read yourself on a periodic basis. Over the years it will save you much time and money, especially if you have more than one dog.

All that is needed by way of equipment is a microscope with 10X power. These can usually be purchased in the toy department in a department store. These microscopes come with the necessary glass slides, equipment and attachments.

After the dog has defecated, take an applicator stick, or a toothpick with a flat end, or even an old-fashioned wooden matchstick, and gouge off a piece of the stool about the size of a small pea. Have one of the glass slides ready with a large drop of water on it. Mix the two together until you have a cloudy film over a large area of the slide. This smear should be covered with another slide, or a cover slip—though I have obtained readings with just the one open slide. Place your slide under the microscope and prepare to focus in on it. To read the slide you will find that your eye should follow a certain pattern. Start at the top and read from left to right, then right back to the left side and then left over to the right once again until you have looked at every portion of the slide from the top left to the bottom right side, as illustrated here:

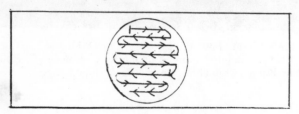

Make sure that your smear is not too thick or watery or the reading will be too dark and confused to make proper identification. On the next page you will find photographs which will show you what to look for when reading the slides to identify the four most common varieties of worms. On the other hand, if you decide that you would rather not make your own fecal examinations, but prefer to have the veterinarian do it, the proper way to present a segment of the stool for him to examine is as follows:

After the dog has defecated, a portion of the stool, say a square inch from different sections, should be placed in a glass jar and

Arrow of Shady Hollow, pictured here at one year of age, winning under the much-respected Judge Albert de la Rie, at the Saint Bernard Specialty show held in Philadelphia. Bred by Dr. Roy Sherman, he is owned by Phyllis Jackson Smith, owner of the Shady Hollow Kennels in Johnston, R.I. Marlene Anderson presents the trophy.

labeled with the dog's name and the name and address of the owner. If the sample cannot be examined within three to four hours after passage, it should be refrigerated. Your opinion as to what variety of worms you suspect is sometimes helpful to the veterinarian and may be noted on the label of the jar you submit to him for examination.

Checking for worms is advisable not only for the welfare of the dog but for the protection of your family, since most worms are transmissible, under certain circumstances, to humans.

"The increasing popularity of the Saint Bernard has necessitated radical changes in hospital personnel."

Best In Show Saint Bernard Champion Kobi's Grand Tyras. "Buster" is pictured in this great win at the Trumbull County Kennel Club show in September 1971, under Judge Ted Wurmser. He is handled by Jack Patterson for owner Robert B. Cox of Agincourt, Ontario, Canada.

# CHAPTER 17

# DICTIONARY OF DOG DISEASES

## AN AID TO DIAGNOSIS
### — A —

ABORTION—When a pregnancy is not right the embryos may be prematurely expelled from the uterus. Usually, the bitch makes a rapid recovery. Abortion can also be the result of an injury or accident which can cause complications. If part of a fetus is left in the uterus, serious infection may occur. The first indication of this will be high fever, dry nose and lethargy. The immediate services of a veterinarian are necessary.

ABSCESS—A skin eruption characterized by a localized collection of pus formed as a result of disintegrating tissues of the body. Abscesses may be acute or chronic. An acute abscess forms rapidly and will more than likely burst within a week. It is accompanied by pain, redness, heat and swelling, and may cause a rise in temperature. An abscess is usually the result of infection of a bacterial nature. Treatment consists of medication in the form of antibiotics and salves, ointments, powders or a poultice designed to bring it to a head. A chronic abscess is a slow-developing headless lump surrounded by gathering tissue. This infection is usually of internal origin, and painless unless found in a sensitive area of the body. The same antibiotics and medications are used. Because abscesses of this nature are slow in developing, they are generally slow in dissolving.

The Saint Bernard Club of America Specialty held at Media, Pa. on June 3, 1956, saw Best of Breed win go to Champion Faust V. Melina, owned and handled by Stanley Bussinger. Judge at this event was Arthur Hesser.

ACARUS—One of the parasitic mites which cause mange.

ACHONDROPLASIA—A disease which results in the stunting of growth, or dwarfing of the limbs before birth.

ADENOMA—A non-inflammatory growth or benign tumor found in a prominent gland; most commonly found in the mammary gland of the bitch.

AGALACTIA—A contagious, viral disease resulting in lowered or no production of milk by a nursing bitch. It usually occurs in warm weather, and is accompanied by fever and loss of appetite. Abscesses may also form. In chronic cases the mammary gland itself may atrophy.

ALARIASIS—An infection caused by flukes *(Alaria arisaemoides)*, which are ingested by the dog. They pass on to the bronchial tract and into the small intestine where they grow to maturity and feed on intestinal contents.

ALLERGY—Dogs can be allergic as well as people to outdoor or indoor surroundings, such as carpet fuzz, pillow stuffings, food, pollen, etc. Recent experiments in hyposensitization have proved effective in many cases when injections are given with follow-up "boosters." Sneezing, coughing, nasal discharges, runny, watery eyes, etc., are all symptomatic.

ALOPECIA—A bare spot, or lack of full growth of hair on a portion of the body; another name for baldness and can be the end result of a skin condition.

AMAUROSIS—Sometimes called "glass eye." A condition that may occur during a case of distemper if the nervous system has been affected, or head injuries sustained. It is characterized by the animal bumping into things or by a lack of coordination. The condition is incurable and sooner or later the optic nerve becomes completely paralyzed.

ANALGESIA—Loss of ability to feel pain with the loss of consciousness or the power to move a part of the body. The condition may be induced by drugs which act on the brain or central nervous system.

ANAL SAC OBSTRUCTION—The sacs on either side of the rectum, just inside the anus, at times may become clogged. If the condition persists, it is necessary for the animal to be assisted in their opening, so that they do not become infected and/or abscess. Pressure is applied by the veterinarian and the glands release a thick, horrible-smelling excretion. Antibiotics or a "flushing" of the glands if infected is the usual treatment, but at the first sign of discomfort in the dog's eliminating, or a "sliding along" the floor, it is wise to check for clogged anal glands.

ANASARCA—Dropsy of the connective tissues of the skin. It is occasionally encountered in fetuses and makes whelping difficult.

ANEMIA—A decrease of red blood cells which are the cells that carry oxygen to the body tissues. Causes are usually severe infestation of parasites, bad diet, or blood disease. Transfusions and medications can be given to replace red blood cells, but the disease is sometimes fatal.

ANEURYSM—A rupture or dilation of a major blood vessel, causing a bulge or swelling of the affected part. Blood gathers in the tissues forming a swelling. It may be caused by strain, injury, or when arteries are weakened by debilitating disease or old age. Surgery is needed to remove the clot.

ANESTROUS—When a female does not come into heat.

ANTIPERISTALSIS—A term given to the reverse action of the normal procedures of the stomach or intestine, which brings their contents closer to the mouth.

ANTIPYRETICS—Drugs or methods used to reduce temperature during fevers. These may take the form of cold baths, purgatives, etc.

ANTISPASMODICS—Medications which reduce spasms of the muscular tissues and soothe the nerves and muscles involved.

ANTISIALICS—Term applied to substances used to reduce excessive salivation.

ARSENIC POISONING—Dogs are particularly susceptible to this type of poisoning. There is nausea, vomiting, stomach pains and convulsions, even death in severe cases. An emetic may save the animal in some cases. Salt or dry mustard (1 tablespoon mixed with 1 teaspoonful of water) can be effective in causing vomiting until the veterinarian is reached.

ARTHRITIS—A painful condition of the joints which results in irritation and inflammation. A disease that pretty much confines itself to older dogs, especially in the larger breeds. Limping, irritability and pain are symptomatic. Anti-

314

Jato's Farmer v. Mar-Will, sired by Ch. Crock's Aiming Hi Double Eagle, owned by R. and C. Thorne of Pinckney, Mich.

inflammatory drugs are effective after X-ray determines the severity. Heat and rest are helpful.

ASCITES—A collection of serous fluid in the abdominal cavity, causing swelling. It may be a result of heavy parasitic infestation or a symptom of liver, kidney, tuberculosis or heart diseases.

ASPERGILLOSIS—A disease contracted from poultry and often mistaken for tuberculosis since symptoms are quite similar. It attacks the nervous system and sometimes has disastrous effects on the respiratory system. This fungus growth in the body tissue spreads quickly and is accompanied by convulsions. The dog rubs his nose and there is a bloody discharge.

ASTHMA—Acute distress in breathing. Attacks may occur suddenly at irregular intervals and last as long as half an hour. The condition may be hereditary or due to allergy or heart condition. Antihistamines are effective in minor attacks.

ATAXIA—Muscular incoordination or lack of movement causing an inhibited gait, although the necessary organs and muscle power are coherent. The dog may have a tendency to stagger.

ATOPY—Manifestations of atopy in the dog are a persistent scratching of the eyes and nose. Onsets are usually seasonal—the dog allergic to, say, ragweed will develop the condition when ragweed is in season, or, say, house dust all year round. Most dogs afflicted with atopy are multi-sensitive and are affected by something several months out of the year. Treatment is by antihistamines or systemic corticosteroids, or both.

— B —

BABESIA GIBSONI (or Babesiosis)—A parasitic disease of the tropics, reasonably rare in the U.S.A. to date. Blood tests can reveal its presence and like other parasitic infections the symptoms are loss of appetite, no pep, anemia and elevations in temperature as the disease advances, and enlarged spleen and liver are sometimes evident.

BALANITIS—The medical term for a constant discharge of pus from the penis which causes spotting of clothing or quarters or causes the dog to clean itself constantly. When bacteria gather at the end of the sheath, it causes irritations in the tissue and pus. If the condition becomes serious, the dog may be cauterized or ointment applied.

BLASTOMYCOSIS—A rare infectious disease involving the kidneys and liver. The animal loses its appetite and vomits. Laboratory examination is necessary to determine presence.

BRADYCARDIA—Abnormal slowness of the heartbeat and pulse.

BRONCHITIS—Inflammation of the mucus lining in the respiratory tract, the windpipe or trachea, and lungs. Dampness and cold are usually responsible and the symptoms usually follow a chill, or may be present with cases of pneumonia or distemper. Symptoms are a nagging dry cough, fever, quickened pulse rate, runny nose, perhaps vomiting, and congested nasal passages which must be kept open. Old dogs are particularly affected. It is a highly transmissible disease and isolation from other animals is important. Antibiotics are given.

BRUCELLA CANIS—An infectious disease associated with abortion in bitches in the last quarter of gestation, sterility or stillbirths. A comparable is testicle trouble in male dogs. It is highly contagious and can be diagnosed through blood tests and animals having the infection should be isolated.

— C —

CANCER (tumors, neoplasia, etc.)—A growth of cells which serve no purpose is referred to as a cancer. The growth may be malignant or benign. Malignancy is the spreading type growth and may invade the entire body. Treatment, if the condition is

Ch. Heilman's Kris von Gero, owned by Dr. and Mrs. E. E. Breyfogle of Massillon, Ohio, wins Best in Show at the Lawton-Fort Sill Kennel Club show in March 1955. Handler is Ed Bracy, judge is Lewis S. Worden, and presenting the trophy is Club President J. Millard Coody.

diagnosed and caught in time, may be successful by surgical methods, drugs, or radioactive therapy. Haste in consulting your veterinarian cannot be urged too strongly.

CANKER (Otitis)—A bacterial infection of the ear where the ear may drain, have a dreadful odor, and ooze a dark brown substance all the way out to the ear flap. Cause of canker can be from mites, dirt, excessive hair growth in the ear canal, wax, etc. A daily cleaning and administering of antifungal ointment or powder are in order until the condition is cured. Symptoms are the dog shaking his head, scratching his ear and holding the head to the side.

CARIES—A pathologic change causing destruction of the enamel on teeth and subsequent invasion of the dentine; in other words, a cavity in a tooth. This may result in bad breath, toothache, digestive disorders, etc., depending upon the severity. Cavities in dogs are rare, though we hear more and more of false teeth being made for dogs and occasionally even root canal work for show dogs.

CASTRATION—Surgical removal of the male gonads or sex organs. An anesthesia is necessary and the animal must be watched for at least a week to see that hemorrhage does not occur. It is best performed at an early age—anywhere from three to nine months. Older dogs suffering from a hormonal imbalance or cancer of the gonads are castrated.

CATARACT—An opaque growth covering the lens of the eye. Surgical removal is the only treatment. Cataract may be a result of an injury to the eye or in some cases may be an inherited trait.

CELLULITIS—Inflammation of the loose subcutaneous tissue of the body. A condition which can be symptomatic of several other diseases.

CHEILITIS—Inflammation of the lips.

CHOLECYSTITIS—A condition affecting the gall bladder. The onset is usually during the time an animal is suffering from infectious canine hepatitis. Removal of the gall bladder, which thickens and becomes highly vascular, can effect a complete cure.

CHOREA—Brain damage as a result of distemper which has been severe is characterized by convulsive movements of the legs. It is progressive and if it affects the facial muscles, salivating or difficulty in eating or moving the jaws may be evident. Sedatives may bring relief, but this disease is incurable.

CHOROIDITIS—Inflammation of the choroid coat of the eye which is to be regarded as serious. Immediate veterinary inspection is required.

COCCIDIOSIS—An intestinal disease of parasitic nature and origin. Microscopic organisms reproduce on the walls of the intestinal tract and destroy tissue. Bloody diarrhea, loss of weight and appetite and general lethargy result. Presence of parasites is determined by fecal examination. Sulfur drugs are administered and a complete clean up of the premises is in order since the parasite is passed from one dog to another through floor surfaces or eating utensils.

COLOSTRUM—A secretion of the mammary glands for the first day or so after the bitch gives birth. It acts as a purgative for the young, and contains antibodies against distemper, hepatitis and other bacteria.

CONJUNCTIVITIS—Inflammation of the conjunctiva of the eye.

CONVULSIONS—A fit, or violent involuntary contractions of groups of muscles, accompanied by unconsciousness. They are in themselves a symptom of another disease, especially traceable to one affecting the brain; i.e., rabies, or an attack of encephalitis or distemper. It may also be the result of a heavy infestation of parasites or toxic poisonings. Care must be taken that the animal does not injure itself and a veterinarian must be consulted to determine and eliminate the cause.

CRYPTORCHID—A male animal in which neither testicle is present or descended. This condition automatically bars a dog from the show ring.

CYANOSIS—A definite blueness seen in and around the mucous membranes of the face; i.e. tongue, lips and eyes. It is usually synonymous with a circulatory obstruction or heart condition.

CYSTITIS—A disease of the urinary tract which is characterized by inflammation and/or infection in the bladder. Symptoms are straining, frequent urination with little results or with traces of blood, and perhaps a fever. Antibiotics, usually in the sulfur category, as well as antiseptics are administered. This is a condition which is of great discomfort to the animal and is of lengthy duration. Relief must be given by a veterinarian, who will empty bladder by means of catheter or medication to relax the bladder so that the urine may be passed.

— D —

DEMODECTIC MANGE—A skin condition caused by a parasitic mite, *Demodex*, living in hair follicles. This is a difficult condition to get rid of and is treated internally as well as externally. It requires diligent care to free the animal of it entirely.

DERMATITIS—There are many forms of skin irritations and eruptions but perhaps the most common is "contact dermatitis." Redness and itching are present. The irritation is due to something the animal has been exposed to and to which it is allergic. The irritant must be identified and removed. Antihistamines and anti-inflammatory drugs are administered, and in severe cases sedatives or tranquilizers are prescribed to lessen the dog's scratching.

DIABETES (Insipidus)—A deficiency of antidiuretic hormone produced by the posterior pituitary gland. It occurs in older animals and is characterized by the animal's drinking excessive amounts of water and voiding frequently. Treatment is by periodic injection of antidiuretic drug for the rest of the animal's life.

DIABETES (Mellitus)—Sometimes referred to as sugar diabetes, this is a disorder of the metabolism of carbohydrates caused by lack of insulin production by the cells of the pancreas. Symptoms are the same as in the insipidus type, and in severe cases loss of weight, vomiting or coma may occur. Blood and urine analysis confirm its presence. It is treated by low carbohydrate diet, oral medication and/or insulin injections.

DIGITOXIN—A medication given to a dog with congestive heart failure. Dosage is, of course, adjusted to severeness of condition and size of the individual animal.

DISC ABNORMALITIES (Intervertebral)—Between each bone in the spine is a connecting structure called an intervertebral disc. When the disc between two vertebrae becomes irritated and protrudes into the spinal canal it forms lesions and is painful. (This is a disease which particularly affects the Dachshund because of its long back in comparison to length of

Ch. Indian Mountain's Winona being awarded her Best of Winners by Judge Gail Devine at the Bronx County Kennel Club. Bred by John and Ruthe Young, Indian Mountain Kennels, Marshalls Creek, Pa. Sired by Ch. Beau Cheval's Padre out of Ryland's Brandywine. Owner-handler Robin Young showed Winona through most of her wins.

legs.) Paralysis of the legs, reluctance to move, and loss of control of body functions may be symptoms. X-ray and physical examination will determine extent of the condition. Massage helps circulation and pain relievers may be prescribed. Surgery is sometimes successful and portable two-wheel carts which support the hindquarters help.

DISTEMPER—Highly transmissable disease of viral origin which spreads through secretions of nose, eyes or direct oral contact.

May be fatal in puppies under 12 weeks. Symptoms of this disease are alternately high and low fevers, runny eyes and nose, loss of appetite and general lassitude, diarrhea and loss of weight. This disease sometimes goes into pneumonia or convulsions if the virus reaches the brain. Chorea may remain if infection has been severe or neglected. Antibiotics are administered and fluids and sedation may be advised by your veterinarian. If the dog has been inoculated, the disease may remain a light case, BUT it is not to be treated lightly. Warmth and rest are also indicated.

DROPSY—Abnormal accumulation of fluid in the tissues or body cavities. Also referred to as edema when accumulations manifest themselves below the skin. In the stomach region it is called ascites. Lack of exercise or poor circulation, particularly in older dogs, may be the cause. While the swellings are painless, excess accumulations in the stomach can cause digestive distress or heart disturbances, and may be associated with diabetes. Occasional diarrhea, lack of appetite, loss of weight, exhaustion, emaciation and death may occur if the condition is not treated.

DYSGERMINOMA—A malignant ovarian tumor. Symptoms are fever, vaginal discharge, vomiting and diarrhea. Tumors vary in size, though more commonly are on the large size and from reports to date, the right ovary is more commonly affected. Radiotherapy may be successful; if not, surgery is required.

— E —

EAR MANGE—Otodectic mange, or parasitic otitis externa. Ear mites suck lymph fluids through the walls of the ear canal. Infections are high where mites are present and a brownish, horrible smelling ooze is present deep down in the canal all the way out to the flap where the secretion has a granular texture. The dog shakes his head, rubs and scrapes. In extreme cases convulsions or brain damage may result. The ear must be cleaned daily and drugs of an antibiotic and anti-inflammatory nature must be given.

ECLAMPSIA—A toxemia of pregnancy. Shortly before the time a bitch whelps her puppies, her milk may go bad. She will pant as a result of high fever, and go into convulsions. The puppies must be taken away from the mother immediately. This is usually the result of an extreme lack of calcium during pregnancy. Also known as milk fever.

ECTROPION—All breeders of dogs with drooping eyelids or exaggerated haws will be familiar with this condition, where the lower eyelid turns out. It can be a result of an injury, as well as hereditary in some breeds, but can be corrected surgically.

ECZEMA—Eczema is another form of skin irritation which may confine itself to redness and itching, or go all the way to a scaly skin surface or open wet sores. This is sometimes referred to as "hot spots." A hormone imbalance or actual diet deficiency may prevail. Find the cause and remove it. Medicinal baths

Champion Cavajone's Baron Aardvark, rough coated male owned by his breeder, Bruce Crabb, Cavajone Kennels, N.H.

and ointments usually provide a cure, but cure is a lengthy process and the condition frequently reoccurs.

EDEMA—Abnormal collection of fluids in the tissues of the body.

ELBOW DYSPLASIA—Term applied to a developmental abnormality of the elbow joints. It is hereditary.

EMPHYSEMA—Labored breathing caused by distended or ruptured lungs. May be acute or chronic and is not uncommon.

EMPYEMA—Accumulation of pus or purulent fluid, in a body cavity, resembling an abscess. Another term for pleurisy.

ENCEPHALITIS—Brain fever associated with meningitis. An inflammation of the brain caused by a virus, rabies or perhaps tuberculosis. It may also be caused by poisonous plants, bad food or lead poisoning. Dogs go "wild," running in circles, falling over, etc. Paralysis and death frequently result. Cure depends on extent of infection and speed with which it is diagnosed and treated.

ENDOCARDITIS—Inflammation and bacterial infection of the smooth membrane that lines the inside of the heart.

ENTERITIS—Intestinal inflammation of serious import. It can be massive or confine itself to one spot. Symptoms are diarrhea, bloody at times, vomiting, and general discomfort. Antibiotics are prescribed and fluids, if the diarrhea and vomiting have been excessive. Causes are varied; may follow distemper or other infections or bacterial infection through intestinal worms.

ENTROPION—A turning in of the margin of the eyelids. As a result, the eyelashes rub on the eyeball and cause irritation resulting in a discharge from the eye. Here again it is a condition peculiar to certain breeds—particularly Chow Chows—or may be the result of an injury which failed to heal properly. Infection may result as the dog will rub his eyes and cause a swelling. It is painful, but can be cured surgically.

ENTEROTOXEMIA—A result of toxins and gases in the intestine. As bacteria increase in the intestine, intermittent diarrhea and/or constipation results from maldigestion. If the infection reaches the kidney through the circulatory system, nephritis results. The digestive system must be cleaned out by use of castor oil or colonic irrigation, and outwardly by

Beau Cheval's Luvi La Mardoug, long-haired bitch co-owned by M. J. Anderson and Thomas Finney of Monroe, Mich. Luvi is linebred through Ch. Kobi v. Steinernhof.

antibiotics.

EOSINOPHILIC MYOSITIS—Inflammation of the muscles dogs use for chewing. Persistent attacks usually lasting one or more weeks. They come and go over long periods of time, coming closer and closer together. Difficulty in swallowing, swelling of the face, or even the dog holding his mouth open will indicate the onset of an attack. Anti-inflammatory drugs are the only known treatment. Cause unknown, outlook grave.

EPILEPSY—The brain is the area affected and fits and/or convulsions may occur early or late in life. It cannot be cured;

however, it can be controlled with medication. Said to be hereditary. Convulsions may be of short duration or the dog may just appear to be dazed. It is rarely fatal. Care must be taken to see that the dog does not injure itself during an attack.

EPIPHORA—A constant tearing which stains the face and fur of dogs. It is a bothersome condition which is not easily remedied either with outside medication or by surgical tear duct removal. There has been some success in certain cases reported from a liquid medication given with the food and prescribed by veterinarians. This condition may be caused by any one or more of a number of corneal irritations, such as nasal malfunction or the presence of foreign matter in the superficial gland of the third eyelid. After complete examination as to the specific cause, a veterinarian can decide whether surgery is indicated.

ESOPHAGEAL DIVERTICULUM—Inflammation or sac-like protrusions on the walls of the esophagus resembling small hernias. It is uncommon in dogs, but operable, and characterized by gagging, listlessness, temperature and vomiting in some cases.

— F —

FALSE PREGNANCY (or pseudopregnancy)—All the signs of the real thing are present in this heart-breaking and frustrating condition. The bitch may even go into false labor near the end of the 63-day cycle and build a nest for her hoped-for puppies. It may be confirmed by X-ray or a gentle feeling for them through the stomach area. Hormones can be injected to relieve the symptoms.

FROSTBITE—Dead tissue as a result of extreme cold. The tissues become red, swollen and painful, and may peel away later, causing open lesions. Ointments and protective coverings should be administered until irritation is alleviated.

FUSOSPIROCHETAL DISEASE—Bad breath is the first and most formidable symptom of this disease of the mouth affecting the gums. Bloody saliva and gingivitus or ulcers in the mouth may also be present, and the dog may be listless due to lack of desire to eat. Cleaning the teeth and gums daily with hydrogen peroxide in prescribed dosage by the veterinarian is required. Further diagnosis of the disease can be confirmed by microscopic examination of smears, though these fusiform bacteria might be present in the mouth of a dog which never becomes infected. Attempts to culture these anaerobes have been unsuccessful.

— G —

GASTRIC DILATION—This is an abnormal swelling of the abdomen due to gas or overeating. Consumption of large amounts of food especially if dry foods are eaten, and then large quantities of water make the dog "swell." The stomach twists so that both ends are locked off. Vomiting is impossible, breathing is hampered and the dog suffers pain until the food is expelled. Dogs that gulp their food and swallow air with it

Ch. Beau Cheval's Fondu Mardoug pictured going Best of Opposite Sex under Judge Ms. George Wessar at the Topeka Kennel Club in October, 1971. Handling is Candy Wait. Fondu is owned by Ben and Ginger Brown, Kansas City, Mo.

are most susceptible. Immediate surgery may be required to prevent the stomach from bursting. Commonly known as bloat.

GASTRITIS—Inflammation of the stomach caused by many things—spoiled food which tends to turn to gas, overeating, eating foreign bodies, chemicals or even worms. Vomiting is usually the first symptom though the animal will usually drink great quantities of water which more often than not it throws back up. A 24-hour fast which eliminates the cause is the first step toward cure. If vomiting persists chunks of ice cubes put down the throat may help. Hopefully the dog will lick them himself. Keep the dog on a liquid diet for another 24 hours before resuming his regular meals.

GASTRO-ENTERITIS—Inflammation of the stomach and intestines. There is bleeding and ulceration in the stomach and this serious condition calls for immediate veterinary help.

GASTRODUODENITIS—Inflammation of the stomach and duodenum.

GINGIVITIS or gum infection—Badly tartared teeth are usually the cause of this gum infection characterized by swelling, redness at the gum line, bleeding and bloody saliva. Bad breath also. Improper diet may be a cause of it. Feeding of only soft foods as a steady diet allows the tartar to form and to irritate the gums. To effect a cure, clean the teeth and perhaps the veterinarian will also recommend antibiotics.

GLAUCOMA—Pressure inside the eyeball builds up, the eyeball becomes hard and bulgy and a cloudiness of the entire corneal area occurs. The pupil is dilated and the eye is extremely sensitive. Blindness is inevitable unless treatment is prompt at the onset of the disease. Cold applications as well as medical prescriptions are required with also the possibility of surgery, though with no guarantee of success.

GLOSSITIS—Inflammation of the tongue.

GOITER—Enlargement of the thyroid gland, sometimes requiring surgery. In minor cases, medication—usually containing iodine—is administered.

— H —

HARELIP—A malformation of the upper lip characterized by a cleft palate. Difficulty in nursing in exaggerated cases can

Headstudy of Beau Cheval's Peer La Mardoug, by photographer-owner Julie Howard of Woodbridge, Va., demonstrates excellent type, color and markings Peer was sired by Ch. Beau Cheval's Padre la Mardoug, and out of Ch. Beau Cheval's Contesa Mardoug. He is a splashed rough.

result in starvation or puny development. Operations can be performed late in life.

HEART DISEASE—Heart failure is rare in young dogs, but older dogs which show an unusual heavy breathing after exercise or are easily tired may be victims of heart trouble, and an examination is in order. As it grows worse, wheezing, coughing or gasping may be noticed. Other symptoms indicating faulty circulation may manifest themselves as the animal retains more body fluids as the circulation slows down. Rest, less exercise, and non-fattening diets are advised and medication to remove excess fluids from the body are prescribed. In many cases, doses of digitalis may be recommended.

HEARTWORM *(Dirofilaria immitis)*—This condition does not necessarily debilitate a working dog or a dog that is extremely active. It is diagnosed by a blood test and a microscopic examination to determine the extent of the microfilariae. If positive, further differentials are made for comparison with other microfilariae. Treatment consists of considerable attention to the state of nutrition, and liver and kidney functions are watched closely in older dogs. Medication is usually treatment other than surgery and consists of dithiazine iodine therapy over a period of two weeks. Anorexia and/or fever may occur and supplemental vitamins and minerals may be indicated. Dogs with heavy infestations are observed for possible foreign protein reaction from dying and decomposing worms, and are watched for at least three months.

HEATSTROKE—Rapid breathing, dazed condition, vomiting, temperature, and collapse in hot weather indicate heatstroke. It seems to strike older dogs especially if they are overweight or have indulged in excessive activity. Reduce body temperature immediately by submerging dog in cold water, apply ice packs, cold enemas, etc. Keep dog cool and quiet for at least 24 hours.

HEMATOMA—A pocket of blood that may collect in the ear as a result of an injury or the dog's scratching. Surgery is required to remove the fluid and return skin to cartilage by stitching.

HEMOPHILIA—Excessive bleeding on the slightest provocation. Only male subjects are susceptible and it is a hereditary disease passed on by females. Blood coagulants are now successfully used in certain cases.

HEPATITIS, Infectious canine—This disease of viral nature enters the body through the mouth and attacks primarily the liver. Puppies are the most susceptible to this disease and run a fever and drink excessive amounts of water. Runny eyes, nose, vomiting, and general discomfort are symptoms. In some cases blood builders or even blood transfusions are administered since the virus has a tendency to thin the blood. This depletion of the blood often leaves the dog open to other types of infection and complete recovery is a lengthy process. Antibiotics are usually given and supplemental diet and blood builders are a help. Vaccination for young puppies is essential.

HERNIA (diaphragmatic)—An injury is usually responsible for this separation or break in the wall of diaphragm. Symptoms depend on severity; breathing may become difficult, there is some general discomfort or vomiting. X-rays can determine the extent of damage and the only cure is surgery.

HERNIA (umbilical)—Caused by a portion of the abdominal viscera protruding through a weak spot near the navel. Tendency toward hernia is said to be largely hereditary.

HIP DYSPLASIA or HD is a wearing away of the ball and socket of the hip joint. It is a hereditary disease. The symptoms of this bone abnormality are a limp and an awkwardness in

Gresham's Redcloud of Ryland, a nine-month-old rough puppy, is owned by Mr. and Mrs. Don Sharp of Flanders, N.J. Sassy is the "trademark" for the Northern New Jersey Saint Bernard Club.

raising or lowering the body. X-ray will establish severity and it is wise in buying or selling a dog of any breed to insist on a radiograph to prove the animal is HD clear. The condition can be detected as early as three months and if proven the dog should have as little exercise as possible. There is no cure for this condition. Only pain relievers can be given for the more severe cases. No animal with HD should be used for breeding.

HOOKWORM—Hookworms lodge in the small intestines and suck blood from the intestinal wall. Anemia results from loss of blood. Loss of weight, pale gums, and general weakness are symptoms. Microscopic examination of the feces will determine presence. Emphasis on diet improvement and supplements to build up the blood is necessary and, of course, medication for the eradication of the hookworms. This can be either oral or by veterinary injection.

HYDROCEPHALUS—A condition also known as "water head" since a large amount of fluid collects in the brain cavity, usually before birth. This may result in a difficult birth and the young are usually born dead or die shortly thereafter. Euthanasia is recommended on those that do survive since intelligence is absent and violence to themselves or to others is liable to occur.

HYDRONEPHROSIS—Due to a cystic obstruction the kidney collects urine which cannot be passed through the ureter into the bladder, causing the kidney to swell (sometimes to five times its normal size) and giving pain in the lumbar region. The kidney may atrophy, if the condition goes untreated.

— I —

ICHTHYOSIS—A skin condition over elbows and hocks. Scaliness and cracked skin cover the area particularly that which comes in contact with hard surfaces. Lubricating oils well rubbed into the skin and keeping the animal on soft surfaces are solutions.

IMPETIGO—Skin disease seen in puppies infested by worms, distemper, or teething problems. Little soft pimples cover the surface of the skin. Sulfur ointments and ridding the puppy of the worms are usually sufficient cure as well.

INTERDIGITAL CYSTS—Growths usually found in the legs.

Ch. Star East Ada, owned by Mrs. Bernard H. Lawson of the Scotholme Kennels in Chester Springs, Pa.

They are painful and cause the dog to favor the paw or not walk on it at all. Surgery is the only cure and antibiotic ointments to keep dirt and infection out are necessary.

INTESTINAL OBSTRUCTIONS—When a foreign object becomes lodged in the intestines and prevents passage of stool constipation results from the blockage. Hernia is another cause of obstruction or stoppage. Pain, vomiting, loss of appetite are symptoms. Fluids, laxatives or enemas should be given to remove blockage. Surgery may be necessary after X-ray determines cause. Action must be taken since death may result from long delay or stoppage.

IRITIS—Inflammation of the iris or colored part of the eye. May be caused by the invasion of foreign bodies or other irritants.

— J —

JAUNDICE—A yellow discoloration of the skin. Liver malfunction causes damage by bile seeping into the circulatory system and being dispensed into the body tissue, causing discoloration of the skin. It may be caused by round worms, liver flukes or gall stones. It may be either acute or chronic and the animal loses ambition, convulses or vomits, sometimes to excess. It may be cured once the cause has been eliminated. Neglect can lead to death.

— K —

KERATITIS—Infection of the cornea of the eye. Distemper or hepatitus may be a cause. Sensitivity to light, watery discharge and pain are symptomatic. Treatment depends on whether the lesion is surface irritation or a puncture of the cornea. Warm compresses may help until the veterinarian prescribes the final treatment. Sedatives or tranquilizers may be prescribed to aid in preventing the dog from rubbing the eye.

KIDNEY WORM—The giant worm that attacks the kidney and kidney tissue. It can reach a yard in length. The eggs of this rare species of worm are passed in the dog's urine rather than the feces. These worms are found in raw fish. It is almost impossible to detect them until at least one of the kidneys is completely destroyed or an autopsy reveals its presence. There is no known cure at this point and, therefore, the only alternative is not to feed raw fish.

— L —

LEAD POISONING—Ingestion of lead-based paints or products such as linoleum containing lead is serious. Symptoms are vomiting, behavior changes and/or hysteria or even convulsions in severe cases. It can be cured by medication if caught early enough. Serious damage can be done to the central nervous system. Blood samples are usually taken to determine amount in the blood. Emetics may be required if heavy intake is determined.

LEPTOSPIROSIS—This viral infection is dangerous and bothersome because it affects many organs of the body before lodging itself in the kidneys. Incubation is about two weeks after exposure to the urine of another affected dog. Temperature, or subtemperature, pain and stiffness in the hindquarters are not uncommon, nor is vomiting. Booster shots after proper vaccination at a young age are usually preventative, but once afflicted, antibiotics are essential to cure.

LOCKJAW (tetanus)—Death rate is very high in this bacterial disease. Puncture wounds may frequently develop into lockjaw. Symptoms are severe. As the disease progresses high fever and stiffness in the limbs become serious though the dog does not lose consciousness. Sedatives must be given to help relax the muscles and dispel the spasms. When the stiffness affects the muscles of the face, intravenous feeding must be provided. If a cure is effected, it is a long drawn out affair. Lockjaw bacteria are found in soil and in the feces of animals and humans.

LYMPHOMA (Hodgkins disease)—Malignant lymphoma most frequently is found in dogs under four years of age, affects the lymph glands, liver and spleen. Anorexia and noticeable loss of weight are apparent as well as diarrhea. Depending on area and organ, discharge may be present. The actual neoplasm or tumorous growth may be surrounded by nodules or neoplastic tissue which should be surgically removed under anesthesia.

## — M —

MAMMARY NEOPLASMS—25 per cent of all canine tumors are of mammary origin. About half of all reported cases are benign. They are highly recurrent and, when cancerous, fatalities are high. Age or number of litters has nothing to do with the condition itself or the seriousness.

MANGE—The loss of a patch of hair usually signals the onset of mange, which is caused by any number of types of microscopic mites. The veterinarian will usually take scrapings to determine which of the types it is. Medicated baths and dips plus internal and external medication is essential as it spreads rapidly and with care can be confined to one part of the body. Antibiotics are prescribed.

MASTITIS (mammary gland infection)—After the birth of her young, a bitch may be beset by an infection causing inflammation of the mammary glands which produce milk for the puppies. Soreness and swelling make it painful for her when the puppies nurse. Abscess may form and she will usually run a fever. Hot compresses and antibiotics are necessary and in some instances hormone therapy.

MENINGITIS—Inflammation affecting the membranes covering the brain and/or spinal cord. It is a serious complication which may result from a serious case of distemper, tuberculosis, hardpad, head injury, etc. Symptoms are delirium, restlessness,

To illustrate dog and bitch, notice masculinity of Barllo v Greta of Hollow Acres as he looms above his small dam, feminine-looking Beau Cheval's Greta v Tablo. Both dogs are owned by Mr. and Mrs. Thomas Ryan, Hollow Acres Farm, Worcester, Pa. Son is improvement over his dam.

high temperature, and dilated pupils in the eyes. Paralysis and death are almost certain.

METRITIS—This infection, or inflammation of the uterus, causes the dog to exude a bloody discharge. Vomiting and a general lassitude are symptoms. Metritis can occur during the time the bitch is in season or right after giving birth. Antibiotics are used, or in severe cases hysterectomy.

MONORCHIDISM—Having only one testicle.

MOTION SICKNESS—On land, on sea, or in the air, your dog may be susceptible to motion sickness. Yawning, or excessive salivation, may signal the onset, and there is eventual vomiting. One or all of the symptoms may be present and recovery is miraculously fast once the motion ceases. Antinauseant drugs are available for animals which do not outgrow this condition.

MYELOMA—Tumor of the bone marrow. Lameness and evidence of pain are symptoms as well as weight loss, depression and palpable tumor masses. Anemia or unnatural tendency to bleed in severe cases may be observed. The tumors may be detected radiographically, but no treatment has yet been reported for the condition.

— N —

NEONATAL K-9 HERPESVIRUS INFECTION—Though K-9 herpesvirus infection, or CHV, has been thought to be a disease of the respiratory system in adult dogs, the acute necrotizing and hemorraghic disease occurs only in infant puppies. The virus multiplies in the respiratory system and female genital tracts of older dogs. Puppies may be affected in the vaginal canal. Unfortunately the symptoms resemble other neonatal infections, even hepatitis, and only after autopsy can it be detected.

NEPHROTIC SYNDROME—Symptoms may be moist or suppurative dermatitis, edema or hypercholesteremia. It is a disease of the liver and may be the result of another disease. Laboratory data and biopsies may be necessary to determine the actual cause if it is other than renal disease. Cure is effected by eradicating the original disease. This is a relatively uncommon thing in dogs, and liver and urinal function tests are made to determine its presence.

NEURITIS—Painful inflammation of a nerve.

NOSEBLEED (epistaxis)—A blow or other injury which causes injury to the nasal tissues is usually the cause. Tumors, parasites, foreign bodies, such as thorns or burrs or quills, may also be responsible. Ice packs will help stem the tide of blood, though coagulants may also be necessary. Transfusions in severe cases may be indicated.

— O —

ORCHITIS—Inflammation of the testes.

OSTEOGENESIS IMPERFECTA—or "brittle bones" is a condition that can be said to be both hereditary and dietary. It may be due to lack of calcium or phosphorus or both. Radiographs show "thin" bones with deformities throughout the skeleton. Treatment depends on cause.

OSTEOMYELITIS (enostosis)—Bone infection may develop after a bacterial contamination of the bone, such as from a compound fracture. Pain and swelling denote the infection and wet sores may accompany it. Lack of appetite, fever and general inactivity can be expected. Antibiotics are advised after X-ray determines severity. Surgery eliminates dead tissue or bone splinters to hasten healing.

OTITIS—Inflammation of the ear.

— P —

PANCREATITIS—It is difficult to palpate for the pancreas unless it is enlarged, which it usually is if this disease is present. Symptoms to note are as in other gastronomic complaints such as vomiting, loss of appetite, anorexia, stomach pains and general listlessness. This is a disease of older dogs though it has been diagnosed in young dogs as well. Blood, urine and stool examination and observation of the endocrine functions of the dog are in order. Clinical diseases that may result from a serious case of pancreatitis are acute pancreatitis which involves a complete degeneration of the pancreas, atrophy, fibrous and/or neoplasia, cholecystitis. Diabetes mellitus is also a possibility.

PATELLAR LUXATION—"Trick knees" are frequent in breeds that have been "bred down" from Standard to Toy size, and is a condition where the knee bone slips out of position. It is an off again, on again condition that can happen as a result of a jump or excessive exercise. If it is persistent, anti-inflammatory drugs may be given or in some cases surgery can correct it.

PERITONITIS—Severe pain accompanies this infection or inflammation of the lining of the abdominal cavity. Extreme sensitivity to touch, loss of appetite and vomiting occur. Dehydration and weight loss is rapid and anemia is a possibility. Antibiotics should kill the infection and a liquid diet for several days is advised. Painkillers may be necessary or drainage tubes in severe cases.

PHLEBITIS—Inflammation of a vein.

PLACENTA—The afterbirth which accompanies and has been used to nourish the fetus. It is composed of three parts; the chorion, amnion, and allantois.

POLYCYTHEMIA VERA—A disease of the blood causing an elevation of hemoglobin concentration. Blood-letting has been effective. The convulsions that typify the presence can be likened to epileptic fits and last for several minutes. The limbs

The grounds of the Hospice in Switzerland.

are stiff and the body feels hot. Mucous membranes are congested, the dog may shiver, and the skin has a ruddy discoloration. Blood samples must be taken and analyzed periodically. If medication to reduce the production of red blood cells is given, it usually means the dog will survive.

PROCTITIS—Inflammation of the rectum.

PROSTATITIS—Inflammation of the prostate gland.

PSITTACOSIS—This disease which affects birds and people has been diagnosed in rare instances in dogs. A soft, persistent cough indicates the dog has been exposed, and a radiograph will show a cloudy portion on the affected areas of the lung. Antibiotics such as aureomycin have been successful in the known cases and cure has been effected in two to three weeks' time. This is a highly contagious disease, to the point where it can be contracted during a post mortem.

PYOMETRA—This uterine infection presents a discharge of pus from the uterus. High fever may turn to below normal as the infection persists. Lack of appetite with a desire for fluids and frequent urination are evidenced. Antibiotics and hormones are known cures. In severe cases, hysterectomy is done.

## — R —

RABIES (hydrophobia)—The most deadly of all dog diseases. The Pasteur treatment is the only known cure for humans. One of the viral diseases that affects the nervous system and damages the brain. It is contracted by the intake, through a bite or cut, of saliva from an infected animal. It takes days or even months for the symptoms to appear, so it is sometimes difficult to locate, or isolate, the source. There are two reactions in a dog to this disease. In the paralytic rabies the dog can't swallow and salivates from a drooping jaw, and progressive paralysis eventually overcomes the entire body. The animal goes into coma and eventually dies. In the furious type of rabies the dog turns vicious, eats strange objects, in spite of a difficulty in swallowing, foams at the mouth, and searches out animals or people to attack—hence the expression "mad dog." Vaccination is available for dogs that run loose. Examination of the brain is necessary to determine actual diagnosis.

RECTAL PROLAPSE—Diarrhea, straining from constipation or heavy infestations of parasites are the most common cause of prolapse which is the expulsion of a part of the rectum through the anal opening. It is cylindrical in shape, and must be replaced within the body as soon as possible to prevent damage. Change in diet, medication to eliminate the cause, etc. will effect a cure.

RETINAL ATROPHY—A disease of the eye that is highly hereditary and may be revealed under ophthalmoscopic examination. Eventual blindness inevitably results. Dogs with retinal atrophy should not be used for breeding. Particularly prominent in certain breeds where current breeding trends have tended to change the shape of the head.

RHINITIS—Acute or chronic inflammation of the mucous membranes of the nasal passages. It is quite common in both dogs and cats. It is seldom fatal, but requires endless "nursing" on the part of the owner for survival, since the nose passages must be kept open so the animal will eat. Dry leather on the nose though there is excessive discharge, high fever, sneezing, etc., are symptoms. Nose discharge may be bloody and the

A wood carving of a mother Saint Bernard and her puppies. This master-piece was done in 1950, taking thirteen hundred man hours to hand carve from one block of wood. It is a prized possession of Saint Bernard fanciers Mary Lou and Donald Dube.

animal will refuse to eat making it listless. The attacks may be recurrent and medication must be administered.

RICKETS—The technical name for rickets is osteomalacia and is due to not enough calcium in the body. The bones soften and the legs become bowed or deformed. Rickets can be cured if caught in early stages by improvement in diet.

RINGWORM—The dread of the dog and cat world! This is a fungus disease where the hair falls out in circular patches. It spreads rapidly and is most difficult to get rid of entirely. Drugs must be administered "inside and out!" The cure takes many weeks and much patience. Ultraviolet lights will show hairs green in color so it is wise to have your animal, or new puppy, checked out by the veterinarian for this disease before introducing him to the household. It is contracted by humans.

ROOT CANAL THERAPY—Injury to a tooth may be treated by prompt dental root canal therapy which involves removal of damaged or necrotic pulp and placing of opaque filling material in the root canal and pulp chamber.

— S —

SALIVARY CYST—Surgery is necessary when the salivary gland becomes clogged or non-functional, causing constant salivation. A swelling becomes evident under the ear or tongue. Surgery will release the accumulation of saliva in the duct of the salivary gland, though it is at times necessary to remove the salivary gland in its entirety. Zygomatic salivary cysts are usually a result of obstructions in the four main pairs of salivary glands in the mouth. Infection is more prevalent in the parotid of the zygomatic glands located at the rear of the mouth, lateral to the last upper molars. Visual symptoms may be protruding eyeballs, pain when moving the jaw, or a swelling in the roof of the mouth. If surgery is necessary, it is done under general anesthesia and the obstruction removed by dissection. Occasionally, the zygomatic salivary gland is removed as well. Stitches or drainage tubes may be necessary or dilation of the affected salivary gland. Oral or internal antibiotics may be administered.

SCABIES—Infection from a skin disease caused by a sarcoptic mange mite.

SCURF (dandruff)—A scaly condition of the body in areas covered with hair. Dead cells combined with dried sweat and sebaceous oil gland materials.

The Bernard Lawsons of the Scotholme Kennels captured this shot to use on their Christmas cards. The dogs are Scotholme's Mr. Reliable and Ch. Pandora's Lady Moriah.

SEBORRHEA—A skin condition also referred to as "stud tail," though studding has nothing to do with the condition. The sebaceous or oil-forming glands are responsible. Accumulation of dry skin, or scurf, is formed by excessive oily deposits while the hair becomes dry or falls out altogether.

SEPTICEMIA—When septic organisms invade the bloodstream, it is called septicemia. Severe cases are fatal as the organisms in the blood infiltrate the tissues of the body and all the body organs are affected. Septicemia is the result of serious wounds, especially joints and bones. Abscess may form. High temperature and/or shivering may herald the onset, and death occurs shortly thereafter since the organisms reproduce and spread rapidly. Close watch on all wounds, antibiotics and sulfur drugs are usually prescribed.

SHOCK (circulatory collapse)—The symptoms and severity of shock vary with the cause and nervous system of the individual dog. Severe accident, loss of blood, and heart failure are the most common cause. Keep the dog warm, quiet and get him to a veterinarian right away. Symptoms are vomiting, rapid pulse, thirst, diarrhea, "cold, clammy feeling" and then eventually physical collapse. The veterinarian might prescribe plasma transfusion, fluids, perhaps oxygen, if pulse continues to be too rapid. Tranquilizers and sedatives are sometimes used as well as antibiotics and steroids. Relapse is not uncommon, so the animal must be observed carefully for several days after initial shock.

SINUSITIS—Inflammation of a sinus gland that inhibits breathing.

SNAKEBITE—The fact must be established as to whether the bite was poisonous or non-poisonous. A horse-shoe shaped double row of toothmarks is a non-poisonous bite. A double, or two-hole puncture, is a poisonous snake bite. Many veterinarians now carry anti-venom serum and this must be injected intramuscularly almost immediately. The veterinarian will probably inject a tranquilizer and other antibiotics as well. It is usually a four-day wait before the dog is normal once again, and the swelling completely gone. During this time the dog should be kept on medication.

SPIROCHETOSIS—Diarrhea which cannot be checked through

normal anti-diarrhea medication within a few days may indicate spirochetosis. While spirochete are believed by some authorities to be present and normal to gastrointestinal tracts, unexplainable diarrhea may indicate its presence in great numbers. Large quantities could precipitate diarrhea by upsetting the normal balance of the organ, though it is possible for some dogs which are infected to have no diarrhea at all.

SPONDYLITIS—Inflammation and loosening of the vertebrae.

STOMATITIS—Mouth infection. Bleeding or swollen gums or excessive salivation may indicate this infection. Dirty teeth are usually the cause. Antibiotics and vitamin therapy are indicated; and, of course, scraping the teeth to eliminate the original cause. See also GINGIVITIS.

STRONGYLIDOSIS—Disease caused by strongyle worms that enter the body through the skin and lodge in the wall of the small intestine. Bloody diarrhea, stunted growth, and thinness are general symptoms, as well as shallow breathing. Heavy infestation or neglect leads to death. Isolation of an affected animal and medication will help eliminate the problem, but the premises must also be cleaned thoroughly since the eggs are passed through the feces.

SUPPOSITORY—A capsule comprised of fat or glycerine introduced into the rectum to encourage defecation. A paper match with the ignitible sulfur end torn off may also be used. Medicated suppositories are also used to treat inflammation of the intestine.

— T —

TACHYCARDIA—An abnormal acceleration of the heartbeat. A rapid pulse signaling a disruption in the heart action. Contact a veterinarian at once.

TAPEWORM—There are many types of tapeworms, the most common being the variety passed along by the flea. It is a white, segmented worm which lives off the wall of the dog's intestine and keeps growing by segments. Some of these are passed and can be seen in the stool or adhering to the hairs on the rear areas of the dog or even in his bedding. It is a difficult worm to get rid of since, even if medication eliminates segments, the head may remain in the intestinal wall to grow again. Symptoms are virtually the same as for other worms:

Debilitation, loss of weight, occasional diarrhea, and general listlessness. Medication and treatment should be under the supervision of a veterinarian.

TETANUS (lockjaw)—A telarius bacillus enters the body through an open wound and spreads where the air does not touch the wound. A toxin is produced and affects the nervous system, particularly the brain or spine. The animal exhibits a stiffness, slows down considerably and the legs may be extended out beyond the body even when the animal is in a standing position. The lips have a twisted appearance. Recovery is rare. Tetanus is not common in dogs, but it can result from a bad job of tail docking or ear cropping, as well as from wounds received by stepping on rusty nails.

THALLOTOXICOSIS or thallium poisoning—Thallium sulfate is a cellular-toxic metal used as a pesticide or rodenticide and a ready cause of poisoning in dogs. Thallium can be detected in the urine by a thallium spot test or by spectrographic analysis by the veterinarian. Gastrointestinal disturbances signal the onset with vomiting, diarrhea, anorexia, stomach cramps. Sometimes a cough or difficulty in breathing occurs. Other intestinal disorders may also manifest themselves as well as convulsions. In mild cases the disease may be simply a skin eruption, depending upon the damage to the kidneys. Enlarged spleens, edema or nephrosis can develop. Antibiotics and a medication called dimercaprol are helpful, but the mortality rate is over 50 per cent.

THROMBUS—A clot in a blood vessel or the heart.

TICK PARALYSIS—Seasonal attacks of ticks or heavy infestations of ticks can result in a dangerous paralysis. Death is a distinct reality at this point and immediate steps must be taken to prevent total paralysis. The onset is observed usually in the hindquarters. Lack of coordination, a reluctance to walk, and difficulty in getting up can be observed. Complete paralysis kills when infection reaches the respiratory system. The paralysis is the result of the saliva of the tick excreted as it feeds.

TOAD POISONING—Some species of toads secrete a potent toxin. If while chasing a toad your dog takes it in his mouth, more than likely the toad will release this toxin from its

345

parotid glands which will coat the mucous membranes of the dog's throat. The dog will salivate excessively, suffer prostration, cardiac arrhythmia. Some tropical and highly toxic species cause convulsions, that result in death. Caught in time, there are certain drugs that can be used to counteract the dire effects. Try washing the dog's mouth with large amounts of water and get him to a veterinarian quickly.

TONSILLECTOMY—Removal of the tonsils. A solution called epinephrine, injected at the time of surgery, makes excessive bleeding almost a thing of the past in this otherwise routine operation.

TOXEMIA—The presence of toxins in the bloodstream, which normally should be eliminated by the excretory organs.

TRICHIASIS—A diseased condition of the eyelids, the result of neglect of earlier infection or inflammation.

— U —

UREMIA—When poisonous materials remain in the body, because they are not eliminated through the kidneys, and are recirculated in the bloodstream. A nearly always fatal disease—sometimes within hours—preceded by convulsions and unconsciousness. Veterinary care and treatment are urgent and imperative.

URINARY BLADDER RUPTURE—Injury or pelvic fractures are the most common causes of a rupture in this area. Anuria usually occurs in a few days when urine backs up into the stomach area. Stomach pains are characteristic and a radiograph will determine the seriousness. Bladder is flushed with saline solution and surgery is usually required. Quiet and little exercise is recommended during recovery.

— V —

VENTRICULOCORDECTOMY—Devocalization of dogs, also known as aphonia. In diseases of the larynx this operation may be used. Portions of the vocal cords are removed by manual means or by electrocautery. Food is withheld for a day prior to surgery and premedication is administered. Food is again provided 24 hours after the operation. At the end of three or four months, scar tissue develops and the dog is able to bark in a subdued manner. Complications from surgery are few, but the psychological effects on the animal are to be reckoned with. Suppression of the barking varies from com-

Simon Ludwig, male Saint Bernard pictured at 11 months. Bred by Mrs. Lyle A. Tracy, Ludwig is owned by Mr. and Mrs. F. Richard Kelley of Lakewood, Colo.

plete to merely muted, depending on the veterinarian's ability and each individual dog's anatomy.

— W —

WHIPWORMS—Parasites that inhabit the large intestine and the cecum. Two to three inches in length, they appear "whip-like" and symptoms are diarrhea, loss of weight, anemia, restlessness or even pain, if the infestation is heavy enough. Medication is best prescribed by a veterinarian. Cleaning of the kennel is essential, since infestation takes place through the mouth. Whipworms reach maturity within thirty days after intake.

# CHAPTER 18

## GLOSSARY OF DOG TERMS

ACHILLES HEEL—The major tendon attaching the muscle of the calf from the thigh to the hock

AKC—The American Kennel Club. Address; 51 Madison Avenue, N.Y., N.Y. 10010

ALBINO—Pigment deficiency, usually a congenital fault, which renders skin, hair and eyes pink

AMERICAN KENNEL CLUB—Registering body for canine world in the United States. Headquarters for the stud book, dog registrations, and federation of kennel clubs. They also create and enforce the rules and regulations governing dog shows in the U.S.A.

ALMOND EYE—The shape of the eye opening, rather than the eye itself, which slants upwards at the outer edge, hence giving it an almond shape

ANUS—Anterior opening found under the tail for purposes of alimentary canal elimination

ANGULATION—The angles formed by the meeting of the bones

APPLE-HEAD—An irregular roundedness of topskull. A domed skull

APRON—On long-coated dogs, the longer hair that frills outward from the neck and chest

BABBLER—Hunting dog that barks or howls while out on scent

BALANCED—A symmetrical, correctly proportioned animal; one with correct balance with one part in regard to another

BARREL—Rounded rib section; thorax; chest

BAT EAR—An erect ear, broad at base, rounded or semicircular at top, with opening directly in front

BAY—The howl or bark of the hunting dog

BEARD—Profuse whisker growth

BEAUTY SPOT—Usually roundish colored hair on a blaze of another color. Found mostly between the ears

BEEFY—Overdevelopment or overweight in a dog, particularly hindquarters

BELTON—A color designation particularly familiar to Setters. An intermingling of colored and white hairs

BITCH—The female dog

BLAZE—A type of marking. White stripe running up the center of the face between the eyes

BLOCKY—Square head

BLOOM—Dogs in top condition are said to be "in full bloom"

BLUE MERLE—A color designation. Blue and gray mixed with black. Marbled-like appearance

BOSSY—Overdevelopment of the shoulder muscles

BRACE—Two dogs which move as a pair in unison

BREECHING—Tan-colored hair on inside of the thighs

BRINDLE—Even mixture of black hairs with brown, tan or gray

BRISKET—The forepart of the body below the chest

BROKEN COLOR—A color broken by white or another color

BROKEN-HAIRED—A wiry coat

BROKEN-UP FACE—Receding nose together with deep stop, wrinkle, and undershot jaw

BROOD BITCH—A female used for breeding

BRUSH—A bushy tail

BURR—Inside part of the ear which is visible to the eye

BUTTERFLY NOSE—Parti-colored nose or entirely flesh color

All aboard! Beau Cheval's Typhoon, sired by Beau Cheval's Masked Baron x Beau Cheval's Showgirl. A shorthaired male puppy eight weeks old.

Closeup of Ch. Sanctuary Woods Gulliver, owned by Beatrice Knight.

BUTTON EAR—The edge of the ear which folds to cover the opening
of the ear

CANINE—Animals of the Canidae family which includes not only
dogs but foxes, wolves, and jackals

CANINES—The four large teeth in the front of the mouth often
referred to as fangs

CASTRATE—The surgical removal of the testicles on the male dog

CAT-FOOT—Round, tight, high-arched feet said to resemble those
of a cat

CHARACTER—The general appearance or expression said to be
typical of the breed

CHEEKY—Fat cheeks or protruding cheeks

CHEST—Forepart of the body between the shoulder blades and
above the brisket

CHINA EYE—A clear blue wall eye

CHISELED—A clean cut head, especially when chiseled out below the eye

CHOPS—Jowls or pendulous lips

CLIP—Method of trimming coats according to individual breed standards

CLODDY—Thick set or plodding dog

CLOSE-COUPLED—A dog short in loins; comparatively short from withers to hipbones

COBBY—Short-bodied; compact

COLLAR—Usually a white marking, resembling a collar, around the neck

CONDITION—General appearance of a dog showing good health, grooming and care

CONFORMATION—The form and structure of the bone or framework of the dog in comparison with requirements of the Standard for the breed

CORKY—Active and alert dog

COUPLE—Two dogs

COUPLING—Leash or collar-ring for a brace of dogs

COUPLINGS—Body between withers and the hipbones indicating either short or long coupling

COW HOCKED—When the hocks turn toward each other and sometimes touch

CRANK TAIL—Tail carried down

CREST—Arched portion of the back of the neck

CROPPING—Cutting or trimming of the ear leather to get ears to stand erect

CROSSBRED—A dog whose sire and dam are of two different breeds

CROUP—The back part of the back above the hind legs. Area from hips to tail

CROWN—The highest part of the head; the topskull

CRYPTORCHID—Male dog with neither testicle visible

CULOTTE—The long hair on the back of the thighs

CUSHION—Fullness of upper lips

DAPPLED—Mottled marking of different colors with none predominating

DEADGRASS—Dull tan color

DENTITION—Arrangement of the teeth

DEWCLAWS—Extra claws, or functionless digits on the inside of the four legs; usually removed at about three days of age

DEWLAP—Loose, pendulous skin under the throat

DISH-FACED—When nasal bone is so formed that nose is higher at the end than in the middle or at the stop

DISQUALIFICATION—A dog which has a fault making it ineligible to compete in dog show competition

DISTEMPER TEETH—Discolored or pitted teeth as a result of having had Distemper

DOCK—To shorten the tail by cutting

DOG—A male dog, though used freely to indicate either sex

DOMED—Evenly rounded in topskull; not flat but curved upward

DOWN-FACED—When nasal bone inclines toward the tip of the nose

DOWN IN PASTERN—Weak or faulty pastern joints; a let-down foot

DROP EAR—The leather pendant which is longer than the leather of the button ear

DRY NECK—Taut skin

DUDLEY NOSE—Flesh-colored or light brown pigmentation in the nose

ELBOW—The joint between the upper arm and the forearm

ELBOWS OUT—Turning out or off the body and not held close to the sides

EWE NECK—Curvature of the top of neck

EXPRESSION—Color, size and placement of the eyes which give the dog the typical expression associated with his breed

FAKING—Changing the appearance of a dog by artificial means to make it more closely resemble the Standard. White chalk to whiten white fur, etc.

FALL—Hair which hangs over the face

FEATHERING—Longer hair fringe on ears, legs, tail, or body

FEET EAST AND WEST—Toes turned out

FEMUR—The large heavy bone of the thigh

FIDDLE FRONT—Forelegs out at elbows, pasterns close, and feet turned out

FLAG—A long-haired tail

FLANK—The side of the body between the last rib and the hip

FLARE—A blaze that widens as it approaches the topskull

FLAT BONE—When girth of the leg bones is correctly elliptical rather than round

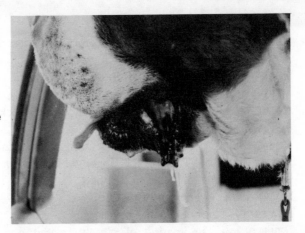

Deep flews account for the "slobbering Saint."

FLAT-SIDED—Ribs insufficiently rounded as they meet the breast-bone

FLEWS—Upper lips, particularly at inner corners

FOREARM—Bone of the foreleg between the elbow and the pastern

FOREFACE—Front part of the head; before the eyes; muzzle

FROGFACE—Usually overshot jaw where nose is extended by the receding jaw

FRINGES—Same as feathering

FRONT—Forepart of the body as viewed head-on

FURROW—Slight indentation or median line down center of the skull to the top

GAY TAIL—Tail carried above the top line

GESTATION—The period during which bitch carries her young; 63 days in the dog

GOOSE RUMP—Too steep or sloping a croup

GRIZZLE—Blueish-gray color

GUN-SHY—When a dog fears gun shots

GUARD HAIRS—The longer stiffer hairs which protrude through the undercoat

HARD-MOUTHED—The dog that bites or leaves tooth marks on the game he retrieves

HARE-FOOT—A narrow foot

HARLEQUIN—A color pattern, patched or pied coloration, pre-dominantly black and white

HAW—A third eyelid or membrane at the inside corner of the eye

HEEL—The same as the hock

HEIGHT—Vertical measurement from the withers to the ground; or shoulder to the ground

HOCK—The tarsus bones of the hind leg which form the joint between the second thigh and the metatarsals.

HOCKS WELL LET DOWN—When distance from hock to the ground is close to the ground

HOUND—Dogs commonly used for hunting by scent

HOUND-MARKED—Three-color dogs; white, tan and black, predominating color mentioned first

HUCKLEBONES—The top of the hipbones

HUMERUS—The bone of the upper arm

INBREEDING—The mating of closely related dogs of the same

Shorthaired bitch, Beau Cheval's Shannan Mardoug, is daughter of huge Ch. Beau Cheval's Shamrock, out of Beau Cheval's Toldya.

standard, usually brother to sister

INCISORS—The cutting teeth found between the fangs in the front of the mouth

ISABELLA—Fawn or light bay color

KINK TAIL—A tail which is abruptly bent appearing to be broken

KNUCKLING-OVER—An insecurely knit pastern joint often causes irregular motion while dog is standing still

LAYBACK—Well placed shoulders

LAYBACK—Receding nose accompanied by an undershot jaw

LEATHER—The flap of the ear

LEVEL BITE—The front or incisor teeth of the upper and low jaws meet exactly

LINE BREEDING—The mating of related dogs of the same breed to a common ancestor. Controlled inbreeding. Usually grandmother to grandson, or grandfather to granddaughter.

LIPPY—Lips that do not meet perfectly

LOADED SHOULDERS—When shoulder blades are out of alignment due to overweight or overdevelopment on this particular part of the body

LOIN—The region of the body on either side of the vertebral column between the last ribs and the hindquarters

LOWER THIGH—Same as second thigh

LUMBER—Excess fat on a dog

LUMBERING—Awkward gait on a dog

MANE—Profuse hair on the upper portion of neck

MANTLE—Dark-shaded portion of the coat or shoulders, back and sides

MASK—Shading on the foreface

MEDIAN LINE—Same as furrow

MOLERA—Abnormal ossification of the skull

MONGREL—Puppy or dog whose parents are of two different breeds

MONORCHID—A male dog with only one testicle apparent

MUZZLE—The head in front of the eyes—this includes nose, nostrils and jaws as well as the foreface

MUZZLE-BAND—White markings on the muzzle

MOLAR—Rear teeth used for actual chewing

NOSLIP RETRIEVER—The dog at heel—and retrieves game on command

NOSE—Scenting ability

NICTITATING EYELID—The thin membrane at the inside corner of the eye which is drawn across the eyeball. Sometimes referred to as the third eyelid

OCCIPUT—The upper crest or point at the top of the skull

OCCIPITAL PROTUBERANCE—The raised occiput itself

OCCLUSION—The meeting or bringing together of the upper and lower teeth.

OLFACTORY—Pertaining to the sense of smell

OTTER TAIL—A tail that is thick at the base, with hair parted on under side

OUT AT SHOULDER—The shoulder blades are set in such a manner that the joints are too wide, hence jut out from the body

OUTCROSSING—The mating of unrelated individuals of the same breed

OVERHANG—A very pronounced eyebrow

OVERSHOT—The front incisor teeth on top overlap the front teeth of the lower jaw. Also called pig jaw

PACK—Several hounds kept together in one kennel

PADDLING—Moving with the forefeet wide, to encourage a body roll motion

PADS—The underside, or soles, of the feet

PARTI-COLOR—Variegated in patches of two or more colors

PASTERN—The collection of bones forming the joint between the radius and ulna, and the metacarpals

PEAK—Same as occiput

PENCILING—Black lines dividing the tan colored hair on the toes

PIED—Comparatively large patches of two or more colors. Also called parti-colored or piebald

PIGEON-BREAST—A protruding breastbone

PIG JAW—Jaw with overshot bite

PILE—The soft hair in the undercoat

PINCER BITE—A bite where the incisor teeth meet exactly

PLUME—A feathered tail which is carried over the back

POINTS—Color on face, ears, legs and tail in contrast to the rest of the body color

POMPON—Rounded tuft of hair left on the end of the tail after clipping

PRICK EAR—Carried erect and pointed at tip

PUPPY—Dog under one year of age

Oil painting of Red Cloud, by artist Marian Sharp of Flanders, N.J.

QUALITY—Refinement, fineness

QUARTERS—Hind legs as a pair

RACY—Tall, of comparatively slight build

RAT TAIL—The root thick and covered with soft curls—tip devoid of hair or having the appearance of having been clipped

RINGER—A substitute for close resemblance

RING TAIL—Carried up and around and almost in a circle

ROACH BACK—Convex curvature of back

ROAN—A mixture of colored hairs with white hairs. Blue roan, orange roan, etc.

ROMAN NOSE—A nose whose bridge has a convex line from forehead to nose tip. Ram's nose

ROSE EAR—Drop ear which folds over and back revealing the burr

ROUNDING—Cutting or trimming the ends of the ear leather

RUFF—The longer hair growth around the neck

SABLE—A lacing of black hair in or over a lighter ground color

SADDLE—A marking over the back, like a saddle

SCAPULA—The shoulder blade

SCREW TAIL—Naturally short tail twisted in spiral formation

SCISSORS BITE—A bite in which the upper teeth just barely overlap the lower teeth

SELF COLOR—One color with lighter shadings

SEMIPRICK EARS—Carried erect with just the tips folding forward

SEPTUM—The line extending vertically between the nostrils

SHELLY—A narrow body which lacks the necessary size required by the Breed Standard

SICKLE TAIL—Carried out and up in a semicircle

SLAB SIDES—Insufficient spring of ribs

SLOPING SHOULDER—The shoulder blade which is set obliquely or "laid back"

SNIPEY—A pointed nose

SNOWSHOE FOOT—Slightly webbed between the toes

SOUNDNESS—The general good health and appearance of a dog in its entirety

SPAYED—A female whose ovaries have been removed surgically

SPECIALTY CLUB—An organization to sponsor and promote an individual breed

SPECIALTY SHOW—A dog show devoted to the promotion of a single breed

SPECTACLES—Shading or dark markings around the eyes or from eyes to ears

SPLASHED—Irregularly patched, color on white or vice versa

SPLAY FOOT—A flat or open-toed foot

SPREAD—The width between the front legs

SPRING OF RIBS—The degree of rib roundness

SQUIRREL TAIL—Carried up and curving slightly forward

STANCE—Manner of standing

STARING COAT—Dry harsh hair; sometimes curling at the tips

STATION—Comparative height of a dog from the ground—either high or low

STERN—Tail of a sporting dog or hound

STERNUM—Breastbone

STIFLE—Joint of hind leg between thigh and second thigh. Sometimes called the ham

STILTED—Choppy, up-and-down gait of straight-hocked dog

STOP—The step-up from nose to skull between the eyes

STRAIGHT-HOCKED—Without angulation; straight behind

SUBSTANCE—Good bone. Or in good weight, or well muscled dog

SUPERCILIARY ARCHES—The prominence of the frontal bone of the skull over the eye

SWAYBACK—Concave curvature of the back between the withers and the hipbones

TEAM—Four dogs usually working in unison

THIGH—The hindquarter from hip joint to stifle

THROATINESS—Excessive loose skin under the throat

THUMB-MARKS—Black spots in the tan markings on the pasterns

TICKED—Small isolated areas of black or colored hairs on a white background

TIMBER—Bone, especially of the legs

TOPKNOT—Tuft of hair on the top of head

TRIANGULAR EYE—The eye set in surrounding tissue of triangular shape. A three-cornered eye

TRI-COLOR—Three colors on a dog, white, black and tan

TRUMPET—Depression or hollow on either side of the skull just behind the eye socket; comparable to the temple area in man

TUCK-UP—Body depth at the loin

TULIP EAR—Ear carried erect with slight forward curvature along the sides

TURN-UP—Uptilted jaw

TYPE—The distinguishing characteristics of a dog to measure its worth against the Standard for the breed

UNDERSHOT—The front teeth of the lower jaw overlapping or projecting beyond the front teeth of the upper jaw

UPPER-ARM—The humerus bone of the foreleg between the shoulder blade and forearm

VENT—Tan-colored hair under the tail

WALLEYE—A blue eye also referred to as a fish or pearl eye

WEAVING—When the dog is in motion, the forefeet or hind feet cross

WEEDY—A dog too light of bone

WHEATEN—Pale yellow or fawn color

WHEEL-BACK—Back line arched over the loin; roach back

WHELPS—Unweaned puppies

WHIP TAIL—Carried out stiffly straight and pointed

WIRE-HAIRED—A hard wiry coat

WITHERS—The peak of the first dorsal vertebra; highest part of the body just behind the neck

WRINKLE—Loose, folding skin on forehead and/or foreface

# CHAPTER 19

# PURSUING A CAREER IN DOGS

One of the biggest joys for those of us who love dogs is to see someone we know or someone in our family grow up in the fancy and go on to enjoy the sport of dogs in later life. Many dog lovers, in addition to leaving codicils in wills, are providing for veterinary scholarships for deserving youngsters who wish to make their association with dogs their vocation.

Unfortunately, many children who have this earnest desire are not always able to afford the expense of an education that will take them through veterinary school, and they are not eligible for scholarships. In recent years, however, we have had a great innovation in this field—a college course for those interested in earning an Animal Science degree, which costs less than half of what it costs to complete veterinary courses. These students have been a boon to veterinarians, and a number of colleges are now offering the program.

Any one who has crossed the threshold of a veterinarian's office during the past decade will readily concur that, with each passing year, the waiting rooms become more crowded and the demands on the doctor's time for research, consultation, surgery and treatment are consuming more and more of the working hours over and above regular office hours. The tremendous increase in the number of dogs and cats and other domestic animals, both in cities and in the suburbs, has resulted in an almost overwhelming consumption of our time.

Until recently most veterinary help consisted of kennel men or women who were restricted to services more properly classified as office maintenance rather than actual veterinary assistance. Needless to say, their part in the operation of a veterinary office is both essential and appreciated; as are the endless details and volumes of paper work capably handled by office secretaries and receptionists.

Beau Cheval's Smartee Mardoug, from last litter sired by Ch. Beau Cheval's Tablo, out of Indian Mountain's Madre v Padre. Smartee loves to sit on the sofa at Beau Cheval and knows it's o.k. to do so on the one in the office.

However, still more of the veterinarian's duties could be handled by properly trained semiprofessionals.

With exactly this service in mind, several colleges are now conducting two-year courses in Animal Science for the training of such semiprofessionals, thereby opening an entire new field for animal technologists. The time saved by the assistance of these trained semiprofessionals will relieve veterinarians of the more mechanical chores and will allow them more time for diagnosing and general servicing of their clients.

"Delhi Tech," the State University Agricultural and Technical College at Delhi, New York, has already graduated several classes of those technologists, and many other institutions of learning are offering comparable two-year courses at the college level. Entry requirements are usually that each applicant must be a graduate of an approved high school, or take the State University Admissions Examination. In addition, each applicant for the Animal Science

Technology program must have some previous credits in mathematics and science, with chemistry an important part of the science background.

The program at Delhi was a new educational venture dedicated to the training of competent technicians for employment in the biochemical field and has been generously supported by a five-year grant, designated as a "Pilot Development Program in Animal Science." This grant has provided both personnel and scientific equipment with obvious good results, while being performed pursuant to a contract with the United States Department of Health, Education and Welfare. Delhi is a unit of the State University of New York and is accredited by the Middle States Association of Colleges and Secondary Schools. Their campus provides offices, laboratories and animal quarters, and they are equipped with modern instruments to train their technicians in laboratory animal care, physiology, pathology, microbiology, anesthesia, X-ray and germ-free techniques. Sizeable animal colonies are maintained in airconditioned quarters, and include mice, rats, hamsters, guineapigs, gerbils and rabbits, as well as dogs and cats.

First year students are given such courses as Livestock Pro-

Cat nap at a dog show! Photographer Evelyn Shafer caught this informal moment during a day at a dog show sponsored by the Eastern Dog Club annual show back in 1953.

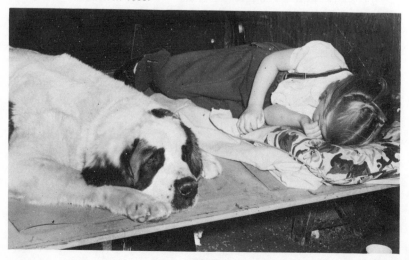

362

Pastel portrait of
Ch. Beau
Cheval's Tablo la
Mardoug at age 9.
Robert Hickey,
artist.

duction, Dairy Food Science, General, Organic and Biological Chemistry, Mammalian Anatomy, Histology, and Physiology, Pathogenic Microbiology, Quantitative and Instrumental Analysis, to name a few. Second year students matriculate in General Pathology, Animal Parasitology, Animal Care and Anesthesia, Introductory Psychology, Animal Breeding, Animal Nutrition, Hematology and Urinalysis, Radiology, Genetics, Food Sanitation and Meat Inspection, Histological Techniques, Animal Laboratory Practices and Axenic Techniques. These, of course, may be supplemented by electives that prepare the student for contact with the public in the administration of these duties. Such recommended electives include Public Speaking, Botany, Animal Reproduction and other related subjects.

In addition to Delhi, there are at least a dozen other schools, in California, Maine and Maryland, now offering training for animal technologists. Students at the State University of Maine, for instance, receive part of their practical training at the Animal Medical Center in New York City, under the tutelage of Dr. Robert Tashjian and his highly qualified staff. Dr. John R. McCoy,

Saints of all ages have their breakfast in kitchen of Marlene Anderson in 1961. All puppies are roughs.

Secretary of the New Jersey Veterinary Medical Association, recently petitioned Rutgers University, on behalf of the veterinaries of the state, for the development of just such a college program. It is hoped that more and more states will follow this lead since the need is immediate in the animal technology field. Veterinarians are most enthusiastic about the possibilities offered by these new resources being made available to our profession.

Under direct veterinary supervision, the following duties are just some of the procedures in an animal hospital that can be executed by the semiprofessional.

- Recording of vital information relative to a case. This would include such information as the client's name, address, telephone number and other facts pertinent to the visit. The case history would include the breed, age of the animal, its sex, temperature, previous client, etc.

- Preparation of the animal for surgery.
- Preparation of equipment and medicaments to be used in surgery.
- Preparation of medicaments for dispensing to cilents on prescription of the attending veterinarian.
- Administration and application of certain medicines.
- Administration of colonic irrigations.
- Application or changing of wound dressings.

Headstudy of a Saint puppy sired by Ch. Riot von Heidengeis, and owned by the Cavajone Kennels, Merrimack, N.H.

- Cleaning of kennels, exercise runs and kitchen utensils.
- Preparation of food and the feeding of patients.
- Explanation to clients on the handling and restraint of their pets, including needs for exercise, house training and elementary obedience training.
- First-aid treatment for hemorrhage, including the proper use of tourniquets.
- Preservation of blood, urine and pathologic material for the purpose of sending them to a laboratory.
- General care and supervision of the hospital or clinic patients to insure their comfort.
- Nail trimming and grooming of patients.

High school graduates with a sincere affection and regard for animals, and a desire to work with veterinarians and perform such clinical duties will fit in especially well. Women particularly will be useful since, over and beyond the strong maternal instinct that goes so far in the care and the "recovery" phase when dealing with animals, women will find the majority of their duties well within not only their mental—but their physical—capabilities. Since a majority of the positions will be in the small animal field, their dexterity will also fit in very well. Students, with financial restrictions that preclude their education and licensing as full-fledged veterinarians, can in this way pursue careers in an area that is close to their actual desire. Their assistance in the pharmaceutical field, where drug concerns deal with laboratory animals, covers another wide area for trained assistance. The career opportunities are varied and reach into job opportunities in medical centers, research institutions and government health agencies; and the demand for graduates far exceeds the current supply of trained personnel.

As far as the financial remunerations, yearly salaries are estimated at an average of $5000 as a starting point. As for the estimate of basic college education expenses, they range from $1800 to $2200 per year for out-of-state residents, and include tuition, room and board, college fees, essential textbooks and limited personal expenses. These personal expenses, of course, will vary with individual students.

Veterinary Councils all over the country are discussing ways they can help and are offering suggestions and opinions on the training of these semiprofessionals.

# DARK EYES

## By Bruce N. Chapman

### I

You sit silently
Looking into those dark, trusting eyes.
Softly you scratch him.
The head cocks appreciatively
And he makes a deep
Almost purring sound.
So much contentment
From so little effort.
Sitting there beside him
He is larger than life,
Truly enormous
And yet so gentle
You cannot help but see
He is worthy of his name,
For in all respects
He is a Saint.

### II

Years after he is gone
You will remember
Those dark trusting eyes
Into which you first looked
When he was young.
They glittered then with a devilment
Born of curiosity—
Nothing would escape him.
He was to smell and taste of everything,
A world rich in sights and sounds—
So many strange and delectable odors.
What a fine place
For a young Saint to explore
What a splendid way
To carry on with the excitement
And joy of being a dog.

He would smell and chew
And chase and bark
Each and every light-long day
Into the night
And you would sit and watch
Sharing many a joyful discovery.
What treasures then did he bring you?
An old shoe?
A stick?
A rock?
Whatever the find,
He was proud to show.
You will recall too
How he grew.
The awkward months
When you were convinced
That he was beyond all hope,
When every leg had a mind its own
Or so it seemed.
You look now at his early pictures
And smile,
For he was as they said,
A most unsightly mess.
With the passing of time,
Long after you decided
To love him for all his faults,
You were to find
The worst had come and gone.
Time was kind,
Puppy manners gave way to poise
And even your friends had to admit
It was now quite certain,
He was a Saint.
With strength and assurance
He moved through your world,
A world you gladly shared.

He enjoyed your presence,
Would sit beside you for hours
Willing to protect
With all his life
Should the need arise.
In turn, you fed and kept him healthy,
Not only accepting, but seeking his company
For he was in every sense
A friend, someone to be trusted,
Someone to share your life.
Years after he is gone
You will still remember—
The bonds of such a friendship
Have no limits.

Sanctuary Woods Orianna, 10 weeks old, sired by Sanctuary Woods Sequoyah ex Fidelas Adela. Owners Ann and Chuck Zayes, Tranquility, Bedminster, Pa.

Saint Bernard fancier Richard Tang with "friends" at a show. Saint has a few inches on the Shetland pony.

Two Saints find out what's inside the keg—Ch. Cinderella von Ava Banz and her mother, Ch. Ava of High Tor, living it up for the holidays. These two champion bitches are owned by Vera and Art Hyman, Englewood, N.J.

Tuckered trio basks in sun and finds napping contagious . . .
Mardonof's Jack de Karamuru and Jill de Karamuru pictured with Dr.
Duveen's lovely daughter in Rio de Janeiro, Brazil.

Beau Cheval's
Snowbound
practices show
stance in living
room, while
handler Julie
Howard assumes
kneeling position
to bring more
attention to the
dog.

The Murphy girls, Patti, Lynda and Kathy, pose in their backyard in August of 1963 with Mardonof's Rigga von Stacks.

Share and share alike ... Mardonof's Nana von Image shares dinner with the other baby in the family. Both are owned by the Mardonof Kennels, North Attleboro, Mass.

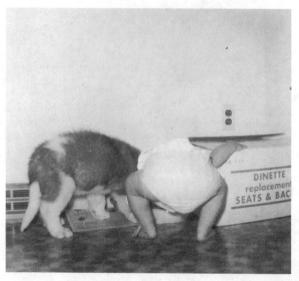

Strange bedfellow . . . for the Knorr children, Tammy and Greg.

Ch. Beau Cheval's Tia Maria stepped into the shallow end of the pool, liked its coolness so well, she decided to stay and catch a nap. She was sired by Beau Cheval's Gaylord out of Cleo St. Now, and she produced Ch. Beau Cheval's Bonni Maria, among others of quality.

A Christmas "Hi!" from Miss Marshall of Absecon, N.J. Her puppy is nine-week-old Beau Cheval's Courage.

Monopolizing the kitchen floor, Beau Cheval's Zee Zee Rider takes a snooze. He's owned by the Collins family, who live in Springfield, Pa.

Dawn Anderson has an armful with Beau Cheval's Can-Do.

All over the world ...children in Switzerland with their pet Saints.

Spacious old stone home of Marlene and Douglas Anderson in Wycombe, Pa., the site of Beau Cheval Kennels where Saint Bernards wandering about the grounds and pool are a familiar sight to visitors.

View of the trophy room at Beau Cheval Kennels, Wycombe, Pa., owned by Marlene and Douglas Anderson.

# INDEX

Listed here are associations, clubs, historical references, kennels, dogs mentioned in the text, as well as pictured (see page numbers boldface type) and all subjects of interest to the readers. Owners, breeders, judges, handlers, dogs' sires, dams and titles are included in captions and so are not repeated in this index.

Von Falkenstein, 30
Von Immenberg, 29
Von Lotten Kennels, 28
Von Rigi Kennels, 29
Von Sauliamt Kennels, 34, 42
Von Sood Kennels, 29

# W

Waldeck Kennels, 56
weaning puppies, 168-172
Westminster Kennel Club, 244
Westminster Dog Show winner,
  **25, 133**
whelping, 156-164
whelping box, 156-157
"whitehead," 112, 120-121
Willow Point's
  Dontchano, **122**
  Ezekiel v. Padre, **177**
  Ezra V Padre, **208**
wood carving of mother and
  puppies, **341**
worm eggs, 306
worm medication, 307

worms, 102-103
worm testing, 305, 309
Wory v Sauliamt, **260**
Wunderbar Von Narbenholt, **133**

# X

X Illo vom Vogelheim, **204**
X-rays for dysplasia, 302

# Z

Zenta vom Bismarkturm, **38**
Zimmerli, Hans, 54
Zippity, **269**
Zwing-Uri Kennels, **34**
Zwinghof Golden Eagle v Jumbo, 62
Zwinghof Jeannen x Xesbo, 62
Zwinghof Jumbo v Xesbo, 62
Zwinghof Moon Minx, 62
Zwingh of Xesbo v Gero's Wonna, 62
Zwinghof Quicksilver, 62
Zwinghof Tawny Luck v Zwingo, 62
Zwinghof Valerie v Zwing, 62
Zwinghof Wonna Joggi, 62
zygotes, 173, 175